MEDIA, POLITICS AND THE NETWORK SOCIETY

ISSUES in CULTURAL and MEDIA STUDIES

Series Editor: Stuart Allan

Published titles

MEDIA, POLITICS AND THE NETWORK SOCIETY

Robert Hassan

OPEN UNIVERSITY PRESS

Open University Press
McGraw-Hill Education
McGraw-Hill House
Shoppenhangers Road
Maidenhead
Berkshire
England
SL6 2QL

email: enquiries@openup.co.uk.
world wide web: www.openup.co.uk

and Two Penn Plaza, New York, NY 10121-2289, USA

First published 2004

A catalogue record of this book is available from the British Library

ISBN 0 335 21315 4 (pb)   0 335 21316 2 (hb)

Library of Congress Cataloging-in-Publication Data
CIP data has been applied for

Typeset by RefineCatch Limited, Bungay, Suffolk
Printed in the UK by Bell & Bain Ltd, Glasgow

For Kate, Theo and Camille

CONTENTS

SERIES EDITOR'S FOREWORD

A new world is beginning to take shape before our eyes, the world of the 'network society' to use Manuel Castells' evocative phrase. Social theorists such as Castells argue that the network society is the social structure of the Information Age, being made up of networks of production, power and experience. Its prevailing logic, while constantly challenged by social conflicts, nevertheless informs social action and institutions throughout what is an increasingly interdependent world. The Internet, he points out, 'is the technological tool and organizational form that distributes information power, knowledge generation and networking capacity in all realms of activity'. As a result, he adds, to be 'disconnected, or superficially connected, to the Internet is tantamount to marginalization in the global, networked system. Development without the Internet would be the equivalent of industrialization without electricity in the industrial era.' It follows, then, that the use of information by the powerful as a means to reinforce, even exacerbate, their structural hegemony is a pressing political concern. Celebratory claims about the 'global village' engendered by new media technologies ring hollow, especially when it is acknowledged that the majority of the world's population have never even made a telephone call, let along logged on to a computer. Critical attention needs to be devoted to the processes of social exclusion – the very digital divide – at the heart of the network society.

Robert Hassan's *Media, Politics and the Network Society* takes up precisely this challenge. The network society is more than the Internet, he points out; it encompasses everything that does and will connect to it, creating in the process an information ecology where the logic of commodification constitutes its life-blood. The information and communication technology (ICT) revolution that has shaped this process from the outset, he maintains, did not emerge in a political, economic or cultural vacuum. Rather, it is inextricably tied to the cultural dynamics of 'neoliberal globalization' as an ideological force, one that is changing the role and nature of the media in modern societies. Accordingly, a number of emergent struggles over who owns and controls access to the very infrastructure of the network society are examined here. ICTs, Hassan suggests, are serving as the weapons of choice for a new generation of activists intent on rewiring the network society in more politically progressive terms. Through new forms of 'technopolitics', fresh ideas are being generated and collectively negotiated with an eye to launching global protests and boycotts, of which the impact on everyday life is remarkably profound at times. In assessing the issues at stake for cultural and media studies, Hassan argues that the first decade of the twenty-first century is witnessing the beginnings of a critical, 'informationized' resistance to the hegemony of neoliberal capitalism – not least, as he shows, from within the network society itself.

The *Issues in Cultural and Media Studies* series aims to facilitate a diverse range of critical investigations into pressing questions considered to be central to current thinking and research. In light of the remarkable speed at which the conceptual agendas of cultural and media studies are changing, the series is committed to contributing to what is an ongoing process of re-evaluation and critique. Each of the books is intended to provide a lively, innovative and comprehensive introduction to a specific topical issue from a fresh perspective. The reader is offered a thorough grounding in the most salient debates indicative of the book's subject, as well as important insights into how new modes of enquiry may be established for future explorations. Taken as a whole, then, the series is designed to cover the core components of cultural and media studies courses in an imaginatively distinctive and engaging manner.

Stuart Allan

ACKNOWLEDGEMENTS

This book, like my first, was made possible primarily through the space, time (and salary) provided by the Institute for Social Research at Swinburne University in Melbourne, Australia. Thanks again, then, should go to its Director, David Hayward, for his trust, faith and patience – and for leaving me to get on with it. Thanks also to Denise Meredyth for putting me in contact with the Series Editor at Open University Press, Stuart Allan. A specific debt of gratitude goes to Stuart for his unstinting cheerfulness and help in the development of the book. I could not have done it without him.

ABBREVIATIONS

BBS	Bulletin Board Systems
BSE	Bovine Spongiform Encephalopathy
CCP	Chinese Communist Party
CERN	European Organization for Nuclear Research
COMINT	communications intelligence
CSAE	Committee for the Study of the American Electorate
DEC	Digital Equipment Corporation
EU	European Union
FLAG	Fibre Optic Link Around the Globe
GM	genetic modification
GPL	general public licence
GPS	Global Positioning Satellite
GUI	Graphical User Interface
IFJ	International Federation of Journalists
IMF	International Monetary Fund
IP	Internet Protocol
ISP	Internet Service Provider
LAN	Local Area Network
MSC	Multimedia Super Corridor
NAFTA	North American Free Trade Agreement
NGO	non-governmental organization
NSA	National Security Agency
NTIA	National Telecommunications and Information Administration
OS	operating system
PET	Personal Electronic Transactor
R & D	research and development

TCP	Transmission Control Protocol
UNDP	United Nations Development Programme
UNEP	United Nations Environmental Programme
WEF	World Economic Forum
WHO	World Health Organization
WTO	World Trade Organization

INTRODUCTION

We live in an age of information, in a networked society. What is the nature of this thing? How did it evolve and what sustains it? What, moreover, are its effects upon media, upon cultural production and upon politics? These are the principal questions that this book will deal with. In response to these sorts of questions many have predicted wonderful times ahead for life in the **network society**. Others, less numerous, foresee only doom and gloom. These are either the worst of times or the best of times, according to the differing poles of perception regarding the networked world. These are also the partisan positions. Alternatively, one can ignore competing claims altogether and just get on with one's own life. This is what most people do. And this is understandable. One of the features of the rise of the network society has been its *rapidity*. Life has accelerated to the point where there is hardly the time to *consider* such questions, much less have a ready answer to, or reflective opinion on, them. Life is fast and so life can be hard. Jobs need to be got and kept, rent paid, kids fed. There's no time to think in terms of root causes and branching effects. Besides, life in the network society can have its undoubted ameliorative effects upon frazzled brain and tired body. For example, after work or school we can relax at home and slip a DVD movie into the player, or insert a Playstation game and blast away at something virtual. We can text-message a friend, log on to the **Internet** and buy dinner, getting someone else to prepare and deliver it. And while in **cyberspace** we can email a friend, lurk or participate in chat rooms, view pornography, make a bid for that kitsch 1950s Japanese toy robot on eBay, or download via **broadband** the latest (bootlegged) Hollywood blockbuster, while waiting for waiting for the pizza delivery to arrive. In other words, we can let the network wash over us. We can opt to savour its fruits while we can and try to cope with its nasty surprises if and when they arrive. This is the neutral position.

This book presents an analysis of the network society and considers the above questions from a critical position. It takes as given that its readers have moved beyond the partisan and neutral positions and believe that there is more to the network society than being able to vote Josh, Jamie, Janey or Josie off the *Big Brother* set with the press of a button on a mobile phone; or of being able to avail oneself of the wonders of the Internet – from gaining a degree, to compiling a vast musical library of one's own from free downloaded **MP3s**. This book is premised upon the idea that these networking activities in themselves are neither good nor bad; but they do *mean* something, and they say something about the sort of society we live in. They are part of much larger, interconnected dynamics and it is important that we understand what these are, and the ways in which they affect us. Why is it important?

It is no exaggeration to say that the evolution of the network society is a world-historical development. Not since the Industrial Revolution of the eighteenth and nineteenth centuries has capitalist society experienced such far-reaching economic and technological change. And never has such change happened so fast. The Industrial Revolution was rapid by the standards of its time. Blindingly fast, even, but that revolution took many decades, indeed generations, to ripple through economies, industries, cultures, politics and societies. Now, however, it is hard to find points of real similarity in our present-day network society with that of the world as it was as recently as the 1970s or 1980s, so completely has it changed. We work differently, we learn differently, we think differently. We do so many things that would have been unimaginable twenty years ago. What is more, we take all this for granted. Now, I realize this sort of talk hovers dangerously close to network society-cliché, but it has to be said again and again to emphasize and to remind ourselves of the newness of the world we live in. Sons and daughters of earlier generations could at least recognize many aspects of their parents' world. Their media, cultures and politics were broadly similar and readily recognizable. Contrastingly, young people born in the 1990s and coming to adolescence and adulthood any time soon will have major difficulties in relating to what was a very recent pre-digital world. This was a world in which the social and economic organizing principals of **Fordism** were dominant to the extent that they had become what David Harvey (1989) called a 'whole way of life'. This was a world, for example, where a 'free-market economy' would have been widely viewed as a form of barbarism, a world where computers were slow and cumbersome and were applied very selectively in industry and in research, a world where we were connected by means of a 'telephone' (a word that is already dying through neglect) which came in a choice of blue, black, white or beige and which sat, expensive and immobile, in the hallway next to the pot plant.

So why the focus upon media, culture and politics when trying to understand the network society, when the network society is, as I will show below, fundamentally an economic and technological phenomenon? Allow me to sketch these reasons schematically for the moment and then deal with them in some detail in the chapters below. I focus on these because primarily it is these realms, in complex combination, that make the economic and the technological possible. And it is these realms, moreover, that have been most radically transformed due to the rise of the network society. Economics and technological development are closely linked processes and have their own powerful imperatives, of course. However, these are only brought to bear and legitimized in society through the interactions of media, culture and politics.

Take the role of the media. In modern societies, the ideas that constitute the basis upon which society is formed and developed are transmitted through (mainly) mass media. This is an endlessly contested terrain, but it is also one that has observable dynamics and identifiable preponderances. It is here that the increasingly intricate interactions of what Antonio Gramsci called 'organic intellectuals' have their effects. For Gramsci, organic intellectuals emerge as the organisers of ideological preponderance, or **hegemony**, for the bourgeoisie, that is to say, the owners and controllers of capital. Through their access to mass media forms, they are those who are able, as Zygmunt Bauman (1992: 1) put it, to:

> . . . articulate the worldview, interests, intentions and historically determined potential of a particular class; who elaborate the values which needed to be promoted for such a potential to be fully developed; and who legitimise the historical role of a given class, its claim to power and to the management of the social process in terms of those values.

These are the journalists, the artists, designers, managers, radio talk-back hosts, newspaper proprietors, academics and so on, who help shape the ruling ideas that feed directly into the forms of economic organization and levels of technological development that dominate within society.

In terms of culture, Raymond Williams, a social, cultural and technology theorist who has had a seminal effect upon the cultural studies discipline, and whose ideas will interweave this narrative, famously argued that 'culture is ordinary' (1958b: 6). Culture is produced, he maintained, through the everyday dynamics that suffuse all social life. These generate the symbols and the representations that shape identity and help us to attribute meaning to the world and our place within it. Cultural production, being both 'ordinary' and vital to the constitution and shape of society, has been transformed by the networking of society. *Forms* of media, media practices and media institutions, it will be immediately obvious, play a significant role in cultural production. It is *in* and *through* these that ideas are transmitted, traditions passed on, ideologies disseminated, hegemonies consolidated, and where the symbols, customs, norms and values that go to make up 'the cultural' are created, contested and manipulated.

Lastly, the political process, primarily institutional politics and the processes of **civil society** more generally, has traditionally been the power-dynamic between these interacting forces of media and culture within society. It is through politics that the major society-shaping ideas and the forms of cultures get worked out, where they become legitimized and possibly hegemonic – or made taboo or marginal (illegal or sub-cultural). This overarching process, as I see it, is profoundly *dialectical*.

In short, parentheses, a working definition for the dialectical process may be useful at this point as it underscores much that follows in this book. The word *interaction* is sometimes used here as a synonym for dialectic and this captures the dynamics of the process – but there is more. The word dialectic is derived from the Greek word for a process of continual interrogation through open-ended dialogue or debate. A debate begins with a proposition (thesis), then the examination of a contrary view (antithesis), and then the arrival at a new view that incorporates elements to both sides (synthesis). In the Marxist tradition this basic philosophical framework was developed, passing through Hegel's more spiritual meaning, into what was called 'dialectical materialism' (the application of this reasoning to real-world criteria). For Marx this was in the dialectic of history that was being played out in the struggle between the bourgeoisie and the proletariat that would eventually be resolved in the 'synthesis' of communism. In cultural studies, the dialectic has been imbued with a critical element, or the arrival at synthesis through critical reflection, or what Fredric Jameson called 'stereoscopic thinking' – or the ability to think through both sides of the argument and develop a new perspective (1992: 28).

The focus of this book is not overtly concerned with the historical class struggle, but with a critical interpretation of the dialectical interactions between media, culture and politics in the context of the network society. For Jean Baudrillard these take place in what he has called a 'dialectical tension or critical movement' (2003: 2). These 'tensions' or 'movements' are the interplay of the semi-autonomous 'spaces' where the dialectic constantly evolves, where they interact and affect each other. And just as importantly, there exists the space for *difference* in forms of media, in ideology, in culture and in politics where the operation of the dialectic acts as the basic precursor for dynamism, for diversity and for change.

So far, so well-known, one may think. This, surely, is the bread and butter stuff of media studies, cultural studies and politics. It is. But the rise of the network society has changed these dynamics and placed the interactions of media, culture and politics on to a new level, to the level of digitization and **informationization**, and this 'digital dialectic', to borrow a term from Peter Lunenfeld (2000), is having a profound effect upon them. Understanding these is the principal aim of this book. In a book called *Critique of Information* (2002) Scott Lash argues that informationization has squeezed out these spaces, cancelled out the poles of difference and obliterated the realms of transcendence and immanency that constituted the fluid mechanics of the dialectic and of the possibility of the creation of other ways of being and seeing. Through the processes of informationization, Lash maintains, media, culture and politics now exist as digital information upon a 'machinically mediated' (2000: 9) plane where there is 'no outside anymore' (2000: 10), no spaces for the dialectic to operate as it once did. Informationization is creating a network society and an information order where the 'differences' within media, within cultural production and within politics are disappearing. The consequences are possibly extraordinary, the effects far-reaching and their significance world-historical. It is these claims and this logic that this book will explore.

Chapter 1 deals with the fundamental question, 'What is the network society?' Most of us will have heard the expression, but what exactly constitutes its dynamics? How and why did it evolve, and what sustains it? After a brief history of the evolution of the Internet, the discussion moves to what I see as the principal organizing features of the network society. I argue these to be techno-economic and *ideological* in origin and to be evolving through interconnecting realms or 'scapes' that exist on the same digital plane. These are discussed in separate sub-chapters and are headed: Digital Technology, Digital Capitalism, Digital **Globalization** and Digital Acceleration. Illustration of these scapes gives form and function to the dynamics of the information order and sets the context for the rest of the book.

Chapter 2 looks at the informationization of media and culture. It begins with some grounding discussion on the meanings of the terms 'media' and 'culture'. From there it moves to an analysis of the '**dialectics** of media-culture' and how the spaces in which they operate are being colonized and constricted through the process of informationization. The chapter ends with some considerations that preface the later chapters on politics and civil society in the network society. In this final part it is argued that although the spaces of dialectical interaction and difference are disappearing and being colonized by the system of neoliberal globalization and informationization, there will always exist spaces of difference where domination and colonization will be resisted and from where other ways of being and seeing can emerge.

The third chapter opens with an empirical look at the development of 'wiring' the world into a networked society. The extent of the process is mind-boggling, with around 39 million miles of fibre optic data cabling in the US alone. I argue that part of the astonishing success of this wiring is our innate need to communicate with each other, a function of what Marx called our 'species being' that is profoundly social. In other words, humans are essentially social beings who are driven to communicate. Thus the opportunity to do this more effectively, more quickly and with more people constitutes for most people an irresistible urge. Ostensibly, then, rapid inter-connectivity of the world appears as something that is unalienating, exciting and 'progressive'. The chapter goes on to argue, however, that the particular logic of the *neoliberalized network society* means that, ironically, the more we 'connect' in the virtual network the more we are in danger of 'disconnecting' from more proximate relationships. The chapter ends with an analysis of those more palpably negative aspects of life inside (or 'outside' for many) the network society, such as the '**digital divide**', the transformed nature of warfare through informationization and the rise of a concomitant and problematic 'surveillance society' alongside the networked one.

Chapter 4 begins with a slightly different approach in the attempt to illustrate the effects of 'Life.com', or the suffusing of **ICTs** into every nook and cranny of culture and society. This is done through the writing of a couple of imagined scenarios that describe a fictionalized 'day in wired life' of two characters whose lives are shaped profoundly by their everyday interaction with ICTs. The intention is to illustrate as vividly as possible what 'life' in the network society is like, and do this in a way that can be more successful than through the more traditionally academic narrative. The chapter then switches focus back to more conventional mode and involves an analysis of the consequences (actual and possible) of our increasingly profound interaction with ICTs in the network society. I argue that the information technology revolution and the rise of the network society is much more than simply a new social relationship with technology. It is inaugurating a new ontology – literally a new way of being – both in the physical world and in the network of networks. This is considered through critical appraisal of the theories and works of Nicholas Negroponte and his 'bits and atoms' projects at the Massachusetts Institute for Technology (MIT) Media Lab. The explicit aim of the Lab's research (and the Center for Bits and Atoms which opened at MIT in 2001) is to 'explore how the content of information relates to its physical representation, from atomic nuclei to global networks' (*MIT News* 2001). This theme of linking (literally) the human with the network is extended through an analysis of Donna Haraway's theories of the technology-meets-flesh '**cyborg**'. In the light of work at MIT and elsewhere and the deep suffusion of ICTs into everyday life, the analysis considers whether it is appropriate to speak of the cyborg as actually existing in our present-day world, or whether it is still the stuff of *Terminator*-type science fiction.

The final chapters (5 to 7) move the focus to the role of politics and how their traditional dynamics have been transformed (and are now in a deep state of flux) due to the effects of informationization. It begins with the argument that 'civil society', the realm from where political forces emerge, has been colonized by the dual-dynamics of neoliberal globalization and the information technology revolution. This is reshaping our civil society into one that has lost much of its transformative and diversity-creating powers. Commodification, consumerism and the effects of 'digital acceleration' in economy, culture and society have struck at the heart of what Robert Putnam calls '**social capital**'. It is this digital 'killing of social engagement', as Putnam terms it, that has emasculated civil society, orienting it towards the market, and that is inculcating a widespread passivity concerning the abilities of ordinary people to change things. Accordingly political participation and 'social engagement' of all kinds that go to make traditional civil society are hardly registering a pulse. The old civil society, the one that took its shape and form in the nineteenth and twentieth centuries, is near comatose and unable to deliver a vibrant democracy and a media, cultural and political diversity anywhere in the world, so completely has the neoliberal/ICT revolution enfeebled it. The book concludes by identifying resistant spaces within civil society in the information order. It looks at the complex dynamics that propel the so-called '**global civil society movement**'. This is a coalition of the disparate and the desperate that range from middle-class church groups, environmentalists of every class strata and trade unionists, to ordinary people from all walks of life who feel the erosion of civil society to be retrogressive, unfair or simply 'wrong' in some unspecified way. What unites these is a deep-seated antipathy towards the logic of **neoliberalism** and the free-market. What enables them to organize together is their shared recognition that the network society is here to stay, and that ICTs, not parliamentary politics or the old ways of a now-corrupted civil society, can be the tools of change. They share the idea that, if used democratically, used primarily for people and not profit, then new ideas, new knowledges, new ways of being and new ways of seeing can take hold and will transform the neoliberalized and rationalized network society into a more fair and sustainable one.

The Dickensian dichotomy alluded to at the beginning of this introduction is a false one. What I have tried to show in what follows is that these are neither the best nor the worst of times. To be sure, we live in an age of extremes of emotion and of opinion. And like Dickens's description of the French Revolution, our own time is '. . . the age of wisdom, the age of darkness, the epoch of belief [and] the epoch of incredulity'. Above all, however, we are in the midst of an open-ended period of immense *transformation*, a dual-revolution of neoliberal globalization and information technology. Media, culture and politics have changed, but, within the flux of change, democratic continuities reveal themselves and become accentuated. Renewal is taking place. These spaces of renewal are, at one and the same time, *networked* spaces of media, of cultural production and of political contestation in the creation of a new civil society. However, renewal is nascent and the future uncertain, notwithstanding the fact that neoliberalism and the information technology revolution are built upon shifting sands. Nonetheless, in the absence of a creditable and widespread alternative vision for the construction of a better society, neoliberalism and its technological imperatives will continue to stagger from crisis to crisis. What is certain is that the continued adoption of a neutral position by the majority of the inhabitants of the network society will assure neoliberalism's uncontested ideological rule and its ongoing economic and technological shaping of the network society in its own image. Understanding the network society, its political economy, its history, its continuities from the pre-digital age, and their agencies for change, is but the first step away from neutrality and passivity and an uncertain (but certainly bleak) digital future. Understanding the network society is also the first step towards autonomy and towards empowerment and progressive activism within it. It is in this spirit that I'd like the reader to consider what follows.

1 | WHAT IS THE NETWORK SOCIETY?

What we were dreaming about was profound global transformation. We wanted to tell the story of the companies, the ideas and especially the people making the Digital Revolution. Our heroes weren't politicians and generals or priests and pundits, but those creating and using technology and networks in their professional and private lives . . . you.

(Louis Rossetto, *Wired*, 6.01, January 1998)

The revolution has been normalized

Writing a couple of years prior to the largely unanticipated **dotcom** crash of 2001, Rossetto was reflecting, in the quotation above, upon what was then a widely held confidence in the exciting possibilities that information and communication technologies (ICTs) held for almost *everything*. Surveying the scene a few years after the crash, the **NASDAQ** stocks that measure the health of the ICT industries may be somewhat less robust, but faith in the ultimate triumph of the 'Digital Revolution' remains undiminished in most quarters of government, business, and society in general. Rather more diminished, however, is the high-octane rhetoric of 'heroes' and of entrepreneurial individualism that routinely accompanied talk of the rapidly evolving network society. For most of the 1990s, in magazines such as *Wired*, in the business press almost everywhere and in feature articles in almost every newspaper across the world, almost every week, one could find articles that lauded the heroes of the nascent Digital Revolution. Bill Gates of Microsoft was the foremost idol. Tales of how, in 1980, he purchased for a mere $50,000 from an obscure programmer called Tim Patterson the MS-DOS operating system for IBM PCs and how he cannily opted to keep the licensing rights for himself instead of selling them to IBM, thus making a mega-fortune as the PC revolution took off, became the stuff of legend. Energetic entre-preneurs and slothful dreamers alike were stunned by Gates's seeming perspicacity, and salivated at the size of his actual (and rapidly growing) bank balance. Coming a close second, arguably, in the hero-worship stakes was Steve Jobs of Apple Cor-poration, with Andy Grove of Intel coming in a somewhat distant third. Grove's brush with techno-celebrity, though, stemmed more from his aggressive business style that seemed to fit the 1990s *zeitgeist*, as opposed to the somewhat more prosaic attributes of his microprocessors. For the more discerning, that is to say, those who saw the ICT revolution in rather more existential terms, the guru/hero of choice was Nicholas Negroponte of **MIT Media Lab**. Negroponte both funded and wrote articles for *Wired* magazine that rapidly became the journal for the digital *cognoscenti*. Negroponte is an interesting and influential character in this particular story of the network age and will be discussed in more detail in Chapter 4.

It was Gates, however, who responded most prominently to the general adulation with the publication of two books: *The Road Ahead* (1995) and *Business @ the Speed of Thought* (with – in the new spirit of the times – *The Road Ahead* CD-ROM included) (1999). These tracts were designed to impart his wisdom to the masses; a handing down, in the manner of Moses, of his set-in-stone theories on the nature of ICTs and their relationship to what was now being called the '**New Economy**'. This was a new and highly flexible form of economic organization that arose in the late 1970s from the ashes of Fordism (Harvey 1989). This Brave New Economy is lubricated by ICTs and was claimed to produce, after two hundred years of trial and error, what Gates called 'friction free capitalism' (1995). Both books were massive best-sellers. However, quite quickly after their publication and after a flurry of similarly oriented but much less successful books by other authors, it seemed that there was less enthusiasm for heroes of the Digital Revolution. We felt less motivated or inspired by the digital entrepreneurs and what they had to say, and the media felt less inclined to give them the plaudits that once regularly came their way. Why such a sudden change?

Part of the answer may have to do with the nature of digital networks and with computerization more generally. In the competitive environment of neoliberal eco-nomic globalization, *acceleration*, or the need for increasingly more powerful com-puter processing capability, is everything. If you can do it faster in a world where 'time is money', and 'money is time', you can therefore do it more cheaply and be in prized possession of the killer app that can beat the competition. Indeed, as Neil Postman argues, the computer-driven speed-up of almost every movement in the economy and in society's institutions soon became a dynamic of *acceleration for its own sake*. As Postman sees it, this has led much of society to view computer technology as 'both the means and end of human creativity' (1993: 61). As a result of this shift up several gears of acceleration, the first romantic phase of the Digital Revolution took place within the blinking of an eye. So quickly, indeed, that we've barely registered its passing. We've internalized it, though, and ICTs are now beginning to suffuse almost every nook and cranny of cultural and economic life. DVD players, 3G videophones,

Sony Playstation, and the highways and byways of the Internet itself used to thrill with their fiendish cleverness and unlimited potential. Now they are just everyday things – precisely due to their deep suffusion into our everyday lives. The feelings of wonderment that earlier generations had for television and radio lasted for many years; our collective fascination with the next killer app, by contrast, can be measured in days, or hours, or even seconds – the timespan of those 'cool' IBM ads showing what their new PC can do for your restaurant or flower shop. The very rapidity of their introduction and suffusion has fed into the speediness of our familiarity and blasé-ness with them.

In less than ten short years we have been blizzarded by the Internet, email, mobile phones, personal digital assistants (**PDAs**), scanners, digital video cameras, home, school and work-based networked PCs and so forth. These interconnectable processes and applications represent both an astonishing technological leap of quantum dimensions and the demotic digital fabric of our daily lives. The stuff of the revolution has become mundane. We crave the new, but exhibit a paradoxical impatience with it as it continually oozes from our popular culture. For example, not long ago mobile phones were viewed as chic and exotic accessories for the sophisticated. Now, as Irvine Welsh describes them in his 2001 novel *Glue*, they are crass and ubiquitous, detested 'schemie (housing estate residents') toys'. Manuel Castells, however, is more sociologically neutral, though hardly less constrained, in his appreciation of the depth, breadth and significance of the revolution. In the opening passages of *The Internet Galaxy* (2001) he writes that

> The Internet is the fabric of our lives. If IT is the present-day equivalent of electricity in the industrial era, in our age the Internet could be likened to both the electrical grid and the electric engine because of its ability to distribute the power of information throughout the entire realm of human activity.

Castells uses the term 'the Internet' to denote 'the network society' and this is a distinction I shall take up below. The point I want to make here, however, is that the applications and devices that connect from the Internet and connect us to it are growing in number and in sophistication all the time. These are deepening and widening the realm of the network and the growing numbers of people connected to it and who make it a 'society'.

The difference between today and the 'heroic' first phase of the revolution is that the time of the Gatesean individualist pioneer is fading fast, like the memory trace of the latest XBOX ad. Ironically, in the age of the *individual*, the network society is concerned more with the incorporation of *masses* of people, with distributed systems, interconnecting networks, processes, business-to-business and people-to-people. In short, digital networks have become an integral (nay, central) part of modern capitalism. Over the space of what was a very short Phase One of the Digital Revolution, it now seems almost unimaginable to envisage a form of capitalism, economic globalization and much of social and cultural life that does not have digital networks at its centreless centre. The revolution, in other words, has been normalized.

Meanwhile, our revolutionaries, in the main, have sunk back into salubrious corporate obscurity, with the media taking an interest only when *Forbes* magazine's rich-list comes out. Tim Patterson didn't get past obscurity, much less into the pages of *Forbes*. However, the famous trailblazers, the made-it-to-print-and-screen digital pioneers of the Information Superhighway, as the Internet was briefly called, have become standard-issue capitalists in the mould of a Rupert Murdoch or a Warren Buffett. Bill Gates still makes the news, though, but for different reasons. Indeed, the veneration enjoyed by Gates has turned into a certain notoriety; and he probably has lost the ethical and moral authority to write convincingly of the unalloyed good that ICTs represent for capitalism and for people in general. Microsoft, as it became hyper-successful, began to be seen more as the overweening bully as opposed to the quintessence of the American Way; the litigious stifler of innovation and rapacious buyer of rivals' ideas. For example, an episode of *The Simpsons* caricatures Gates as a money-grabbing thug who deals with competition in the same way that the Mafia do. And unfortunately for Gates and Microsoft, in the real world outside Springfield there is still plenty of traction in his 'friction-free capitalism', and he and his company have become snagged in a good deal of it. In 2001, the US Justice Department came close to ordering that Microsoft Corporation be broken up, so as to dilute its alleged monopoly practices in the PC software market. At the time of writing, detailed and protracted wrangling goes on in North America and in Europe. So far this has resulted in partial victories for both Microsoft and those states and countries that brought antitrust complaints. Nonetheless, Microsoft, while denying that it is a monopoly, proposed a class action settlement amounting to around one billion dollars in cash and computer products to go to the 12,000 most deprived schools in the US. It was not immediately clear, however, how the pushing of Microsoft training, software and services down to the furthermost reaches of the network society food chain would improve perceptions of monopoly practices. And it was a point not lost on lawyers involved in the case. Gene Crew, an antitrust lawyer representing plaintiffs from California, argued that: 'this is a very clever marketing device' whereby 'Microsoft can use its software to further entrench itself in the education market, which is the one market where Apple really competes' (Public Broadcasting Service 2001).

The anguish, tribulation and satirizing suffered by Gates and Microsoft is not really the issue, however. The point I want to make here is that our Digital Revolutionaries are no longer heroes. The majority no longer views them as trailblazers taking us to a brave new digital and frictionless world of plenty. What is important to understand – and this is a point that will be unnecessary to make to future generations – is that ICTs have become part of the fabric of capitalism, part of economic globalization, and part of the processes of everyday life for hundreds of millions of people around the world. Something *big* has happened. It has happened (and will continue to happen) with such speed and comprehensiveness that most of us barely notice it or consider its consequences.

Noticing it 1: the rise of the network society

Since the beginning of the 1990s at least, there have been many books written about the emergence of the network society and its implications for the economy, for culture and for society. Some of these descriptions and analyses, such as David Harvey's *The Condition of Postmodernity* (1989), have been implicit – and necessarily so – as the nature and contours of the emerging digital networks were not sufficiently clear at the time of writing to enable the formulation of definite conclusions. Others, such as Manuel Castells's *The Rise of the Network Society* (1996) and *The Internet Galaxy* (2001), Dan Schiller's *Digital Capitalism* (1999), *Web.Studies* by David Gauntlett *et al.* (2000) and James Slevin's *The Internet and Society* (2001) are much more explicit, having had the benefit of hindsight when describing and analysing the genesis and development of the process.

Given the surfeit of material on the rise of the network society, there is not much point in rewriting it once more within these pages. We can skip much of the minutiae. Instead, I will briefly describe the bare bones of the widely accepted facts to give an idea of the principal dynamics involved. After my short description I will look in more detail at what I believe to be the most significant factors involved. In doing this I will unpack what I take to be the most salient elements from a range of sources in the literature to form a single narrative that will outline the formation and development of the network society. This brief analysis will be a useful starting point that will comprise a framework to help conceptualize the arguments and analyses on media, culture and politics contained in the rest of this book.

A few facts on the history of the Internet and the network society

What we experience as the Internet today has its genesis in early 1960s US Cold War thinking by the Defense Advanced Research Projects Agency (**DARPA**). The aim was to develop computer information and command-and-control systems that could survive nuclear attack by the Soviet Union. The problem was that the networked computer systems in use at the time were based upon the 'star' topology whereby many net-worked machines relied upon a centralized computer. If the centralized computer were hit, then the whole network would fail. A new technique called 'packet switching' was found to be a way to avoid such total collapse. Packet switching was made possible through what is termed a Transmission Control Protocol (TCP). This protocol breaks up messages into digital pieces, 'packets', that can be sent individually, by differing routes if needed, to their destination where they are then reassembled into the original message. In theory, information can thus be routed around the damaged part of the system to arrive safely at the intended recipient, keeping the network functional.

The factual history stemming from this seminal development tends once more to revolve around individualistic 'heroes', this time of the proto-geek variety that inhabited the research labs. These individuals came not only from US defence agencies, but also from the major universities. They were driven just as much by the intellectual challenges laid out by J.C.R. Licklider of MIT than by any Cold War dream to outsmart the communists. (The USSR had recently launched *Sputnik* into orbit, to the enduring mortification of the US government.) Considered *primus inter pares* within the realms of geekdom, Licklider penned a series of memos in 1962 discussing the feasibility of a 'Galactic Network' through which people could communicate across an interconnected set of computers. This became the basic blueprint for the Internet. Licklider was an MIT man, but the fact that the Internet has its systemic logic rooted in Defense Department imperatives is not unimportant, and I shall return to it presently.

But to resume the present narrative: for much of the 1960s, within the universities or the Defense Labs, or through collaboration between both, what was to become the Internet was busily evolving. Much more thinking, research and further technological development led in 1969 to the formation of **ARPANET**, a computer network of research agencies in the US government and in the major research centres in universities such as MIT, Harvard and Stanford. These began to 'network' (send and receive information) and grow through the decentralized TCP protocol. In 1972 ARPANET demonstrated to the public its data-retrieval, real-time data access and interactive cooperation capabilities at the International Conference on Computer Communication in Washington, DC. It was 1972 when the first email was sent.

In 1974 Vinton Cerf and Bob Khan designed the TCP/IP (Internet Protocol), to put in place the architecture that would develop into the Internet as we know it today. Other developments began to take place on other fronts, bringing networked computers to ever-growing numbers of users outside the defence–university nexus. In 1977 two students from Chicago, Ward Christiansen and Randy Seuss, wrote a program they called XMODEM that allowed the transfer of files from PC to PC. The development of the XMODEM spurred the production of more PCs, which were beginning to become more than a professional computational tool and were bordering on becoming a general consumer product. Indeed, 1977 was something of an extended footnote in the history of the network society. It was in that year that Apple Computer was incorporated; when the first ComputerLand franchise opened as Computer Shack in Morristown, New Jersey; when Bill Gates and Paul Allen signed a partnership agreement to officially create the Microsoft Company; when the first issue of *Personal Computer* (later renamed *PC Magazine*) was published; and when Commodore Business Machines released PET (Personal Electronics Transactor) computer at the (inaugural) West Coast Computer Fair. The PET included a 6502 CPU, 4KB RAM, 14KB ROM, keyboard, display and tape drive – all for $600. In 1978 email developed its inevitable and now-detested excrescence, spam mail, when Digital Equipment Corporation (DEC) decided to send all its ARPANET colleagues a 'reminder' about its upcoming Open Day, when all its new computers would be on display.

The next important development on the road down the Information Superhighway was the design of a program that allowed UNIX users to share and copy files between each other. UNIX was a PC operating system program written by Bell Laboratories in 1974 that was designed by and for programmers. A program for communicating files between different UNIX systems (UUCP) was released in 1978 and allowed the formation of even denser computer networks. These networks began to form the early structure, the 'backbone', of the Internet. However, although PCs were becoming more and more commonplace, for much of the 1980s the Internet was largely unknown. It was still a realm for professionals in the computer industries, in the universities and in government agencies. They used the growing networks to 'network': that is, to share information and research; to 'post' notices to the burgeoning number of BBS (Bulletin Board Systems) and to swap gossip and opinion about, for example, the specifications of the new Apple Macintosh (vintage 1984) and whether $2495 was too much to pay for it; or whether the new (vintage 1985) **Windows** 1.0's Graphical User Interface (**GUI**) was a shameless rip-off from Apple.

In February 1990 ARPANET was decommissioned, having become an obsolete system. However, knowledge of its systems and software, of its protocols and pro-cedures, remained squarely in the public (and, by this time, commercial) domain. Moreover, this period coincided with the deregulation of the telecommunications industry in the US. Industry deregulation, coupled with the growing 'grass-roots' movement that networking had developed, brought the Internet quickly to what might be called a 'phase transition'. This was a point where networking activity reached a critical mass that was about to develop into the Internet we recognize today. This phase transition included the emergence of many new, independent and commercial Internet Service Providers (ISPs) that would enable workplace and home PC users to dial-up to the Internet through their modem connection. This allowed the Internet to expand in an unregulated and amorphous way, adding new nodes in endless configurations to accommodate the needs of the now rapidly expanding numbers of users. In 1993, some three million people were connected to the Internet.

Around this time, the work of Tim Berners-Lee, a software programmer from the Geneva-based European Organization for Nuclear Research (CERN) became a crucial factor in the popularization of the Internet. Indeed, the CERN website advertises itself today as '. . . where the Web was born'. Berners-Lee created the software that enabled the user to send and retrieve information to and from any other computer connected to the Internet, through now-familiar applications called **URL**, **HTTP** and **HTML**. In 1991 Berners-Lee, together with CERN colleague Robert Cailliau, developed a browser-editor that allowed text to be linked (through what they called hypertext) to further, cross-referenced, information on the Internet. They called the system the World-Wide Web (WWW). The commercial potential of the Internet (and the WWW) was beginning to be appreciated and, in the freewheeling, free-market *zeitgeist* of the 1990s, things now began to move quickly.

In 1992, another programmer/hero/geek called Marc Andreesen developed Mosaic, a program (browser) that enhanced the hypertext applications of Berners-Lee. Among other things, Mosaic allowed for text and images to appear on the same screen. This, as one may readily appreciate, represented a quantum leap in the look, the interactivity and the 'feel' of the Internet. Crucially, the software was downloadable for free from the Internet and so millions more began to get online to see what all the fuss was about. Two years later an improved version of Mosaic, renamed Netscape, appeared. Again it was free to users and by 1996 it had 75 per cent of the market. Microsoft belatedly got into the Internet game in a serious way around 1995 with the release of its Windows 95 that had a free browser, Internet Explorer, as part of the package. Spurred by the global hype surrounding Windows 95 (Mick Jagger and Co. reportedly banked 12 million dollars from Microsoft for selling the rights of their song 'Start Me Up'), the number of Internet-connected users rose to nearly 15 million. The phase transition had begun in earnest, kicking off what Castells called the '. . . extraordinary human adventure' (2001: 9). Thus the late 1990s saw the Internet 'explosion', the dotcom boom and the sprawling ubiquity of networks upon networks. These quickly enmeshed within its orbit the realms of industry, education, leisure, entertainment and home life; bringing us to the point we are at today – individuals and masses immersed within the logic of ICTs.

Noticing it 2: a way to think about networks (not just the Internet)

The above is a brief but serviceable history of the Internet and the network society. So far, so good. But this is only the first step. How should one *think* about the Digital Revolution? How should one make sense of the seemingly all-pervasiveness of ICTs? How should we view our continually accelerating way of life? How do we judge the claims that ICTs have made our lives and our work more efficient, more convenient and more 'connected'? What I want to do here is to engage in some Jamesonian 'stereoscopic thinking'; to make what is implicit in much of our assumptions of the network society, explicit. This is to engage in dialectical thinking, to engage in *critique*: to think, to reflect and to bring deep-seated dynamics to the surface to analyse and comprehend better and, ultimately, to have some sort of control over their effects.

It seems to me that we can identify *four principal dynamics* or interconnecting 'scapes' that need to be made explicit to help us think about how we live in the network society and thus enable us to orient ourselves more effectively within it. I have termed these 'Digital Technology', 'Digital Capitalism', 'Digital Globalization' and 'Digital Acceleration'. These will be discussed in turn.

Digital Technology

When we think about new ICTs, we tend to think about the artefact itself: the 'look' of the new iMac, the 'feel' of the latest Blackberry PDA, or the size of the new model Nokia mobile phone. We also, generally speaking, go past the aesthetics to also consider their utility (we're paying for it, after all). 'Can the mobile receive and send emails?' 'How good are the video graphics?' 'Does the computer allow me to burn downloaded MP3s and MPEGS?' 'How good are the Internet graphics on the PDA?' There is also the 'cool' factor to consider. Countless ads now tell us, implicitly or explicitly, that this or that new device will make us popular, or sexually appealing and that through their acquisition and use we will feel superior, confident, 'connected' and on the cusp of the techno-wave.

Not often do we consider the technology itself: its history, or what McKenzie and Wajcman (1999) call its 'social shaping', or where its uses 'situate' us within society. When we do give the technology any thought at all, we tend to think of it as neutral. However, Neil Postman, in his 1993 book *Technopoly*, argues that technology comes pre-encoded with its own values, its own **embedded ideology**. He writes (1993: 13) that 'embedded in every tool is an ideological bias, a predisposition to construct the world as one thing rather than another, to value one thing over another . . .'. In other words, we perceive the world through the tools and technologies we use. 'Predisposition' is an important term, here. The effects of a single technology on an individual level (gun, knife, mobile phone) are impossible to quantify or make hard-and-fast rules about. However, *systems* of technology and technique may predispose (not compel) us to act in a certain way. Technology theorist Jacques Ellul subtly argued in his *The Technological Bluff*, that 'technical development[s] [are] neither good, bad, nor neutral' (1990: 37) but that, acting as part of a system, they create the technological and ideological environments that condition or 'predispose' us to act in a certain way.

We have seen how the Internet and by extension the network society that we increasingly inhabit has its genesis in Cold War strategic thinking. This has not been made irrelevant through its popularization and ubiquitous non-military uses. In fact, Kevin Robins and Frank Webster, in their *Times of the Technoculture* insist that 'the military origins of the information revolution remain pertinent and pressing' (1999: 150). These martial origins, the authors argue, were based upon '. . . a logic of control and domination' – control over information flows and domination of the enemy (1999: 150). Moreover, the digital logic, the logic of technique, is one of the rationalization and instrumentalization of communications: that is, a stripped-down, goal-oriented mechanism that allows for no 'human error' factor. The logic was and is designed specifically to take out the human factor as much as possible. Human error, in war or in capitalist production, is costly. Ultimately, however, the cost is always borne by humans themselves (soldiers/civilians and workers) through injury, death and unemployment.

The network society more generally is embedded with the military–industrial logics of control, rationalization, instrumentalization and domination. Indeed, in the US especially, many computer scientists, programmers and software engineers cut their teeth in the military, to go on to jobs in the burgeoning private sector (Campbell-Kelly 2003). To be generally accepted and legitimated, however, the effects of militarization have to be ideologically expunged. This means that these elements are painted in the sunny primary colours of 'progress', 'freedom' and 'efficiency'. We tend to notice only the 'utility' and 'aesthetics' of ICTs because, in the main, the media (much of it operating on the same logic and with the same technologies) tell us that this is what is important. What is not overtly disclosed in the technology is that the underlying embedded logic of the on–off, yes–no, binary language of computerization tends, like the miliary itself, to be rigid, to foreclose other ways of seeing, other ways of thinking and other ways of being. So powerful is the ideology that masks this, however, we (mostly) are willing to adapt ourselves to it.

I should state here that this is not an argument for **'technological determinism'** whereby, so the argument goes, technologies themselves *compel* people to act in a certain way. What I am trying to convey here is that if we make ICTs explicit, by submitting them to critique, then what we uncover is an 'ideological determinism'. Here, the ideological preponderance of neoliberal capitalism, with ICTs at its core, allows it to present itself as the only possible reality. What is more, whereas techno-logical determinism presupposes compulsion, ideological determinism in this instance works on the opposite plane – that of *desire*. 'Where do you want to go today?' asks the Microsoft slogan – as if Microsoft did not have a very good idea to begin with. As Langdon Winner (1997: 48), one of the foremost theorists on technology and society, notes:

> For those willing to wait passively while the computer revolution takes its course, technological determinism ceases to become mere theory and becomes an ideal; a desire to embrace the conditions brought on by technological change without judging them in advance.

The passivity Winner speaks of stems not from the technology, but from the ideol-ogy, the 'ideal'. Nevertheless, for ideologies to work they must contain a grain of truth, some glint of recognition that makes the proposition, the 'idea', ring true in the heads of people. And so it is with ICTs. It is *true* that the Internet and the network society that it helps sustain can be a place where fast and efficient communication can be beneficial in all sorts of material ways. It is true, also, as I will discuss in the final chapter, that people can even use ICTs to subvert the dominant ideology. Moreover, users can be extremely creative within the network society, in art, music, design, litera-ture and so on. However, I believe that much of this innovation, this creativity, this subversion, takes place within the bounds of a certain logic, and within the binary and linear constraints of ICTs themselves.

As Terry Eagleton notes, we cannot separate successful ideologies from questions of power – and power works best when it is not obvious and when, in fact, it 'requires a degree of intelligence and initiative from its subjects' (1991: 46). And so it is important to be able to think outside the limitations of ICTs, to look beyond the immediate artefact and its utility. Raymond Williams wrote that

> New technology is itself a product of a particular social system and will be developed as an apparently autonomous process of innovation only to the extent that we fail to identify and challenge its real agencies.
>
> (1974: 135)

Brian Winston has expressed similar ideas more recently with the term 'supervening necessity' (1998: 147). This is the culmination of an array of social forces (political, ideological, economic) that create the conditions, the environment, that 'allow' the technology to come into being. Identifying the agencies and making explicit the supervening dynamics behind the creation of the Internet and the network society remains a fundamental challenge as we embark upon the twenty-first century. Technology does not shape humans in a one-way, deterministic action. It is, as Williams points out, the 'product of a *particular* social system'. Technologically speaking, our social system today is, I think, notwithstanding the continuities from the pre-digital age, one that is historically and particularly unique. No other technology has suffused society to such an extent, with such speed, across every industry, while creating new industries at the same time. The revolution in ICTs, moreover, comes in the context of the absence of any plausibly countervailing worldview. This makes the ideology of neoliberal capitalism even more powerful and compelling. The effect is that capitalist technologies, self-evidently and manifestly, are the only form of 'progress' on offer. And as I just argued, on the surface this does not *seem* tyrannical, it seems *desirable* and we are required to participate and even use our initiative and intelligence. How totalitarian does the iMac look? How repressive the latest Playstation game or personal MP3 player?

Digital Capitalism

We can begin straightaway with what I believe to be an inescapable, though possibly not an immediately obvious fact: that there would be no Internet and no network society (as we know it) without capitalism. That is to say, without big business persistently pushing the envelope our way for reasons that have less to do with *personal* 'freedom', 'creatively' or 'efficiency' and more with *business* freedom to use networks creativity in order for us to buy from them in extremely efficient and profitable ways. And there would be no Internet and network society without it being alleged and promoted by corporate capitalism (and embraced right down to the level of your local post office) to be the most effective way to work more 'efficiently' and 'productively'.

The outcome of the tension between the military–industrial complex *logic* of the network society and its freethinking co-developers in the universities and the science labs was always, in retrospect, a no-brainer. Getting to this point, however, saw a major shift in the way in which capitalism is organized; saw a major transformation in how people organized their working and leisure time (or more accurately, had it organized for them); and saw the inflating and bursting of a enormous, speculative, **dotcom bubble**. This is not to say that the colonization and subsequent refashioning of cyber-space largely in capitalism's own image has not had both negative and positive consequences. As I just noted, the material benefits that have accrued to many in the developed countries are real. The point is the extent to which the *technological momentum* and *ideological preponderance* is on the side of big business. What is significant, what needs to be made explicit is, as Ellen Meiksins-Wood has argued, the extent to which this militates against the possibilities for using ICTs, the Internet and the network society in more socially and environmentally creative and positive ways – not simply in the realms of production and consumption (1998: 162).

As we have seen, from the 1960s until the early 1990s the Internet developed quietly and comparatively sluggishly in the defence labs, in the university campuses and, latterly, in the research departments of telecom and computer companies. However, outside the labs and the campuses during the 1970s and the 1980s a revolution was going on, one that saw a fundamental restructuring of the ways in which capitalism is organized. The 'mode of production' that had characterized capitalism, especially since 1945, was Fordism. The term comes from the name of Henry Ford, US carmaker and autocrat whose factories produced the revolutionary Model T car. 'Any colour you like as long as it's black' was his famous catchphrase, and this said a lot about what Fordist society was about. Fordism was a mode of production based upon long production lines, making standardized goods for mass consumption. It later came to denote what David Harvey (1989) called a 'whole way of life', whereby the mass planning of production for consumption led to the planning of large swathes of the economy. This was called the 'managed' or 'mixed' economy and was the organizing principle for the post-war democracies. Here the market was confined to a subsidiary role in what was deemed (by government) to be the 'leading sectors' of the economy, sectors such as steel, heavy engineering, shipbuilding, large-scale manufacturing and so on. The economy was planned and managed through cooperation between organized labour, big business and government. By 1973, Fordism was in its death-throes. Western economies were in deep economic crisis and the 'partnership' between labour, business and government began to fall apart. The emerging 'neoliberals' blamed this terminal condition on both over-powerful unions and 'interfering' and 'bureaucratic' govern-ment. Long ignored market-oriented economists such as Milton Freidman and Friedrich Hayek were now having their day in the sun. Their ideas on letting the market permeate all facets of society, with its 'hidden hand' of alleged 'efficiency' and 'equi-librium' were taken up by powerful politicians such as Ronald Reagan and Margaret Thatcher, and began to transform the world.

A key component of this was a general process of 'deregulation', or 'letting market forces decide' the nature and scope of production, consumption, wages, the viability of industries and so on. Advanced ICTs were seen as a crucial factor in the transition to post-Fordist 'flexibility' and so computers and automated systems began to come into their own. Previously, governments and unions had intervened to slow down the introduction of ICTs, as they tended to 'displace' jobs. However, the growing strength of neoliberalism and the precipitous decline of organized union power, coupled with increased government unwillingness to get involved in the management of the economy, meant that the removal of what free-market ideologues termed 'rigidities' in the economy could proceed. Accordingly, from the late 1970s onwards the computerization, automation and flexibilization of capitalist production got underway in a thoroughgoing and rapid fashion. This was part of what Castells calls 'the transformation of work and employment' in the Organization for Economic Cooperation and Development (OECD) democracies. These factors contributed to the shift away from old Fordist industries that manufactured 'things', towards a 'service-based' economy. They also dissolved millions of 'old' jobs and created many more new jobs in the far more profitable 'knowledge-based industries and services' that dovetailed exactly with the capacities and capabilities of new ICTs (Castells 1996: 201–79).

As Dan Schiller notes, 'corporate reconstruction around networks was not limited to any sector but was economywide' (1999: 13). This 'economywide' transformation through computerization, networking and automation is what has made the ICT revolution truly revolutionary. ICTs have what has been termed 'enabling' qualities, meaning that they are able to be applied across almost all industries, transforming them and making them ICT-dependent in very short order. For example, the steam engine and the telegraph were certainly revolutionary technologies, but it was decades before their influences rippled out into society more generally. The ICT revolution, by contrast, has been widespread and lightning-fast. Moreover, its prolific logic demands that interconnectivity drives the need for more interconnectivity, across more and more sectors of the economy, bringing more industries, more businesses and more people into its digital thrall.

Using the computer and networking technology that was now becoming available, medium and large businesses rapidly began to automate and interconnect their own processes such as manufacturing, administration, billing, information flows and so on. These in-house networks were called *intranets*. However, although businesses must compete with rivals in the marketplace, they must also collaborate with suppliers, customers and partners in joint ventures. Business-to-business networking was thus a major deepening and widening of the overall networking process. This expansion of the network, and the catalyst for the development of new networking technologies, came about through what are termed *extranets*. 'Extranets', as Schiller (1999: 17) writes,

> ... allowed corporations to expand their shielded activities by linking up with collaborators. Cutting edge network applications (voice and video) were also

expedited within these inhouse corporate systems, ahead of their appearance on the open Internet.

For business, a logical externalization of this development is what we have come to call *e-commerce*. However, as Thomas Frank (2000) argues, in the 1990s *zeitgeist*, many CEOs began to believe much of their own hype regarding the business possibilities of the Internet. Anything was possible through the Internet, it was claimed, much of it implicitly based upon cutting out the 'human factor'. Investors drooled at the idea of cutting their wages bill. This meant more profit for business, and so all sorts of schemes were dreamed up that envisioned millions of mouse-clicking customers who would clamour to the Internet to consume everything from pizzas and CDs to cars and houses. The high street, some of the more radical boosters imagined (or led others to imagine), was to be replaced by the Information Superhighway; and the shopping mall would soon be a thing of the past – a tacky aberrance, the appalling effect of low-tech consumerism. At the same time an Internet economic bubble began to inflate dangerously, much of it due to this ideology of techno-inevitability drummed up through the nexus between Wall Street analysts, Internet 'gurus', industry boosters and the not inconsiderable gullibility of CEOs and shareholders (Frank 2000).

Amazon.com was founded in 1994 as an online bookseller and became the archetypal Internet start-up and prototype for the New Economy. The Internet effect meant that businesses began to do well in the developed countries; profits were rising and the stock markets boomed. Excess capital from what Alan Greenspan, Chairman of the Federal Reserve Board, called an 'irrationally exuberant' stock market was diverted into ten thousand different dotcoms with fifty thousand different sure-fire, make-lots-of-money ideas. Wannabe Bill Gateses who assured investors that they were 'in on the ground' in something that was going to be as big as Microsoft were also in abundant supply in that dizzying decade.

History records that things did not quite turn out the way Wall Street and corporate boardrooms across the world thought they would. Amazon.com is still with us and even managed to turn a profit for the first time in 2002 (a modest five million dollars). But many, many others burned shareholders' money spectacularly on their way to bankruptcy and oblivion as the promise of e-commerce underwhelmed the public at large. Symptomatic of the folly of the dotcom boom was www.boo.com, an online fashion retailer headed by a Swedish couple who had no business track record or Internet experience – just a purportedly cool-sounding domain name and a lot of credulous investors. In 1999/2000 over one hundred million pounds was squandered by www.boo.com in the space of six months before it filed for bankruptcy (Lee 2000).

Paralleling the rise of the Internet bubble was the massive and largely successful effort over the late 1990s and early 2000s to bring the Internet to the people. To make e-commerce work, consumers would have to have easy and low-cost network access.

Thus the drive to make networks part of everyday life began in earnest as going online became cheaper and more convenient almost by the month. Competition to load potential consumers onto the Internet reached a new level with the launch in 1998 of the ISP Freeserve.com that would, for the cost of a local phone call, allow people to go online, browse and, its owners hoped, spend, spend, spend! Again, numbers of Internet users soared, climbing year on year to reach 530 million users in 2001, with a predicted 1.1 billion in 2005 (Computer Industry Almanac 2002).

The jury is still out on whether e-commerce is the wave of the future, notwithstanding the billions of dollars spent and the tens of thousands of jobs created – only to be vaporized in the space of a few crazy years in the effort to make it work. The network society, however, grows at a rate of knots and raw Internet users' data do not paint the whole picture. Millions now inhabit the network society through Internet-enabled mobile phones, PDAs, wireless computers, etc., with new connectible devices coming on to the market constantly. Connectivity and interconnectivity are set only to become denser. Broadband access, the next big killer app, is presently being sold as the next wave to catch, making, so it is promised, dial-up access seem as old and as useful in today's world as the flint axe. Telecom and ISP companies are shaving margins down to almost nothing to get users 'always-on'. And 'always-on', for the CEO, means always ready to sell and always ready to advertise and always ready to entice the user to spend more and more of his or her time (and money) in the commodified cyberspace of the network.

Despite the mania, the reckless investments, the hyperbolic rhetoric, the fact that Freeserve.com is no longer free, and despite the criminal malfeasance on the part of more than a few, the network society is here to stay. Indeed, it can only deepen and broaden its scope, given the prolific logic underpinning it. Reading the development of capitalism historically leads to the conclusion that what is happening in the wake of the dotcom crash is the classic 'shake-out' of the capitalist economy; and in true social-Darwinist style, the strongest will survive and some will in fact thrive. Moreover we can expect the drivers of the network society to become fewer in number and to begin to resemble globalized oligopolies. A few mega-corporations in media, entertainment, IT, telecommunications and so on will dominate and help shape how we live, think and organize our lives (this is already happening, as we shall see). Lots of money has been wasted, but a lot can still be made and so electronic networks will continue to have the technological momentum to shape society in ways that many of us will have little choice in.

Digital capitalism is here to stay. The revolution has gone too far for there to be anything other than the continued informationization of how capitalism (and by extension, society) is organized. And if e-commerce does not succeed in making the high street shops redundant, so what? There is still a bundle to be made in, say, *e-learning* another new 'industry' said to be worth around 4.5 trillion dollars by 2010 (Stewart 2001: 2).

Digital Globalization

Just as there could be no network society (as we know it) without the economic imperatives of capitalism, then so too there could be no globalization (as we know it) without the ICT revolution. The ICT revolution and the processes of globalization have mutually reinforced one another to evolve into a super-charged capitalism. This has resulted from a process of 'convergence' that has its origins in the so-called 'resolution' to the 'crises of capitalism' of the 1970s that we discussed in the previous section. Convergence has brought capitalism to a higher order of organization, complexity and flexibility (Hassan 2000a). To be sure, the processes of globalization itself take certain modes that writers and commentators may give more or less emphasis to – such as the cultural and the political as well as the economic. However, it is my contention that the convergence of neoliberalism and the ICT revolution has meant that the *economic* dimension is the one that carries most of the power and momentum. To a very substantial degree, it underpins and facilitates the 'globalization' of both the cultural and the political. This is not to argue that the economy is the sole driver of the cultural and the political, but simply that the levels of cultural and political globalization attained today would not have been possible without the convergence of ICTs and neoliberal capitalism.

In this section I will try to substantiate the argument that digital globalization is a process underpinned by the economics of neoliberal capitalism. This will show that globalization today is primarily the economic colonization of increasing parts of culture and society, a powerfully dynamic process that has served to *intensify* and *extensify* capitalism in ways that are historically unparalleled. Moreover, this dual process of globalization, or what I have elsewhere called 'inside' and 'outside' globalization (Hassan 2000b), is rapidly creating a world where issues of cultural identity and democratic citizenship are becoming problematic. Let me explain what I mean.

'Globalization', of course, did not begin in the late 1970s. In its economic, cultural and political forms it has been underway for a very long time. Indeed, at an extreme point one could argue that humans began to 'globalize' when they first began to walk upright around a million years ago, and spread out from the savannahs of Africa to colonize the planet in a long and slow process of intercontinental migration (Diamond 1999). Or we could argue that globalization 'really' began in 1492 when Columbus came across the Americas; an unexpected but nonetheless momentous 'discovery' which began the process of (Europeans) being able to conceive of the world not only as a 'planet' – helping, unintendedly, to confirm the works of Ptolemy and Copernicus – but also as a singular space to be colonized and marketized. Or again, we could update globalization's originary point to something more recognizable, that is, to the dynamics of capitalism. This saw the beginnings of systematic global trade and communications and the dynamism we attach to modernity. Thus we find Marx and Engels writing in the *Communist Manifesto* of 1848 that [national industries] are dislodged by new industries . . . that no longer work up indigenous raw material, but raw material drawn from the remotest zones; industries whose products are consumed, not only at home but in every quarter of the globe. In place of old wants, satisfied by the productions of the country, we find new wants, requiring for their satisfaction the products of distant lands and climes. In place of the old local and national seclusion and self-sufficiency, we have intercourse in every direction, universal interdependence of nations.

(Marx and Engels 1975)

Arguably, these are all stages at which we could point to globalization in action; or, perhaps more accurately, stages along the *longue durée* of globalization where it took on very differing constitutive elements. Compared with today, however, these earlier phases in globalization were far less intensive and extensive. Marx and Engels's rather breathless rhetoric aside, the majority of people in the world of 1848 could expect to lead fairly localized existences, essentially unaffected by the 'world' at large. Indeed, the 'world' at large, that is to say, the world as an interconnected and interdependent space that could be conceived of by most people, hardly existed at all. War and revolution (industrial and political) could sweep over them (as they did in Europe in the very year the *Communist Manifesto* was published), but the 'world' at large, the 'world' of capitalism, did not enter every nook and cranny of their social and cultural lives. The dynamics of this earlier time were suffused with their own temporality. Things took longer, and technologies, in relative terms, were much cruder and less insinuating than those of today. Farmers would go on farming, and city dwellers' lives would still revolve around their homes, family, community, work and town. The local and the global would stay fairly separate spheres for a while yet. Indeed, for most of the twentieth century this was still the case. Notwithstanding the domination of capitalism in the west and in many of the developing regions, people across the world could still maintain separate spheres in their lives, where the economic, the cultural, the social, the private and so on, could be clearly delineated.

It is through the convergence of neoliberalism and the ICT revolution that the age-old processes of globalization began to exhibit a *radical* intensity and extensity. We have seen how ICTs are endowed with 'enabling' qualities that allow them to transform not just one industry but many. We have noted, too, the words of Dan Schiller who argued that the effect of 'enabling' ICTs 'was not limited to any sector but was economy-wide' (1999: 13). However, it is more than this again. The revolutions in neoliberalism and ICTs that bring the market into every sphere of social and cultural life have rapidly intensified the experience of being in a single, interconnected, interdependent and commercialized space. In subsequent chapters I will expand upon this central issue of 'intensification' but for now I will illustrate what I mean by way of a quotation. Since the 1990s there have been many attempts at defining what globalization is from a variety of political, economic and cultural perspectives (see, for example, Appadurai 1990; Omahe 1990; Barber 1996; Falk 1999). However, for me, Naomi Klein (2002: xx) states simply and concisely what globalization *is* and what globalization *does*, in the following words. 'The economic euphemism', she notes,

> that goes by the name of 'globalization' now reaches into every aspect of life, transforming every activity and natural resource into a measured and owned commodity . . . It is also about feeding the market's insatiable need for growth by redefining as 'products' entire sectors that were previously considered part of the 'commons' and not for sale. The invading of the public by the private has reached into categories such as health and education, of course, but also ideas, genes, seed, now purchased, patented and fenced off . . .

This has meant that not only has the 'world' come to us through digital globalization, but also that the 'world' is now *part* of us through its colonization of 'every aspect of life'. And as Klein argues, this is a thoroughly commodified world, creating a commodified culture based upon the pervasive ethos of commercialism and the profit motive.

Extensive globalization is the parallel dynamic to the colonization of our local and private spaces by neoliberalism. A way to think about this is to consider that if intensive globalization brings the commercial and uncertain world of neoliberalism to *you personally*, then extensive globalization makes sure that this happens to everyone else, everywhere else, too. ICTs and the border-busting philosophy of neoliberalism are succeeding mightily in bringing the 'global village' vision of McLuhan into reality – but in ways that even the prescience of McLuhan could not have imagined. More precisely, ICTs have 'enabled' the interconnectivity of regions, cities, economies, businesses and individuals and their processes of trade, production and consumption into a networked society, one that now encompasses almost the entire planet. The diverse and pluralistic 'local' is being fundamentally challenged and changed by the predominantly commercial and homogeneous 'global'. This, as one might expect, has not been a smooth process; in fact it is one increasingly fraught with uncertainty and risk. As Anthony Giddens (1997: 4–5) has noted,

> We are at the beginning of a fundamental shakeout of world society, which comes from numerous sources . . . It comes from the impact of technology on global markets and also from the disappearance of the Soviet Union. We are at the beginning of this process and we don't really know as yet where it is going to lead us . . . *If you could say that the west controlled the earlier phases of globalisation, the current phase is one which nobody controls.* (emphasis added)

In a world where no one is in control, extensive globalization, or the imposition of an unstable neoliberal order, is generating much dissonance, disjuncture and uncertainty. In his book *Jihad vs McWorld* Benjamin Barber argues that neoliberal globalization is setting up a dichotomy between the local and the global, between what he terms the 'ancient subnational and ethnic borders from within' and the ideology of 'universalizing markets' (1996: 23). The 'Jihad' in Barber's dichotomy are those peoples, institutions, belief-systems and cultures that are antithetical to the perceived homogeneity of 'McWorld', that is to say, that of the globalization and colonization by the culture and values of the likes of McDonalds, Coca-Cola, the Body Shop and Vodafone. Barber's dichotomy is interesting. What sets it apart from books such as Samuel Huntington's *Clash of Civilisations* – which posits the argument that the two distinct and irreconcilable worlds and societies (Islam and Christianity) are set to become 'the fundamental source of conflict in this new world' (1993: 22) – is that Jihad and McWorld inhabit the *same* world and the *same* society (a networked society) that is trapped in a 'powerful and paradoxical interdependence' (1996: 22). Barber goes on to write that

> . . . Jihad *and* McWorld are at work, both visible sometimes in the same country at the very same instant. Iranian zealots keep one ear tuned to the mullahs urging holy war and the other cocked to Rupert Murdoch's Star television beaming in *Dynasty, Donahue* and *The Simpsons* from hovering satellites. Chinese entrepreneurs vie for the attention of party cadres in Beijing and simultaneously pursue KFC franchises in cities like Nanjing, Hangzou and Xian where twenty eight outlets serve over 100,000 customers a day. The Russian Orthodox church, even as it struggles to renew an ancient faith, has entered a joint venture with California businessmen to bottle and sell natural waters under the rubric Saint Springs Water Company. Serbian assassins wear Adidas sneakers and listen to Madonna on the Walkman headphones as they take aim through their gunscopes at scurrying Sarajevo civilians looking to fill family watercans. Orthodox Hasids and brooding neo-Nazis have both turned to rock music to get their traditional messages out to the new generation, while fundamentalists plot virtual conspiracies on the Internet.

We can add to this litany a new and more dangerous element to emerge from Barber's 'paradoxical interdependence'. In the mid-1990s the terrorist group al-Qa'ida, an Islamic fundamentalist organization that wants to impose a medieval theocracy across large parts of the planet, began to wage war on what they call the 'Crusader–Jewish coalition' of the west – using twenty-first-century means. Al-Qa'ida is a closed network that skulks the open byways of the network society. Satellite phones, augmented by the Internet, email, fax and so on, connect al-Qa'ida cells around the world. When it wants to get its message to the world at large, it sends a videocassette, or an email to CNN, the BBC or to the Al-Jazeera television network – the Arab equivalent of CNN. And al-Qa'ida's *jihadis* also reflect the class nature of the 'paradox' that is Jihad against McWorld. The educated young men with experience of the cosmopolitan worlds of Hamburg, London and New York and who bombed the World Trade Center and the Pentagon in 2001 shared the same fundamentalist worldview as the semi-literate peasants who helped organize the fire-bombings in Bali a year later.

For Barber, McWorld represents the culture and values of the 'new temples of liberty' such as MasterCard, Disney or Louis Vuitton (1996: 23). And today it is increasingly clear that these new gods are being defended in the US, in Britain, in Australia and in other bastions of neoliberalism *in the name of liberty*. Accordingly, the 'war against terrorism' initiated in 2001 by the Bush administration in the US is, in the analysis offered here, a war to ensure the freedom for (US) capital and to expand unfettered wherever and whenever profit, or the expectation of profit, presents itself. And in a world where no one is in control, with an atrophying state system, an increasingly irrelevant United Nations and growing unilateralism, this 'war' is pursued by the trigger-happy governments in the major democratic countries of the world who undermine their own liberal democratic traditions through the introduction of 'emergency' laws that diminish individual and collective freedoms – in the name of the 'war against terror'.

Digital globalization makes all this possible. The ultimate paradox, however, in a globalizing world of increasingly connected individuals, of increasingly seamless and networked markets, of interdependence and interconnected economies, countries and regions is what Zygmunt Bauman (1998: 18) calls a 'new polarization'. It is a world where meaning has spun off from its traditional anchors and is sucked into the virtual ether of the network. I will conclude this section with a quotation from Bauman that I reprint here at some length as it captures well the social, cultural and *ontological* costs of the convergence of neoliberalism and the ICT revolution. He writes:

> . . . rather than homogenising the human condition, the technological annulment of temporal/spatial distances tends to polarize it. It emancipates certain humans from territorial constraints and renders certain community-generating meanings exterritorial – while denuding the territory, to which other people go on being confined, of its meaning and its identity-endowing capacity. For some people it augurs an unprecedented freedom from physical obstacles and unheard-of ability to move and act from a distance. For others, it portends the impossibility of appropriating and domesticating the locality from which they have little chance of cutting themselves free in order to move elsewhere. With 'distances no longer meaning anything', localities, separated by distances, also lose their meanings. This, however, augurs freedom of meaning-creating for some, but portends ascription to meaninglessness for others. Some can now move out of the locality – any locality – at will. Others watch helplessly the sole locality they inhabit moving away from under their feet.

Digital Acceleration

A major feature of this techno-economic auto-momentum – and significant cause of our loss of control – is what James Gleick calls the 'acceleration of just about everything'. Gleick's book, entitled *Faster: The Acceleration of Just About Everything* (2000), is an interesting, if somewhat breezy, account of the many and varied effects upon life in the 'heyday of speed' (2000: 6). The trouble with the book is that after reading it you are no wiser as to *why* we have now all got speed religion and drive in a permanent fast lane. It's implied, though. The effects of computers, the Internet, microprocessors and the digital compression of clock time into nanoseconds permeate the book. Effects, but no real causes. Making the locus of this increase in the velocity of life much more explicit is theorist Paul Virilio. Virilio is a pioneer thinker on the effects of speed upon power, military strategy, culture and the economy (1995a, 1997, 2000). In his *Information Bomb* (2000), Virilio argues that 'instrumental, digital pro-cedures' underpin the acceleration of life, leading to the 'acceleration of reality' (2000: 2–3). And in a little-noticed gem of an Internet article from 1995 entitled 'Speed and Information: Cyberspace Alarm!', Virilio prefigures some of the thoughts that materialize in *Information Bomb*. He links the 'acceleration of reality' with the revolu-tion in ICTs and the shift to neoliberalism. Through digital globalization, he notes, we 'are facing a new phenomenon: loss of orientation [stemming from] liberalization and the deregulation of financial markets' (1995b).

We can build here on Virilio's ideas and situate the locus of acceleration and 'loss of orientation' not simply in ICTs *per se*, or even the Internet, but in the ever-growing thicket of interconnected networks that comprise the neoliberal network society. A metaphor often used to describe networks is as an 'environment', the 'network environment'. I believe the term 'environment' is much more than a handy metaphor. Indeed, it describes the *reality* of what networks constitute, just as much as the 'natural' environment, or 'built' environment do. As John S. Quarterman (2002) argues,

> The Internet is an ecosystem. It is composed of many interacting parts, ISPs, datacenters, enterprises, end-users, each of them drawing sustenance from the others and from raw materials. Each of them needs to make informed decisions. This is an ecology. And this ecology whose life forms are corporations and people is also a market.

Importantly, this 'ecosystem' generates and sustains its own temporality, the digital meter of the network. The more we inhabit the network – on a PC at work or at home, on a PDA on the train, or in the street with a mobile phone clamped to the ear – the more we inhabit its temporally accelerated domain, with its potentially disorienting and frenetic pace. As the influence, scope and depth of digital networks have become more and more encompassing of what we do, the more the thrust of acceleration has its impact. Gleick's book is useful in that we can see how almost every aspect of our lives is being lifted out of the thousand-year-old meter of clock-time (we'd just got used to that) and into the much higher tempo of real-time. However, a more explicit way to think about the locus and pace of acceleration is not through the 'non time' of real-time (which implies total 'instantaneity'), but the much more asynchronous tem-porality I call *network time* (Hassan 2003b). There are many time-durations in the network: for example, there is the ostensibly 'real-time' of the landline or mobile telephone call; the satellite videoconference; the 'instantaneous' or delayed time (depending on when we choose to read it) of email; the relatively fast time of broadband Internet, or the slower time of the dial-up connection and so on. The point is, however, that taken as a networked totality, these represent a generalized *acceleration*. This new temporality has been feeding into culture and society for at least the last twenty years, contributing, more or less quickly, to what Gleick correctly terms the 'acceleration of just about everything'.

Thinking only slightly historically it is easy to see the effects of acceleration almost everywhere. Jeremy Rifkin has studied the effects of network time upon business. For example, trustworthy and traditional products such as typewriters, he notes, used to last for years, even decades. Computers, by contrast, have a shelf-life of a year or two. The PC I write these words on is less than a year old, but already it is showing its age. When first used, the hard drive ran smoothly and silently; now it rattles and groans with signs that seem to indicate that a dust-collecting retirement or landfill oblivion may be on the horizon. The squander of resources is monumental. Acceleration and waste is an under-explored link that I must make a note of when I have the time. Behemoth computer maker Hewlett Packard (itself once stolid and traditional) now makes most of its revenue from products that did not exist a year ago. Japanese consumer products have an average three-month life-cycle, with Sony introducing 5000 new products in 1995. This is not just a ICTs thing. Massively 'enabled' by ICTs, acceleration cuts across every industry, from pharmaceuticals and publishing to burgers and beer. Miller Brewing Corporation (how traditional can you get?) makes ninety per cent of its revenue from beers that did not exist a couple of years ago (Rifkin 2000: 21–2). Supermarket shelves change their displays constantly, with new products disappearing as fast as they appear in the manic and constant turnover that strives to hit upon something that will sell.

This is how business *must* be run under its techno-economic logic. As Howard S. Charney, vice-president of Cisco Systems, said in a speech in March 2000: 'In the Internet Economy, the race is now about the fast versus the slow' (Charney 2000). In the raging pace set by globally networked stock markets and gung-ho CEOs, most corporations are now under extreme pressure to produce results (accurate or otherwise) and do it fast. Annual corporate results now have to be submitted quarterly – and show profit – or the share value is in danger of an 'adverse market reaction'. Much of the 'creative accounting' and out-and-out criminality that has been such a feature of the New Economy has its roots in the immense and constant pressure the new velocity brings. And predictably, the network society cycles of fast product turnaround, fast profit and fast accounting have also incorporated fast *people* turnaround. The Japanese just-in-time system of production has been refined by Anglo-American capitalism to include 'just-in-time staff', or the turning of casualized labour on and off like a tap when required. Hire them fast and fire them even faster.

The network logic of driving products, people, processes faster and faster comes at a cost. And, as Virilio cautions, 'What will be gained from electronic information and electronic communication will necessarily result in a loss somewhere else' (1995b: 1). Zygmunt Bauman puts his finger on something more specific when he argues that 'the trouble with the contemporary condition is that society has stopped questioning itself' (1998: 5). What this amounts to, according to David Shenk, is a 'memory loss', an inability to digest and remember information coming at us increasingly thick and fast – where contexts, instances, events, histories, our cognitive basis for self-reflection, seem to 'vanish in a sea of data' (1997: 48). In his novel *Slowness*, Milan Kundera put the same sentiment somewhat more acutely when he wrote that 'the degree of speed is directly proportional to the intensity of forgetting' (1996: 2).

Such are the effects of network time acceleration. As we shall see in the following chapters, network time, or the 'acceleration of just about everything', also has important consequences for the ever-shifting patternings of media and cultural production in a hyper-connected world. Accordingly, this dimension, together with the inter-penetrating dimensions of digital technology, capitalism and globalization that we have just discussed, constitute, I believe, a useful framework for contextualization, enabling us to make explicit the fundamental changes taking place in the world today.

Before we go on to analyse media, culture and politics in the network society more specifically, I want to say a word or two about whinging.

Pessimism or critique?

The shape, tone and voice of what I have written so far have been deliberate. Some will no doubt call it 'pessimistic', or 'Luddite', or maybe just more whinging when we should be 'optimistic'. Academics and social theorists in particular, when writing on the effects of ICTs in media and culture, are routinely shot down for the intellectual felony of 'being one-sided and too negative' as James Slevin says of Manuel Castells in his *The Internet and Society* (2001: 51). Slevin goes on to issue a call for more balance when weighing up the pros and cons of ICTs within society. Actually, I agree. Much more balance would in fact be a very good thing. What Slevin seems to ignore, however, is that through our media, through our exposure to ICTs at work and elsewhere, we are continually bombarded with optimism. From Bill Gates right down to the now-mandatory weekly IT supplements in most newspapers, optimism oozes from every pore of our network society. As I argued at the beginning of this chapter, the Digital Revolution no longer needs its heroes to disseminate its ideology – the processes are now largely automatic and systemic.

That Slevin ignores questions of ideology is a typical effect of the success of neo-liberalism in projecting informationized capitalism, the deification of the market, and the worship of speed religion as essential ingredients in the ultimate form of human social development. It is also symptomatic of the general malaise, I think, when an otherwise useful book such as Slevin's takes time out to criticize Castells' alleged 'negativity', while ignoring questions of the overwhelming preponderance of ideological 'optimism' that we face at almost every turn. Indeed, for many, to call a work 'negative' or 'pessimistic' becomes a handy device for the dogmatist to dismiss views found to be inconvenient. I don't think Slevin does this on purpose, but the effect is the same. He shoots down thoughtful critique (as pessimism), while leaving issues of ideology and its overwhelming preponderance on the side of rationalizing information technology, capitalism and the market unaddressed.

Nevertheless, as Robins and Webster argue in their *Times of the Technoculture*, the charge of pessimism may have validity if there is 'no alternative to the new technological order', proffered (1999: 8). Read in this way, we can argue that the prevailing optimistic worldview of Bill Gates, of much of academia, of the high-energy IT supplements and of the mass media in general are in fact deeply *pessimistic* in that there is nothing else on offer, no alternatives. What I have tried to do in this first chapter is to make explicit the elements of the power/ideology nexus that underscore perspectives of the network society. This then is not 'pessimism' but *critique*, and critique that argues that there are *always* alternatives, always other ways of being and seeing – we just need the intellectual tools to unearth and recognize this fundamental fact. Raymond Williams puts the issue superbly in his *Politics and Letters* (1979: 252) when he writes:

> However dominant a social system may be, the very meaning of its domination involves a limitation or selection of the activities it covers, so that by definition it cannot exhaust all social experience, which therefore always contains space for alternative acts and alternative intentions which are not yet articulated as a social institution or even project.

More pertinent to the issues at hand, McKenzie Wark (2001:1) writes:

> There may well be an emerging consensus as to how wearying it is to keep up with the 'speed' of the Internet. Why not take Deleuze's advice and try to be 'untimely'? This need not always, as in Virilio, mean . . . counterposing the slowness of reflection to the speed of the media . . . but [of] seeking another rhythm.

Recognition and understanding are only the first steps in creating such a space as Williams argues for, and for having the self-reflexivity to be 'untimely' sometimes, or to find 'another rhythm', as Wark urges. Recognition and understanding is all I propose to offer in these pages. Realizations of alternative projects will always themselves be the outcome of practical social and political processes. Moreover, responsibility rests upon the individual and the individual as part of a collectivity, to conceive, plan and implement conscious (explicit) tactics and strategies for alternatives to the 'new technological order' in his or her own life. It is in this sense I want the following discussion on media, culture and politics in the network society to be understood.

Further reading

Barber, B. (2000) *Jihad vs McWorld*. New York, NY: Times Books.

Castells, M. (1996/97/98) *The Information Age: Economy, Society, and Culture* (three volumes). Oxford: Blackwell.

Castells, M. (2001) *The Internet Galaxy*. New York, NY: Oxford University Press.

Robins, K. and Webster, F. (1999) *Times of the Technoculture*. London: Routledge.

Schiller, D. (1999) *Digital Capitalism*. Cambridge, MA: MIT Press.

Virilio, P. (2000) *Information Bomb*. London: Verso.

2 | THE INFORMATIONIZATION OF MEDIA AND CULTURE

Ever bigger and more encompassing corporate mergers suggest emergent synergies between the Internet and media culture, and thus the information and entertainment industries. These interactions of technology and capital are producing fecund forms of technocapitalism and a technoculture which promise that the new millennium will be full of novelties, innovation, hype, and instability.

changes in (M)/(C)

(Kellner 2003)

This chapter is pivotal and goes to the heart of my understanding of the radically altered dynamics of media and culture in the network society. What I argue is that in their dominant and world-altering forms, these domains, these spaces, have been 'informationalized' by the logic of the neoliberal globalization/ICT revolution nexus, and evolve now on the digital plane of the network. This is an unprecedented development, and its consequences may be significant. It is an important development because the spaces of media and cultural production have evolved historically (in the pre-information age), with their own dynamics. These spaces, to be sure, influenced each other and interacted deeply; but the fact that they could be analytically and empirically separate meant that the 'dialectical tension' (2003: 2) that Baudrillard spoke of could function as the basis for the construction of a critical literacy necessary to enable a level of autonomy and sovereignty within these spaces. Informationization has served to obliterate much of the interstices between these realms, along with the dialectical tension that held the unified whole in place.

To understand this process, I have organized this chapter in the following way and for the following reasons. To begin with I will make more explicit the terms 'media' and 'culture' themselves, to open them up and make them amenable to understanding through the context of theory drawn from elements of the major historical and contemporary literature. From there I will take a slightly historical perspective on the development of the realms of media and cultural production. This brief 'stepping back' will allow us to compare the dynamical processes of media and culture in both the pre-information age and in the age of informationization itself.

So what is 'media' and what is 'culture' anyway?

These terms are so prevalent, so much part of our daily language, that many of us acquire and internalize them without giving much attention to their definitions, meanings and implications. 'Media' we take, vaguely, as meaning 'newspapers', or 'radio', or 'television'; or, more recently, 'the Internet', a technology that is replete with its own various elements of 'multimedia'. We can also personalize the term, with 'the media' meaning, again somewhat vaguely, journalists, or people who work in 'the media', an industry headed by 'media moguls'. It's the same story with the term 'culture'. Often it comes connoted with a fuzzy sense of something that is 'different' to us, or something we have which makes 'us' different to 'others'. And so we can think of (but may have exquisite difficulty in defining), say, 'British culture', or 'American culture', or 'Japanese culture'. The term can also be used fairly readily to describe such things as music styles (world music culture), fashion (street culture), or 'sub-cultures' (skate-boarding, trainspotting, stamp-collecting or punk), or even the 'culture' of an organization. Apart from indicating a sense of 'difference', the word does not connote what *makes* culture, what *sustains* or what can *change* it. In the network society both these terms are now ultra-prevalent and so a basic understanding of their meanings is increasingly vital if we are to understand our new 'mediated world' and its 'globalized culture' – terms that are becoming as hotly disputed as they are widespread.

In fact we do not need to go very far to find meanings, definitions and examples of both 'media' and 'culture' and so their explication will be brief. The exercise, though, is an extremely useful one. It will help make what is implicit in these terms more explicit, and will lay a conceptual groundwork for a better understanding of what these terms mean, and how 'media' and 'culture' interact.

Media

We can start with some definitions. 'Media' is actually a plural form, the plural form of 'medium' – a wordshift that immediately throws up a different way to think about it. 'Medium', as the *Collins English Dictionary* defines it, is 'an intervening substance or agency for transmitting or producing an effect'. We can see it thus clearly beginning to link to related words with similar meanings such as 'intermediary', or 'mediation', or 'median'. These words suggest an 'in between-ness', something 'in the middle', the 'substance or agency' that either transmits or produces an effect between the individual and the world. In short, media is that which connects us to the world and to our environment, allowing us to make an impression upon it – and *vice versa*.

The term 'media' began to gain currency in language during the nineteenth century with the introduction of widespread communication forms such as newspapers. In the early part of the twentieth century, with the emergence of even larger circulations of newspapers, magazines, radio, cinema, etc., people began to speak in terms of 'mass media'. However, the 'substance or agency' definitions are important, as they indissolubly bind up 'media' with 'technology'. For example, a newspaper is a form of media that can be more or less 'mass', depending upon the size of its readership. It is also quite clearly a *technology*, a media technology. Anthropologist Walter Ong describes, in his *Orality and Literacy* (1982), how media technologies such as writing change what it is for us to be human in the world. He developed the concept of the 'sensorium' to describe the totality of the human senses, each of which develop more or less depending upon the cultural, technological and natural environment(s) that the individual lives within. The development of writing had a fundamental effect upon the sensorium. According to Ong, ancient, pre-literate societies were based upon oral communication, causing the ear to be prominent within the sensorium. With the introduction of the technology and medium of writing, however, the sensorium rearranged its priorities in accordance with its changed environment to favour the eye. The advent of writing, in other words, changed the societies into which it had been introduced, from oral societies based upon sound and hearing to visual ones dependent upon the written word (and later printed and electronic images). In this view, media technologies – from a 'simple' technology such as the written word, to the mass complex of images that come to us through photographs, film, videogames etc. – have a powerful effect on how we perceive the world and how we derive meaning from it.

In his famous dictum 'the medium is the message', Marshall McLuhan had earlier made basically the same argument with respect to electronic media, but with a significant difference in emphasis – the dynamics and effects of acceleration. In his *Understanding Media* (1964: 16) he writes that

> the message of any medium or technology is the change of scale or of pace or pattern that it introduces into human affairs. The railway did not introduce movement or transportation or wheel or road into human society, but it accelerated and enlarged the scale of previous human functions, creating totally new kinds of cities and new kinds of work or leisure.

In the social and cultural world everything is media; we apprehend what is 'out there' through mediation. From 'simple' media such as speech, writing and printing, to more complex mass media such as radio, television and the Internet, we experience and understand the world and our place in it through the processes of mediation. In some ways this is a fairly mundane point. But to be able to comprehend the process more fully, to make explicit what is implicit, we need to appreciate the nature of the 'substance and agency' through which we make our mark upon the world and the world makes its mark upon us.

The important point to realize when thinking about communications media is that they are *technologies*. As technologies, we need to understand them on at least two levels. First, as we saw in Chapter 1, technologies are the product of a particular social system; they are social constructions that reflect the nature of the society that created them. And as Williams urges us, we need always to be able to 'identify and challenge [their] real agencies' or they will appear, like the workings of the capitalist economy, as 'neutral' (1974: 135). The development of writing, for example, created a new source of power and a new social division between those who could (and were allowed) to read and write, and those who could not. Secondly, we need also to recognize that although new technologies emerge with a specific intent they carry also a host of 'unintended consequences'. To return to McLuhan once more: acceleration in electronic media creates 'totally new kinds of cities and new kinds of work or leisure', most of them unknowable and more or less positive. What we can add to this, through the insights of Ong and following from the arguments I made in Chapter 1, is that they always have the *potential* to create new ways of seeing the world, new ways of under-standing the world and new ways of being in the world. Again, much of what unfolds will be unknowable and unintended, but will be shaped in large part, nonetheless, by the dominant political, economic and cultural forces that bring the technology (the new media) into being.

Culture

Notwithstanding its ubiquity, a widely acknowledged definition is not easy to pin down. If you ask the question 'what is culture?' the answer will depend largely upon whom you ask. Consider these quotes:

British prime minister, Tony Blair:
[Britain] has overtaken France and Italy to become the fourth largest economy in the world. [It] has the language of the new economy, more brilliant artists, actors and directors than any comparable country in the world, some of the best scientists and inventors in the world, the best armed forces in the world, the best teachers and doctors and nurses, the best people any nation could wish for . . .

President George W. Bush:
September the 11th brought out the best in America, and the best in this Congress. And I join the American people in applauding your unity and resolve. Now Americans deserve to have this same spirit directed toward addressing problems here at home. I'm a proud member of my party – yet as we act to win the war,

protect our people, and create jobs in America, we must act, first and foremost, not as Republicans, not as Democrats, but as Americans.

Pop singer, Madonna:
When I was a child, I always thought that the world was mine, that it was some stomping ground for me, full of opportunities. I always had this attitude that I was going to go out into the world and do all the things I wanted to do.

In their different ways these three individuals speak directly of culture and how their view of the world is shaped by it. Depending on one's perspective, one may cynically deride the quotes by the politicians, as something you would expect them to say, and see Madonna's as 'cool', more 'real' and in tune with the times; more aspirational in terms of the individual. However, politicians consciously target known constituencies, and in these cases, those for whom the cultural stereotypes of patriotism, community and so on resonate strongly. They may read or hear the words of Blair and Bush and find them inspirational – and view Ms Ciccone's as simply vacuous or shallow and typical of today's egoism, selfishness and having no sense of belonging. The point is that their cultural worldview is derived from the *meanings* they give to them, the *resonances* that make these cultural prisms (real or imagined) important to them. Today cultural differences are more or less acknowledged, though not necessarily accepted or understood. Accordingly, we can make fun of, empathize with, be hostile to, or ignore those whose cultural worldview does not resonate with our own.

It wasn't always so complex, so *laissez faire*, or so contestable a site. In the late nineteenth century, for example, the notion of 'culture' did not enter the heads of most people and certainly did not constitute part of everyday language as it does today. However, some did seek to define and understand it, albeit for very particular socio-economic and 'cultural' reasons. The idea of culture in the higher reaches of society was straightforward and immutable. It came with one's class location, with supposedly only those with the correct breeding, manners and deportment of the *upper classes* able to appreciate and understand it and what it was. This was what later became known as 'high culture' and consisted of such things as going to the opera, being able to read and speak Latin, or French, knowing which fork to use at table, which books to read and so on.

Others saw issues of culture as something less fixed and more amorphous. During the mid- to late Victorian era the Industrial Revolution was in full swing and the concomitant rise of modernity and the 'mass society' was perceived as a threat by sections of the intellectual class. Industrialization had necessitated a degree of literacy in the masses and the educated elites saw this as a distinct threat to their rarefied cultural prerogatives. For example, Victorian novelist and intellectual George Gissing lamented the 'pretence' of education afforded by the English 'School-board system' as 'extending and deepening Vulgarity' in Britain (Carey 1992: 93). Substandard education, in other words, was causing society to be 'levelled down', diluting and debasing what was high and noble about British culture. A not dissimilar perspective on culture came from one of Gissing's contemporaries, Matthew Arnold. Arnold was an educator and a believer in the role of state education to raise the moral, social and cultural standards of the masses. He was also a believer in 'high culture' but thought that its attainment was simply a matter of good education that would 'level up' instead. In the Preface to his *Culture and Anarchy* ([1869] 1960), he wrote: 'Culture [is] a pursuit of our total perfection by means of getting to know, on all the matters which most concern us, the best which has been thought and said in the world.' In his well-meaning liberal Victorian way Arnold was saying that the masses deserve (his) culture – primarily because they have no culture of their own that is worthy of the name – and if they did, then it was undoubtedly of the 'vulgar', 'inferior' and 'low' kind.

These views on the essence of culture, expressed as either a hostile elitism or through a benign patronizing, were both common and dominant until at least after the Second World War. In the 1950s and 1960s Marxist historians such as E.P. Thompson and Raymond Williams were keen to explore the *class* dimensions of culture and cultural production and so laid the foundations of a whole academic discipline we know today as 'cultural studies'. In his *The Making of the English Working Class*, Thompson defined culture as society-wide and something 'embodied' in such things as 'traditions, value-systems, ideas and institutional forms' (1968: 7). Thompson's pioneering work led to questions of culture being seen more objectively and sociologically and as being informed by other dimensions such as identity, race, power, geography, consumption, language and class. In other words, cultural production came from *lived experience*. Williams famously expressed this all-encompassing and dynamic view of what consti-tuted culture in a 1958 essay entitled 'Moving from high culture to ordinary culture'. He wrote:

> Culture is ordinary: that is the first fact . . . We use the word culture in these two senses: to mean a whole way of life – the common meanings; to mean the arts and learning – the special processes of discovery and creative effort. Some writers reserve the word for one or other of these senses; I insist on both and on the significance of their conjunction. The questions I ask about our culture are questions about deep personal meanings. Culture is ordinary, in every society and in every mind.
>
> (1958a: 6)

Culture, in other words, is what we 'do' every day; the dual processes of 'meaning' and 'learning' that make up 'a whole way of life'. It is a lived process of meanings and values that appear to us as confirmations for our actions in the world and help us to orient ourselves within it. It is also, as Williams emphasizes, a process of 'learning', which implies that cultural production is an ongoing and evolving dynamic process. Meanings change, values change and so the patternings of culture change, too. It is this *plasticity* of cultural production that is the most important point, I think. Culture is not fixed, but is subject to shaping, reformulation and manipulation by wider forces 'out there' in society and 'in here' through the ways in which we ourselves help shape culture and society through our interactions with it. Moreover, if we learn culture and its meanings, then someone or some 'things' have to *teach* it. This realization takes us back, once more, to questions of power and where it resides in society. Traditionally, the social forces with the power to teach and disseminate culture and its meanings include such elements as family, religion, schools, friends – and *media*.

In a web essay entitled 'Cultural studies, multiculturalism and media culture', cultural theorist Douglas Kellner (2002) shows an acute awareness of the interaction between media and culture and so needs to be quoted at some length. He notes:

> We are immersed from cradle to grave in a media and consumer society and thus it is important to learn how to understand, interpret and criticize its meanings and messages. The media are a profound and often misperceived source of cultural pedagogy: They contribute to educating us how to behave and what to think, feel, believe, fear and desire – and what not to. The media are forms of pedagogy which teach us how to be men and women. They show us how to dress, look and consume; how to react to members of different social groups; how to be popular and successful and how to avoid failure; and how to conform to the dominant system of norms, values, practices and institutions. Consequently, the gaining of critical media literacy is an important resource for individuals and citizens in learning how to cope with a seductive cultural environment. Learning how to read, criticize and resist socio-cultural manipulation can help empower oneself in relation to dominant forms of media and culture. It can enhance individual sovereignty vis-à-vis media culture and give people more power over their cultural environment.

Economic globalization and the ICT revolution have made the world an even more mediated and interconnected place. This is a 'network society', but it is also at the same time a 'media society' where dominant forms of culture are now shaped and produced. This is an extension of Lash's (2002: 10) argument that there is 'no outside anymore' by way of spaces of critique and for the functioning dynamics of media and cultural production. They have become informationized and so we need to change the ways in which we think about media and about culture. As Lash argues, 'social and cultural theory would increasingly take on the form of *media theory*' (2002: 64) (italics in original). This argument sets up an interesting (and for us, vital) question. Do the processes of globalization and the ICT revolution and the informationization of society fragment power and create the basis for new and infinitely diverse cultures and ways of being? Alternatively, is there a definite pull toward the homogenization of culture, toward a uniformity of meanings, values and practices through the monotonous prism of information technology, technology that we neither have any real control over – nor have asked for?

To get some idea of what is at stake we need to spend some time looking at the historical dialectic or *interaction* between media and culture.

The dialectics of media–culture

If just about everything is mediated and culture is ordinary, then the nexus between media and culture must be a very important one. As Roger Silverstone (1999: 13) argues,

> Mediation involves the movement of meaning from one text to another, from one discourse to another, from one event to another. It involves the constant transformation of meanings, both large scale and small, significant and insignificant . . .

Movements of meaning, in other words, like Baudrillard's 'critical movements' (2003: 3), are what shape the patternings of cultural production; and mediation (media technologies) are what both produce meaning and shift them about (Tomlinson 1999). This is a pretty amorphous and shapeless way to think about the process and, as Silverstone goes on to explain, there are identifiable logics and dynamics that shape and form the process in one way or another. Media and cultural studies have had a long history in trying to discover how exactly (or inexactly) these interactions work. Early on, during the 1940s in fact, Theodor Adorno and Max Horkheimer, central characters in the so-called '**Frankfurt School**', argued that capitalism had created a 'culture industry' where mass media produced a ready-made, commodified culture for the masses to consume in a largely one-way process ([1944] 1986). More optimistic and nuanced were theorists such as Raymond Williams and Richard Hoggart who in the 1950s and 1960s pioneered work on the effects of popular media such as newspapers, radio, magazines and pop music on 'working class culture' and how ordinary people *could shape these media and be shaped by them* in an ongoing interaction. Out of this work came the next major cultural studies school, the '**Birmingham School**', whose best-known theorist was Stuart Hall.

The Birmingham School, like the Frankfurt School and like Williams and Hoggart before them, emerged from the broadly neo-Marxist tradition and so looked to the forces of manipulation, domination, hegemony and political economy for theories on how technology and culture interact. For many in the Birmingham School tradition, *ideology* was a powerful factor in the media–culture dialectic. This perspective argues that mass media technologies such as radio, television, newspapers and so on are controlled primarily by a relatively small number of big businesses. Practitioners who work in the media, such as editors and journalists, consciously or unconsciously internalize the 'dominant ideologies' and values of big business and transmit these through the various media vectors to the mass of the population. However, this is not a one-way process. For Hall, media texts (films, newspapers, television, etc.) and their meanings are sites for 'negotiation' and may be 'read' (or consumed) in different ways, according to the individuals' place in the social, economic and political structures. Nevertheless, within the range of meanings on offer, there is usually a 'preferred reading' – preferred by the dominant ideology, that is, but this is still a reading, Hall maintains, that 'cannot be guaranteed' (1981: 135).

Spaces of culture

Implicitly or explicitly, what binds these and other theories of media–culture inter-action is that there exist *spaces* in which the interaction takes place (Featherstone and Lash 1999). These are spaces that are shaped and formed by temporality, his-tory, class, ideology, geography, pre-existing cultural patterns and so on. And these are numerous spaces that, according to Hall, create 'their own conditions of existence' (1981: 135). Quite obviously, these 'spaces' can also be termed 'contexts' and within their dynamics of temporality, history and so on, these intersect to bring about what John Fiske (after Bourdieu 1986) calls a **'cultural competence'** and 'social experience upon the . . . moment of reading' (1987: 19). What post-war cultural studies was able to do in terms of the media–culture dialectic was to reveal that this took place in many different spaces and created a diversity of ways in which the dialectic operated. For example, feminist 'spaces' (see Ang 1996) would thus be expected to have a different perspective on the nature of the media–culture dialectic than would, say, the 'ideological' space (see Stallabrass 1996). Each is informed and shaped by different cultural competences and by potentially limitless different 'social experiences'.

All this 'diversity', however, leaves us with a problem. Either we accept that the media–culture dialectic is all 'context', a sort of 'anything goes' mentality, which does not lead anywhere particularly illuminating, or we pick a context, possibly one to fit with our own biases, say 'ideology', and argue it's all down to that – a similarly fore-closing process in the search for understanding. I do not think the choice has to be such a stark 'either–or' one. Accordingly, over the remainder of this chapter, I want to develop the concept of 'spaces' a bit further. This is necessary if we are to understand how this particular dialectic operates in the context of the totally new environment created by pervasive digital networks. Thus the interactions between media and culture within the network society require a reconceptualization, a gearshift up to a new plane of theorization that is able to incorporate the new dynamics of temporal acceleration, of globalization, of neoliberal capitalism and of the ICT revolution itself. We can begin with an analysis of the nature of mass media and how it has changed with the coming of the network society.

Mass media = mass culture?

How 'mass' is mass media? Consider newspapers. The daily circulation figure for *US Today*, the best-selling newspaper in the United States, was 2,241,677 on 30 September 2001. *The Wall Street Journal* and the *New York Times* are the only two other news-papers that sell more than a million a day. The population of the US is almost 290 million. In Britain, the biggest selling daily newspaper is the rambunctious tabloid, the *Sun*, with daily sales of over 3.5 million during July 2002. The broadsheet and more 'serious' daily, the *Guardian*, came in behind a gaggle of *Sun*-like tabloids, with sales of around 370,000 per day for the same month. The population of Britain is about 60 million. Consider television. The quiz show *The Weakest Link* pulled 17.5 million viewers for CBS in 2001, making it the most watched show on American TV at that time. In Britain, an episode of Channel 4s 'reality show' *Big Brother* was watched by 7.1 million viewers in 2002, or 34 per cent of the country's terrestrial audience on the night of transmission. You get my drift. These figures, those of newspaper sales and television viewers, are not small, they are significant, but when matched against the whole population, they can hardly be described as the 'mass' of the population.

The point to keep in mind is that for all its influences, for all its potential pervasiveness, mass media does not and never has constituted a totality – 'mass' does not equate with 'majority'. It has never been a homogeneous and seamless 'space' that covers the whole of society. Remember, too, that 'media' is a plural term and what is 'mass' is also varied, so that people are able to consume mass media such as television, radio, magazines, journals, newspapers, billboard advertising and so on, in differing forms and at different times. However, it is also important to note that much of what we consume comes from a relative handful of mega-corporate sources. To quote just a couple of examples: Eli Noam, in a paper entitled 'Media concentration in the US' (1996) estimates that the 'big three' commercial television corporations, ABC, CBS and NBC, had collectively 92 per cent of TV viewership in the early 1980s; and in Australia, Jock Given notes that Rupert Murdoch's News Corporation controls 75 per cent of daily newspaper circulation (2001: 7).

These facts should alert us to something that should be obvious. It *would* be obvious if it weren't something that we have largely internalized and naturalized and therefore something we tend not to think about, that is, that mass media is a business and business is about selling and selling is about (in no small part) *illusion*. It is probably a safe bet that it still comes as a bit of an uncomfortable surprise to many people to realize that commercial television (or radio, or print media, for that matter), exists not to bring information and entertainment to people – but to deliver audiences for advertisers. In other words, the actual programme we tune into, be it *Coronation Street, The Late Show with David Letterman* or any of the wall-to-wall sports shows that clutter the airwaves, are 'brought to you by . . .' purely and simply in the attempt to get you to watch their ads and then buy their products.

This somewhat crude and depressing realization recalls what Raymond Williams said as long ago as 1958 in his classic *Culture and Society*. He wrote:

> The conception of persons as masses springs, not from an inability to know them, but from an *interpretation of them according to a formula* . . . The formula, in fact, will proceed from our intention. If our purpose is art, education, the giving of information or opinion, our interpretation will be in terms of the rational and interested being. If, on the other hand, our purpose is manipulation –

the persuasion of a large number of people to act, feel, think, know, in certain
ways – the convenient formula will be that of the masses.

(Williams 1958b: 303)

This 'formula' reveals nothing less than a distain for ordinary people by big business, one that goes back to the beginning of the 'mass society' of the late 1800s. It also
has a shared logic with the 'high culture–low culture' dichotomy of the Victorian
period and beyond. It sees ordinary people as cultureless, stupid and herd-like, an
agglomeration to fear and to loathe (and thus feel superior to), or to manipulate as a
market to sell into. Mass media, seen in this light, is synonymous, then, with mass
marketing – the ad-man's dream of selling without end and markets without limit. The
constant designation of 'the masses' and 'mass media' as a fully formed *reality*, instead
of the *marketing formula* that it is, has been perpetuated by the media itself and
blithely repeated by academics and commentators for decades now. Consequently,
this has tended to overemphasize the power and reach of the mass media. As Williams
also noted in *Culture and Society*, '. . . there is, I believe, no form of social activity
which the use of [mass media] has replaced. At most, by adding alternatives,
[mass media] have allowed altered emphases in the time given to particular activities'
(1958b: 301–2).

There is no doubt that over the space of the twentieth century mass media did
grow and concentrate as an industry – as well as homogenize and commercialize its
content as a result (McChesney 1993). The important point to remember, though, is
that it did not reach into every nook and cranny of culture and society. In between
discrete mass media forms there were still plenty of spaces in which 'social activity',
as Williams puts it, could survive, or thrive, or wither and/or regenerate in another
form. This was culture making in the interstices, inside those spaces where people as
members of classes, of families, of communities, or as individuals could take and
shape the meanings of mass media offerings. They could take them or leave them or
reinterpret them for themselves. It is within these spaces that Fiske's 'cultural
competencies' were constantly developed and honed – or maybe allowed to atrophy;
the point being, as the cultural studies tradition has taught us, is that they *existed*.
Moreover, cultural competency *vis-à-vis* the media and its offerings allowed people to
develop a degree of **media savvy**, a *media literacy* that stemmed from a certain level
of autonomy and distance from the media itself. This, in turn, provided people with
the freedom to construct a world of meanings that may radically diverge from the
'preferred' meanings of the mass media formula. In other words, people were able to
develop what Peter Golding and Graham Murdock term a 'critical political economy
of the media' where consumers are culturally competent enough to recognize the
'interplay between [capitalist mass media] organisation and political, social and
cultural life' (2000: 73).

Hegemony and mass media

It is not all sweetness and critical political economy, though. There was and is a definite trend, a predisposition, in the direction of all of this interaction and it was not in the direction of people, plurality and diversity. The practices of culture making have not been left intact within this particular dialectic. If we see mass media as being a business (give or take a few public broadcasters such as the BBC, PBS and so on) we must also allow that they are part of very big industries that follow, in turn, the general logics of capitalism (Garnham 1990). Accordingly, in their interactions with the offerings of mass media, people, societies, communities and cultures have indeed changed and many of these changes reflect the imperatives of the media industries and the 'dominant ideologies' and value systems of the economic and political interests that control them.

Since the turn of the twentieth century at least, mass media outlets (and capitalist industries in general) have tended toward concentration – toward systems of *oligopoly* where a few big players dominate. This was a tendency, as McChesney (1997) notes, which for much of the last century was 'generally national in scope'. The logic of oligopoly in a 'competitive' economy is brutally simple: the bigger you are, the more market share you have and the more you can dominate and/or incorporate your rivals. And the history of the US media industry, as Dennis W. Mazzocco (1994) has shown, is one of relentless expansion and concentration (deflected only occasionally and temporarily by antitrust laws). With fewer players around the media product tends to have limited diversity – you stick with what sells. In general terms this restricts innovation, choice and difference. An ineluctable consequence is that under the veneer of difference a dreary sameness usually lurks – as much in our choice of car as in our choice of soap opera or newspaper.

If weaned on such essentially bland fare, the process becomes internalized and can seem completely natural. That there may exist other ways of being and seeing, tend not to register or to become explicit. As Mazzocco himself admits in the very first passage of his book, 'As a "television child" of the 1950s and 1960s, much of what I learned and believed about the world was filtered through the corporate myths and illusions of U.S. commercial television and radio' (1994: 9). He perhaps exaggerates somewhat for the sake of making his case, but his arguments are clear: your worldview can be predominantly, perhaps even decisively, moulded and formed through constant exposure to mass media.

Persuasion is a large part of the business of mass media, too: persuading one to buy this, think that, or to find this objectionable and that commonsensical. In politics and in the opinion forming that shape the parameters of our politics, the mass media has also made very definite inroads into the cultures of civil society. Noam Chomsky, mainly through the publication of *Manufacturing Consent*, a book he co-authored with Edward Herman, has become famous (or infamous, depending on where you stand) for his analysis of how mass media works in liberal democracies. What we see, hear and read every day, according to Chomsky, is but a sanitized version of reality, a 'cleansed residue' that has passed through several layers of 'filtering' before it hits our eyes or ears (1994: 2). Chomsky makes no bones about how mass media works. He states that

The mass media serve as a system for communicating messages and symbols to the general populace. It is their function to amuse, entertain, inform and to inculcate individuals with the values, beliefs and codes of behaviour that will integrate them into the institutional structure of the larger society. In a world of concentrated wealth and major conflicts of class interest, to fulfil this role requires systematic propaganda.

(1994: 1)

'The propaganda model', as Chomsky calls it, is much more insinuating than the crude versions that used to emanate from the state-run mass media 'organs' of the former communist countries. The 'filtering system' has been built up and refined over many years, Chomsky maintains, and is today a complex, subtle, flexible and all-pervasive force within the media. He identifies five levels through which 'news' is filtered. These are:

- the size, concentrated ownership and profit-orientation of the dominant mass media firms;
- the need to take advertisers into account in deciding what to print and broadcast. As the mass media's primary source of income, sponsors must not be offended by news or information that would damage their interest or tarnish their image;
- the reliance of the media on information provided by government, business and 'expert opinion';
- the disciplining of media through 'flak', or criticism for articles, programmes, stories, or opinion that stray outside the 'norm', as 'biased' or 'flawed';
- neoliberalism and the market as a national religion and the basis upon which news and opinion is judged. In other words, if news or information is consistently hostile to the market and market values, then it will come in for serious 'flak'.

(1994: 1–35)

This flexible and subtle 'propaganda model' amounts to what Chomsky calls 'agenda setting', whereby the 'elite media', the big owners and controllers, set the news agenda for the rest to follow. He notes:

If you are watching the Associated Press, who grind out a constant flow of news, in the mid-afternoon it breaks and there is something that comes along every day that says 'Notice to Editors: Tomorrow's *New York Times* is going to have the following stories on the front page.' The point of that is, if you're an editor of a newspaper in Dayton, Ohio and you don't have the resources to figure out what the news is, or you don't want to think about it anyway, this tells you what the news is.

(Chomsky 1997)

Agenda setting and filtering, as noted, are subtle and flexible processes. So much so, that news tends to appear as 'objective', reflecting a diversity of opinion and so on. But as Chomsky maintains, this is largely fantasy. Most of what we see, hear and read from the mass media more or less reflects the 'dominant ideology' and its values. A useful way of looking at agenda setting is to see it not as mass media telling you what to think – as did Goebbels's *Propagandaministerium* in Nazi Germany, or the INGSOC government of Orwell's *1984* – but what you can think *about*. Chomsky illustrated this point in the aftermath of 11 September 2001 when he argued that much of US domestic public bewilderment expressed as 'why us?', or 'why do they hate us so much?' was a direct effect of the lack of media critique of US foreign policy. Despite the facts and the histories being widely available, sustained criticism of US foreign policy is largely a taboo subject in US mass media, outside the parameters of what may be discussed or thought about. Consequently, argues Chomsky, most Americans simply could not understand why the bombings occurred. Taking their cue from the President himself, people subscribed in large number to the notion that the terrorist acts were simply the result of the hijackers' irrational 'evil' and inexplicable hatred of America's 'freedoms' (2001: 34–5).

In almost all accounts of mass media effects, media *power* is given as a significant factor. Power to dominate markets, power to set agendas and power to shape opinion and values. It was noted before that mass media industries, generally speaking, were 'national in scope'. However, it will be obvious to many non-American readers, especially, that there has been an unambiguous international dimension to this, in the form of exposure to increasing amounts of US mass media and culture. This has primarily been ensured through the pre-eminence of American economic and political power. And as industries (culture industries), the dynamics of cultural and media imperialism flowed naturally as part of the logic of globally expanding US capitalism (Mattelart 1979). Accordingly, spaces of local (non-American) cultural production have been colonized by 'foreign' culture and none more so than by American culture. As Jonathan Weber (2002) put it,

> No company conveys more powerfully the image of a conquering cultural army than Walt Disney. Its founder was a true-blue patriot who saw himself as a proselytizer for the values of the American heartland. The company's products and services – unlike, say, fast-food hamburgers or sugary soft drinks – are not merely symbolic of the American way of life, but contain as part of their essence a set of beliefs about good and evil and human aspiration. Disney, moreover, has throughout its history been extremely shrewd about building mutually reinforcing products across many different kinds of media, with theme parks and TV shows, movies and merchandise, all working together in service of the Disney way.

Of course, Disney is only one vector for the transmission of 'American cultural imperialism'. There are many others that we all can recognize and probably consume every day. American B52s may conduct high explosive incendiary bombing of Iraq, Afghanistan and anywhere else they feel the need; but American culture industries also engage in what Naomi Klein (2000) calls 'brand bombing'. McDonald's, Starbucks, Nike, Gap and the continual stream of US-centric Hollywood 'blockbusters' and television programmes ensure that most of us feel we 'know' that place without ever having gone there. Revealingly, this brand recognition and feeling that significant elements of US mass culture are part of our own cultural landscape does not easily work the other way. For example, conspicuous by their absence in the average US strip mall are plenty of non-US mass cultural icons such as Boots the chemist, Carrefour supermarkets, Vegemite spread, Wimpy hamburgers, David Jones stores and so on – brands and icons instantly recognizable in large parts of Britain, continental Europe, East Asia and Australia.

Networked media, networked culture: the disappearance of the dialectic

> Any new medium forms an environment that casts deep cultural shadows.
> (Nguyen and Alexander 1996: 101)

Chapter 1 offered some ways to think about networks and the network society. Much of this chapter has looked at media and culture as 'spaces' that interact to form and shape each other within the context of a mass media society. The objective has been to show the dynamics of these spaces, in general terms, before their 'informationization' caused them to merge and (now) to evolve of the same digital plane.

To get to this point, let us continue the discussion, then, by tracing (and occasionally retracing) the contours of the network society and then try to reach some conclusions regarding *this* as both a *media space* and a *culture space*. In particular, this section will argue that the 'spaces' of media and culture that interact and enable the production of both diverse cultures and a cultural competence *vis-à-vis* the media are *disappearing* due to the suffusion of the processes of informationization into the deepest realms of society. The chapter will end with some reflections on the social and cultural implications of these developments.

We have seen how, through the convergence of the formerly discrete ICT technologies of computers, satellites, cables and telephony, the basis for digital networks was laid down. We have seen, too, how this was primarily driven by ideology (the ideology of neoliberalism) and by the economics of market fundamentalism, inaugurating, in the process, the start of what came to be termed economic 'globalization'. In terms of its mass media dimension this entailed a shift to truly *global* media networks where the 'generally national' character of media development shifted rapidly to another (digital and global) plane. As Herman and McChesney (1997: 10) put it,

> The emergence of a truly global media system is a very recent development, reflecting to no small degree the globalisation of the market economy. Although global media are only one part of the overall expansion and spread of an increasingly integrated and global corporate system, they complement and support the needs of nonmedia enterprises.

'Integration' is key to the processes Herman and McChesney describe. It places media (entertainments, news, magazines and so on) on the same digital and global-izing logic as, say, education, or services, or manufacturing, or the stock market or almost anything else you can think of. An effect of sharing a similar technological and ontological plane with capitalism has meant that the once-vaunted 'special case' of the media and of the role of journalism as its 'critical' and 'objective' element, in particu-lar, is diminishing. As Katherine Ainger succinctly puts it in the *New Internationalist* magazine (2001):

> The media have not been 'pro-globalization' so much as an integral part of the process. For most journalists neoliberalism is not an economic ideology whose fundamental assumptions can be challenged, but simply 'reality'.

Moreover, the reduction of the traditional barriers to trade in goods and services meant that over the 1990s media enterprises, just like other industries that caught the techno-wave early, were able to grow rapidly and increasingly viewed the whole world as their potential marketplace. 'The dominant players', Herman and McChesney (1997: 41) note, now 'treat the media markets as a single global market with local subdivisions'. The new media strategy to 'think global, act local' is made possible only through the use of interconnected and integrated networks of ICTs. This, in turn, is globalization made into a reality, through what Dan Schiller has termed 'digital capitalism', where economic processes are becoming comprehensively digitized through the revolutionary forces of networked capitalism. Schiller forensically describes the 'networking of the global market system' into a single, seamless whole that is tailor-made for and by giant conglomerates. A combination of free-market policies by governments around the world and the opportunities afforded by information technologies themselves has meant that media companies, possibly more than any other industry, were able to thrive and dominate, to become what Schiller calls 'vertically integrated megamedia' (1999: 99).

What is 'vertical integration'? Prior to the rise of neoliberalism and economic globalization, 'horizontal integration' is what most large media (and other cor-porations) aimed for. This was basically to stick to your own backyard in terms of developing the business. For example, television production companies would concern themselves, as prudence would demand, with *production*. They would strive to hone an expertise and possibly a dominating position within the television production niche. Television production would be what they 'do'. Moreover, there were laws in many countries that would restrict businesses from going any further, anyway. 'Vertical integration', on the other hand, evolved out of the neoliberal mantra of free competition and the 'right' for the owners and controllers of capital to get into any business they thought might turn a profit. Primarily this has meant that any self-respecting and globally ambitious television production company would also want to buy into *distribution* as well, that is, acquire a TV station. This is because to be able to control content *and* distribution makes for a very powerful player across the whole TV industry. And if size matters in a merger-mad free-market system, it is impossible to stop at the limits of one's own backyard. Indeed it is no longer useful or accurate to look at traditional media sectors such as 'television' in isolation any longer, so seamless has the media industry become. As McChesney (1999) argues,

> . . . looking at specific media sectors fails to convey the extent or the nature of the system today, for no longer are media firms intent on horizontal integration. Today, they seek 'vertical integration,' not only producing content but also owning distribution. Moreover, they are major players in media sectors not traditionally thought to be related. These conglomerates own some combination of television networks, TV show production, TV stations, movie studios, cable channels, cable systems, music companies, magazines, newspapers and book publishing firms.

In much the same vein and propelled by exactly the same logic, globally recognized 'brands' like Manchester United football club cannot now be content simply with fielding a team every Saturday (or Monday, or Sunday, or whenever the television agreement dictates). Vertical integration demands that the team as 'the product', or the 'content', must be integrated with the 'distribution' through its TV station, MUTV. As a 'brand' it must also share with its famous players, who are also 'brands', the 'image rights' that accrue through the merchandising of innumerable 'branded' goods in its 'megastore' and the mandatory website. In the age of globalized media, football must now depend less on people paying at the turnstile and more on television and sponsorship rights, on hugely overpriced replica shirts, on branded paraphernalia such as soft toys, duvet sets, wristwatches, coffee mugs and on almost anything else the marketers can think of. In fact, so tempting was the Manchester United set-up that Rupert Murdoch's News Corporation tried to take it over in 1998 to secure for itself an even larger share of the 'sports media' market. It was stopped only through some extraordinary grass-roots hostility to the selling-off of the club's perceived 'traditions' and 'culture' to vulgar commercial interests – a process, ironically, that had been underway for years prior to the predatory attentions of that particular media conglomerate.

The relative weakness of rules on cross-media ownership by governments more or less happy with a *laissez-faire* approach has allowed hyper concentration of global media in the hands of a few behemoths. Schiller sees this as an ongoing global power game where 'multibillion dollar properties – film studios, broadcast networks, programme packagers, cable systems, satellite channels – change hands like marbles' (1999: 99). McChesney (1999) has looked at this marble swapping in more detail. He notes that

> The mega-media firms have enjoyed a staggering rate of growth in the last decade. In 1988, Disney was a $2.9 billion a year amusement park and cartoon company; in 1998, Disney had $22 billion in sales. In 1988, Time was a $4.2 billion publishing company and Warner Communications was a $3.4 billion media conglomerate; in 1998, Time Warner did $26 billion of business. In 1988, Viacom was a measly $600 million syndication and cable outfit; the new Viacom is expected to do $22 billion worth of business in the coming year. Moreover, each of these firms averages at least one equity joint venture – sharing actual ownership of a company – with six of the eight other media giants. Rupert Murdoch's News Corporation has at least one joint venture with each of them. AT&T Liberty owns nearly 10 per cent of both News Corporation and Time Warner. This looks more like a cartel than it does the fabled competitive marketplace.

What is happening through these processes? In what way is networked media different from traditional mass media – and what does this change mean for the spaces of difference that are vital for the production of cultural diversity? The difference, as the arguments that thread throughout this book would suggest, is the effect of neo-liberalism and the ICT revolution. Echoing what I argued earlier in the discussion on globalization, what the 'media' is and what it does has been *intensified* and *extensified* through the convergence process. What this means, as Scott Lash argues in his *Critique of Information* (2002: viii), is that the network society is at the same time a media society. No longer are the media industries analytically and practically different (if only in degree) from other industries. Information technologies are flattening them all onto a single, digital plane. What I shall describe in Chapter 4 as 'mediatized culture' is able, through increasingly dense interconnectivity, to seep into every nook and cranny of social and cultural life. It is dissolving the spaces of difference where cultural diversity is produced. In this digital realm, Givenchy is culturally on a par with CNN in terms of its social, cultural and economic logic; McDonald's with Motorola; Subway with Manchester United and so on. We now live in an age, argues Lash, where 'social and cultural life has been pervaded by the media' and 'what was once "society" is just as much media as it is society . . . and what was once "culture" is just as much media as culture' (2002: 66–7).

As the network society becomes more and more all-encompassing then so also does the operation of the media–culture dialectic diminish. There are simply fewer 'spaces' and less 'distance' for it to operate as it once did. This poses significant issues for advocates of the idea that globalization and the network society are inaugurating the beginning of a new era of cultural diversity and cultural hybridity, where difference builds on difference to produce new and ever changing forms of culture (for example Rheingold 2000).

Stuart Hall reminds us, rightly, that 'global culture requires and thrives on difference' (1997: 211). However, within the network society, 'difference' in the form of real and substantive alternatives in worldview, in the meanings derived from symbols and practices, are increasingly hard to find. The spaces of difference that produce cultural diversity are being colonized by the onward march of informationization much more rapidly and comprehensively than traditional mass media was able to. As Paul du Gay (Hall 1997: 210) has put it,

> ... the new electronic media not only allow the stretching of social relations across time and space, they also deepen this global interconnectedness by annihilating the distance between people and places, throwing them into intense and perpetual contact with one another in a perpetual present ...

In the global culture that emanates from the network society, one based upon the 'annihilation of distance', difference tends to be weak and surface-level, such as halal meat for your McHappy Meal in Kuala Lumpur, or a West Indian accent delivering the news on the BBC World Service.

This is exacerbated by another factor. In Chapter 1 we discussed some of the issues involved in a network society that generates its own 'digital acceleration' – that of network time. Cultures, traditionally, have evolved and have been shaped, in part, by what Barbara Adam calls 'temporal rhythms'. These are the 'multitude of times' which suffuse consciousness, memory, narrative and physiology and 'which interpenetrate and permeate our daily lives' (1995: 12). This cultural production, according to Adam, is 'contextually situated'. These contexts (or spaces) serve as the basis for the production of a potential infinity of diversity in human culture. The arrival of clock time and the spread of capitalism made many significant inroads into this diversity by putting society onto a more instrumental-rational basis. However, the processes of economic globalization and the ICT revolution have put the process of colonization onto another plane altogether (Hassan 2003a). As media and computer theorist Mads Haahr (2001) has argued,

> We often fail to realize that our interaction with the world is a feedback loop: a circle we can choose to make either benevolent or vicious. As participants in an active culture, we take and we give – this is the core of our interaction with the surroundings. This dual flow of action is everywhere: in language (hear/say), in technology (sensors/feedback), economics (demand/supply), biology (stimulus/ response) and computers (input/output). Our current cultural patterns encourage an accelerated mode of interaction: one that expects the rate not only to be high but also to grow. We teach ourselves that speed is good, that a fast-paced lifestyle (busi-ness) is a sure sign of success and that if we can run/work/create faster than

our peers, we will do better than them. But acceleration is a risky characteristic on which to base a culture, because a continually tightening feedback loop will eventually become too tight to work well. For the feedback loop to work at a human level, we need time to reflect and digest; to distill information into knowledge; to turn experiences into experience.

To a significant degree, then, culture has become media and media has become culture, with their common denominator being interconnected and temporally accelerative information technologies. Culture has become mediatized – *digitally mediatized*. Furthermore, the process of cultural homogenization has its corollary, that of *fragmentation*. It is a profound contradiction within the network society, that as it deepens our interconnectivity with each other, then so too does it fragment and alienate us (Castells 1996: 3). The shrinking of time and space through the Internet, email and so on means increasingly we can have more in common with communities of interest that may span the entire planet than with our sibling, neighbour or friend. Quite possibly, our sibling, neighbour or friend may share our interests, but in the increasingly accelerated life in the network society we simply do not have as much time or opportunity to 'connect' with them any longer in the non-digital sense.

There is another shift underway due to the disappearance of the dialectic due to informationization. The media savvy that people were able to develop through the application of Fiske's 'cultural competencies', the skill of discernment fashioned through a critical distance, is being replaced by a '**techno savvy**' that contains no critical distance. Here the focus is instrumentally upon gaining the skills to 'navigate' the network and to optimize our life chances within the bounds set by the logic of the network society itself. This loss of cultural competence is also a diminution of the ability to critique the technologies that many of us have become so expert in and *au fait* with, or to understand in any deep sense what these may mean for us, for our communities, polities and societies.

Going, but not gone

There is of course hope in all this. The 'disappearing dialectic' that was part of the title of the previous section is not the same as the 'disappeared dialectic', and I think Lash overdetermines the process somewhat by arguing that 'there is no outside anymore'. This is definitely the direction in which we are going, but it is doubtful if we would ever reach this extreme point. We have seen how the suffusion of the spaces of difference by the neoliberalism–ICT revolution is, at its root, a process of domination. This is domination through the ideological, political, economic and cultural projects of neoliberalism to place the market and capitalism more generally at the centre of human existence. A consequence, of course, is to relegate other ways of being and seeing to the margins or to oblivion. The processes of informationization are central to this.

However, domination, as Williams (1979: 252) reminds us, can never be total, and there will always exist spaces where what he terms 'alternative acts and alternative intentions' may take place. Moreover, we are only at the beginnings of the formation of the network society. This means that there still exist spaces at the interstices where reflection and critique may be developed in the creation of a media savvy and a personal and collective cultural competence. Nevertheless, what is undoubtedly true is that these spaces are more difficult to find and to inhabit.

In the fields of these *Kulturkampfen*, many still recognize and resist cultural domination when they see, hear or read it. Such recognition can act as a spur for others to question and critique their own culture/media interactions. For example, French theatre director Ariane Mnouchkine condemned Paris Disneyland as a 'cultural Chernobyl' (Weber 2002). Others, however, are not so quick to reject the 'alien' culture outright. They try to emphasize what is positive in the culture clash and what may in fact be signs of growing cultural synthesis that is creating yet more diversity. In an interview, 'traveller and writer' Pico Iyer (1996) noted how people are not only able to accept cultural and media influences from the US and elsewhere, but actively recreate them for themselves. For example:

> In Japan they play baseball, but they smile when they strike out and they don't slide into second base because they don't want to offend the opposition. In India . . . they were making five different remakes of Rambo . . . and one of them even had a woman in the title role.

Iyer speaks here in the language of classical cultural studies when he emphasizes that people and cultures do not simply absorb, sponge-like, and in its totality, the cultural imperium of the dominant power. There is an interaction, a dialectic, in operation.

Nonetheless, the 'culture shaping' that Iyer speaks of seems to me basically a *defensive reaction*, a withdrawal and attempt to cope with a process of cultural incursion that cannot easily be stopped. And retreat in war can easily lead to being overrun and routed. Like the example of the halal meat-filled McHappy Meal in Kuala Lumpur, it is inevitable that Malaysians who are increasingly exposed to the global culture through the Internet, cable TV and so on will one day wonder if they may be missing out on something 'cool' in the 'Two 100% beef patties, sesame seed bun, American cheese slice, Big Mac sauce, lettuce, pickles, onions, salt and pepper' that comprise the global Big Mac. My guess is that the halal meat, Japanese baseball and female Rambo compromises are actually cases of cultures in retreat – a wearing down of the diverse local by the overpowerful and homogeneous global. Similar cultural microdramas are being played out all over the world today, and many in the cultural studies and media studies disciplines are missing the point by viewing such retreats as evidence of 'postmodern' cultural empowerment and diversity instead.

In Chapters 5, and 7 I will discuss ways in which the cultural retreat may be stemmed and the initiative regained to push back the forces of domination and recover spaces of difference where plurality and diversity can operate. In the culture wars being conducted through media technologies, as we shall see, offensive 'tactics' and 'strategies' offer much more promise in the search for plurality and diversity than does compromise, retreat and incorporation. For now, however, I want to conduct a more empirically based assessment of the network society, to try to get some understanding of its radical intensity and extensity, and how the physical means for the informationization of media and culture has evolved.

Further reading

Golding, P. and Murdock, G. (2002) Culture, communications and political economy, in J. Curran and M. Gurevitch (eds) *Mass Media and Society*. London: Arnold.

Kellner, D. (2002) *Cultural Studies, Multiculturalism and Media Culture*. www.gseis.ucla.edu/faculty/kellner/papers/SAGEcs.htm

Lash, S. (2002) *Critique of Information*. London: Sage Publications.

McChesney, R.W. and Herman, E.S. (1997) *The Global Media: The New Missionaries of Corporate Capitalism*. London; Washington, DC: Cassell.

Tomlinson, J. (1999) *Globalization and Culture*. Cambridge: Polity Press.

ADDICTED TO DIGITAL: THE WIRED WORLD

I connect therefore I am.

(Leer 2000: 157)

Connecting . . .

The planet is wired. Hundreds of thousands of kilometres of undersea fibre optic cable connect the continents with invisible digital garlands of super-thin glass and plastic. This digital network has no originary point and no terminus; it has no beginning and no end: its logic is connection upon connection, upon connection. However, for the sake of description, let us begin in Porthcurno in England, where the 28,000-kilometre Fibre-Optic Link Around the Globe (FLAG) cable begins. From here it snakes and wends its way southeast through the Straits of Gibraltar to Italy and across the Mediterranean to North Africa. It pops up out of the water at Port Said in Egypt and runs overland across the North African and Arabian deserts to Dubai in the United Arab Emirates. At this point the cable submerges once more across the length of the Indian Ocean to the Bay of Bengal, north along the bottom of the Andaman Sea, a short dry run across Thailand and then northeast through the South China Sea to Hong Kong. From there the FLAG cable runs under the North Pacific Ocean to Japan.

A 30,000-kilometre transpacific network begun in 1997 will link China, Japan and Korea to the west coast of the US. At the continent's eastern seaboard, numerous transatlantic links connect North America to western Europe, to complete the global circuit. Sub-links branch off from these mainlines to connect Southeast Asia, Australasia and South America. Indeed, the network will soon incorporate the South Pole. In late 2002 it was reported that the American National Science Foundation issued a request for industry to bid to build the trans-Antarctic fibre optic link. It is planned to be in use by 2009 (Whitehouse 2002). From these global 'backbones', regions, countries, cities, businesses, universities, government bureaucracies, regional governments, district councils, communities and individuals link to the network through their own growing local telecommunications systems. The fibre optic system that girds and criss-crosses the planet is of course augmented and made still denser through wireless communication, satellite links, cable systems and the standard-issue copper wire telephone link that brings the Internet and network connectivity to, potentially, almost everywhere.

The network is physical and real but for most of us it exists as an unseen abstraction. For millions upon millions of people the network has become the McLuhanesque unconscious extension of our bodies. We have become receivers and transmitters of information (network nodes) who give little thought as to how it comes to us or flows from us. Nevertheless, that eagerly expected email containing a JPEG of your newborn niece from San Francisco, the thirty-second digital movie from a cousin's twenty-first party on Bondi Beach, that bootlegged Oasis MP3 you've just downloaded from Kazaa, or even the spam mail offering instant riches that you delete automatically has reached your hard drive and your consciousness though fairly exotic and amazing routes. Describing one leg of the digital journey, Susan Dumett (1998) writes:

> The e-mail I send semi-regularly to a friend in London has a rigorous itinerary. After maneuvering through a perplexing network of land-based routers and wires, it dives into the Atlantic Ocean along a single fibre optic cable. As it travels along continental shelves, at depths of more than 14,000 feet, through tempestuous currents and in some places even under the ocean floor, it fights for space on the cable with a multitude of data transmissions including voice, Internet and video before landing in the inbox on my friend's desktop PC.

In the developed world, interconnectivity is becoming the core of our lives. In the US alone, 39 million miles of fibre-optic line criss-cross the country, long enough to string around the planet 1566 times (Brenner 2003: 54). Like potable water, it has become something we vitally need, but only tend to think about it when it's not there. Many of us now know the frustration at work or at home when the network is disrupted, or is running slow or has shut down altogether. We feel the growing annoyance when that little 'loading' bar at the bottom of a download screen is not moving toward '100%' fast enough; when we stand at a supermarket checkout with a trolley-full of items and no cash, only to be told the EFT link is down; and that vein on your temple fairly throbs when the mobile phone breaks up mid-sentence when you've moved too far from a radio column. And it's not as if this frustration is baseless, or it really does not matter. It does. In the accelerated network society, individuals, institutions, corporations and governments transact massive amounts of business through it. Jobs depend on it, livelihoods are sustained through it and much learning and skills acquisition is conducted over it. For example, building sub-contractors went digital a long time ago, buying mobile phones so as to be sure that they could be on call for the next job and be connected to enable them to make a bid for another one. Students need to have a fair degree of computer literacy to be able to study and increasingly need to have their own computer and Internet link to make study practicable at all. In the US, especially, a laptop computer is becoming almost mandatory in many campuses, *literally* so in others, indicating that you simply cannot participate fully in university life without one.

This rapid digital wiring of the world has wrought some profound changes. Twenty years ago computers and digital networks did not much exist. Nor did they matter very much. Today it is no exaggeration to say that these are absolutely central to economic life. A 2002 US government document called *The National Strategy to Secure Cyberspace*, states:

> By 2002, our economy and national security are [now] fully dependent upon information technology and the information infrastructure. A network of networks directly supports the operation of all sectors of our economy – energy (electric power, oil and gas), transportation (rail, air, merchant, marine), finance and banking, information and telecommunications, public health, emergency services, water, chemicals, defense industrial base, food, agriculture and postal and shipping.
>
> (US Government 2002: 9)

For bureaucratic prose, it is hard to be much more unequivocal or unambiguous than this. The world's most advanced economy, and all the others who are trying to catch it up, are staking just about everything on this 'network of networks', including, as we shall see, our national defence systems. We call it the New Economy. The ICT revolution is much more than about simply using computers to do what we do more efficiently – most of us don't do what we did any more. The Old Economy was based upon a fairly rigid Fordist standardization, which meant that what was not mass-produced tended to be expensive. The New Economy is based upon flexibility and is thus able to produce highly specialized goods and services without losing economies of scale. This in itself constitutes a thoroughgoing revolution in the capitalist mode of production; making possible the seemingly illogical conjunction of what Robert Reich (2002) calls 'mass specialization'. Moreover, the Old Economy was an economy based upon owning and controlling material 'things' such as factories, plant, machinery and physical labour, to produce steel, cars, fridges, ships, footwear, textiles and so on. Of course these 'things' are still important, but much of the production of these 'things' now takes place in developing countries, which consumers in the rich developed countries buy cheaply. Look at the back of your Palm Pilot or mobile, or at the inside of your trainers, or the label on the inside of the back of your shirt. If you are from a 'fully developed' country in North America, western Europe or Australasia, chances are it's imported – from China, from Mexico, from Vietnam or wherever the cheapest labour may currently be found.

Around twenty years ago, the developed countries made what was, for many, a painful transition to the New Economy. This is a very different mode of production from its sluggish and ponderous predecessor, Fordism. Jeremy Rifkin (2000: 30–50) calls it the '**weightless economy**'. This is based upon ethereal things such as ideas, knowledge and information, stuff that knows no physical boundaries and is unaffected by geography or climate. In what reads as a manifesto for the New Economy, *Wired* magazine in its publication entitled *Encyclopaedia for the New Economy* (*Wired* 2002) proclaims:

> When we talk about the New Economy, we're talking about a world in which people work with their brains instead of their hands. A world in which communications technology creates global competition – not just for running shoes and laptop computers, but also for bank loans and other services that can't be packed into a crate and shipped. A world in which innovation is more important than mass production. A world in which investment buys new concepts or the means to create them, rather than new machines. A world in which rapid change is a constant. A world at least as different from what came before it as the industrial age was from its agricultural predecessor. A world so different its emergence can only be described as a revolution.
>
> The fact that Bill Gates is the world's richest man belies a huge shift in the values of capitalism. Microsoft has annual sales of US$11 billion and most of its assets walk in and out of the doors wearing T-shirts. Yet the stock market values the company at well over $150 billion – far more than either IBM (sales $76 billion, market cap $100 billion) or General Motors (sales $160 billion, market cap $50 billion). Why? Because the rules of competition are changing to favour companies like Microsoft over the paragons of the industrial age.

Terms such as 'New Economy' and 'weightless economy' are useful to convey certain aspects of the economic, social and technological changes, as well as to give an indication of the 'paradigm shift' that has taken place. However, as the arguments contained throughout this book would suggest, what they describe could more accurately be termed a *network society*. The distinction is important, because these revolutionary processes suffuse more than just a slice of life. We are talking about more than the 'economy'. We are talking about the technological transformation of culture, society and politics, too. As Frederic Jameson wrote, this ICT-powered form of globalization is also colonizing areas of life '. . . hitherto sheltered from it [globalisation] and indeed for the most part hostile to and inconsistent with its logic' (1996: 9).

We can get more of an appreciation of this process, perhaps, when we realize that *life itself* has become deeply commodified and infused by the logic of both ICTs and the market. Biotechnology is a science discipline that depends upon high-powered computers to do the awesome number crunching that gene sequencing requires. Indeed, the famous 2000 Genome Project draft completion of the human genome could not have been done without mammoth computing power. However, as scientists, aided by computers, gain more knowledge about the very essence of living organisms, the more the market follows in their wake. 'Intellectual property' – the privatization of human creativity and innovation – has been a feature of capitalism since its earliest beginnings. However, under the rule of neoliberalism and the market economy it has exploded to engulf every aspect of life. Through advances in biotechnology, life itself, the genetic 'the heritage of humanity', is rapidly being cordoned off, privatized and made ready for the market. In an article for *Le Monde Diplomatique*, John Sulston, the 2002 Nobel Prize winner for his discoveries in genetics, gave us a sense of the scale of this commercial frenzy in biotechnology when he noted that 'the number of applications for gene patents on human and other organisms has now passed the half-million mark' (2002: 12). The world has been transformed in these and many other fundamental ways over the last generation, and without the digital wiring of the world and the network society it has created, such transformation would have been impossible.

CyberAsia

Castells (1996) argues that the network society is characterized by 'flows'. These 'flows' of capital, information, culture and flexible production systems respect no geographic boundaries and they constitute the very lifeblood of globalization. Accordingly, the rest of the non-OECD world, that is to say the 'emerging markets' of South America, China and Southeast Asia, are rapidly being connected and incorporated into the network society. Indeed, the original 'tiger economies' such as Taiwan, Hong Kong, Singapore and South Korea are, in their cities at least, even more 'wired' than, say, Spain or Italy or France. Internet density is growing swiftly in much of Asia with, for example, 46 per cent of Singapore residents having domestic access to broadband Internet (IDA Singapore 2001: 6), whereas only 18 per cent of Spaniards have domestic access of any kind (Nielsen Net Ratings 2002). The trend, however, is that *everywhere* the move toward digital interconnectivity is growing. For much of Asia it is a race to connect and to catch up with the global leaders such as the North Americans and the western European countries such as Britain, Sweden, Germany and Finland. Governments and business leaders of the so-called 'second generation tigers' in the Asian region such as Malaysia, Indonesia and Thailand are keenly aware of the importance of ICTs as key to their development. Accordingly, political support and capital investment in ICTs to informationize their economies is given high priority. The extent of this commitment can be seen in the multi-billion dollar Malaysian Multimedia Super Corridor (MSC). This is a fantastically ambitious project that aims to make the Kuala Lumpur region a magnet for the world's 'technopreneurs' and the 'digital hub' for the whole of Southeast Asia. It has attracted many of the major IT companies such as Microsoft, Sun Microsystems and Intel (see for example, www.mdc.com.my).

The digital addiction is worldwide and a frantic race to connect and to catch up takes place at almost all developmental levels. China, for example, could be considered a 'third generation tiger', but the scale and the pace of the digital interconnectivity involved in that country seems set to eclipse the rest of Asia – and perhaps the world. Under the political, social, cultural and technological deep freeze that was China in 1979 there were only 2.03 million telephones for a population of almost a billion people. By 1998 the number of telephones had increased to 100 million and only four years later, in 2002, this had 'doubled to 200 million with 65 million of these being mobile phones' (*People's Daily Online* 2002). This surging and seemingly unstoppable growth in telephony is only one aspect of China's growth in connectivity. In a remarkable document that analyses the diffusion of the Internet in China, William Foster and Seymour E. Goodman from the Center for International Security and Cooperation at Stanford University, wrote:

> The Internet is diffusing rapidly and extensively throughout China. Five thousand users in 1994 grew to over eight million by the end of 1999. Between January and July of 2000, that number grew from 8.9 to 16.9 million. Although it is unlikely that the number of users will continue to double every six months, if growth can be sustained at anywhere near that level – a big 'if' – in several years China will have more Internet users than any other country on earth.
>
> (2000: 2)

A big part of the 'big if' is the Chinese Communist Party (CCP) and its one-party rule over that country. Nevertheless, the CCP intends to incorporate the Internet and digital networks into its strategic economic development plans and help it to become a significant element in the network society. Then-president Jiang Zemin is quoted in Foster and Goodman (2000: xii) as saying that 'Internet technology is going to change the international situation, military combat, production, culture and economic aspects of our daily life significantly.' He omitted to mention 'politics' in his list, of course, and the CCP struggles, vainly, to control what growing numbers of Mainland Chinese read, see and hear on the Internet. For example, Chinese users love the Google Internet search engine because it reads Chinese characters. In mid-2002 the Chinese government blocked access to Google and also tried to limit access to the CNN and BBC websites (Sloan 2002). However, for Chinese users with a minimum of Internet knowledge and a willingness to defy their government, it was simply a matter of a few mouse-clicks to detour around those sites blocked and limited by the authorities and search or browse through a Google, CNN and BBC **mirror-site** instead. Censoring the Internet's content, especially its political content, seems set to be a constant (and ultimately unsuccessful) rearguard action for the CCP.

Given the enormous potential of the Chinese economy, as well as its obvious attraction as a market for ICT companies, the 'resolution' to this particular dilemma is going to be one of the more important and interesting aspects of the wired world in the years to come.

Roll with it

The immense and rapid growth of the network is based in large part upon a *positive feedback loop*. This can perhaps be best illustrated by looking at positive feedback loop theory in economics. The idea is simple enough and states that as people earn more money, so they will spend more. This in turn grows the economy, creating more jobs, which makes for more spending consumers, which grows the economy yet more, and so on it goes, onwards and upwards. In communications technology we can trace the positive feedback effect back, I think, to McLuhan's 'the medium is the message' thesis that we discussed in Chapter 2. There is something special about the nature of human communication. In general we can argue that if people are able to communicate something in a more convenient or immediate way, then they will. Couple this with the idea that information technologies themselves almost compel one to use them and the momentum becomes both powerful and addictive. How many of us, for example, have entered the mobile phone market telling ourselves 'I'll just keep it for emergencies' and then find ourselves using it constantly, for almost anything other than the 'emergency' that in most cases never comes? In offices people send emails to colleagues sitting just a few feet away, and students surreptitiously text-message each other in class, not simply because it's fun, or they have anything particularly important to say – but because they can.

We need to communicate. We are social beings and communication is part of our 'species-essence', as Marx called it. This human trait is very good for the ICT industries. ICTs are prolific, almost self-generating. As more connections are made, then more connections are needed; and as connectivity becomes part of more aspects of our lives, then the more we need increased means of communication to keep pace with our perceived communication needs. The idea that we need to be contactable at all times translates into big business and ambitious projects. In 2002 ICT giants AT&T, IBM and Intel announced plans to increase the density of interconnectivity yet further, with the creation of a nationwide broadband network of wireless 'hotspots'. These hotspots will allow individuals or businesses to access the network almost anywhere, anytime. As Jay Wrolstad (2002) explains it, 'The ultimate goal . . . is to have hotspots within a five-minute walk of any business in an urban setting, or within a five-minute drive in rural areas.' What this logic means in our own lives can be expressed in other (if somewhat biblical) terms: the office computer begets the home computer which begets the PDA which begets the broadband wireless connection which begets the Internet homepage which begets the Hotmail account which begets the scanner which begets the 3G enabled mobile phone which begets the MP3 player which begets the CD/RW unit and so on it goes, *ad infinitum*.

There is another, unstated 'ultimate goal' for ICT companies, however, and this is the creation of an environment, a world, where there is no escape from the urge to connect. This is a deeper and deadly serious business logic whereby ICT industries envision a planet deeply suffused by interconnectivity. As we shall soon see, the research and development (R&D) wings of the ICT industry are working daily to bring this vision to reality.

Seeing the writing on the wall, so to speak, and using the Internet as their example, information technology theorists Mark Weiser and John Seely Brown have characterized this process of ICT suffusion as the development of what they term 'ubiquitous computing' (1997: 5). They write:

> Today the Internet is carrying us through an era of widespread *distributed computing* towards the relationship of *ubiquitous computing*, characterised by deeply embedding computation in the world.

'Ubiquitous computing', of course, is not simply the Internet. It is everything that connects to and from it. Computing is everywhere, from 'smart' refrigerators that can go online, to Global Positioning Satellite (GPS) enabled cars that tell us exactly where we are in time and in space. 'Ubiquitous computing' also means powerful computing at our fingertips (or thumbs). That mobile phone in your pocket or bag, for example, has more computing power than the Apollo 11 space flight that put the first men on the moon in 1969. Similarly, the processing power of the Microsoft Xbox or Playstation in the bedroom would probably multiply the power of Apollo 11's on-board systems by a factor of ten or more.

The positive feedback loop means also a hyper-diffusion of ICTs pushing outward into every region and country in the world. I've already mentioned the fibre optic cable that is going to be stretched across the South Pole. This hyper-diffusion is also aided and abetted by the innate need we have to communicate with each other and our seemingly irresistible fascination with gadgets that help us do it more efficiently. A colleague emailed me an article on the topic of ICT diffusion that clearly illustrates the power of the feedback loop and of the process of 'deeply embedding' connectivity into every nook and cranny across the world. The story came from BBCWorld.com (2002) and concerns the rapid appearance of the latest mobile phones in Afghanistan. Up until 2001 that country was under the rule of the Taliban, an Islamic theocracy with a medieval mindset that banned everything from cinema and television to soccer and radio as 'unIslamic'. Telephones of any kind were almost non-existent. Today, those Afghanis who are able to afford it are happily using mobile phones like veterans. The western engineer involved in setting up the telecom infrastructure said that the project took only three months to complete and that wireless data technology would follow shortly. This will enable Kabul residents to surf the Internet, use WAP and 3G communications technologies and many other applications and devices. Almost overnight, Afghanistan (or its capital, Kabul, at least) had been transformed from a repressive theocracy stuck somewhere in the eleventh century to a country on the verge of being a member of the wired world.

Get a life(style)

This positive feedback loop is, of course, augmented massively by the ideology of globalization, of free markets, of no borders for information and of the over-arching corporate vision of the planet as a single, seamless and interconnected market-place. Those relatively few corporations who have networked our world have risen meteorically from nothing, or from relative obscurity, to become part of our daily existence as the brands and images of the wired life. In the 1970s and 1980s, for those who can still remember those pre-digital decades, our corporate consciousness, whenever it would occasionally (if ever) come to the fore, would have been dominated by old industry titans such as Chevron, British Petroleum, Shell, General Motors, General Electric and Ford. Today, so deeply have the New Economy 'weightless' corporations such as Nokia, Apple, Sun Microsystems, Compaq, Dell and Microsoft insinuated themselves into our lives, that it is difficult not to be *daily* aware of those that construct our digital world and network consciousness. We are nodes in the network they create. Recall that meant-to-be-soothing little Microsoft boot-up jingle and logo that greets hundreds of millions of users as their working day or online leisure time begins; or the Internet Explorer logo that spins irritatingly and continuously in the top right-hand corner of the browser, intermittently blurring planet earth with the 'Windows' logo. One does not need to be a Derridean expert to deconstruct its underlying meaning: the whole world is Microsoft and Microsoft is the whole world.

Something else differentiates these New Economy builders from the old and further indicates how deeply the process of informationization has become part of our world and us. Not many of its customers would argue that Chevron or General Motors is (or was) 'cool' or represents a 'lifestyle' – not even Chevron or GM themselves would argue this. However, Vodafone *is* 'cool', and is a 'lifestyle'. Its website says so. A moving banner ad tells the website visitor that Vodafone is 'groovy' and so, by implication, if you purchase one of their handsets or phone plans, will *you* be? (www.vodafone.com). Likewise, Nokia Corporation from Finland pitches itself as the quintessence of Scandinavian 'cool' design, a sort of Bang and Olufsen for the digerati, an inventor of sleek products with beautiful blonde-haired users and purveyor of a lifestyle that the whole world can buy into. Apple Corporation's applications and services, in the 'coolest' possible way, of course, will 'synchronize your digital life' by linking PDA, mobile phone, iTunes MP3 player and iMac into a symphony of inter-connectivity (www.apple.com). These are randomly picked examples that represent the very tip of what is a colossal iceberg. What they also represent is Kleinian 'brand bombing' on a global scale, a digital pounding of our consciousness with the idea that what we buy is not merely a computer, or a CD containing a software application, or a mobile handset, or a personal digital assistant, but an *idea* and a *lifestyle* (Frank 2000; Klein 2000). This 'dialectic of desire' feeds directly into the feedback loop, strengthen-ing the scope and power of informationization by linking ICTs and the network society with who we imagine ourselves to be; by linking them, in fact, with our very being.

A wired world of risk?

Where is all this feverish networking leading us? The extent and depth of digital networked communication is, as Peter Lunenfeld puts it, 'unique in the history of technological media' (2000: xix). The problem we face is that we have nothing to measure this network society against and so are every day stepping into an unknown and very unpredictable future. The feedback loop, the competition inherent in capitalist accumulation and our own intense love affair with information technologies has put this process of wiring the world on autopilot. Ulrich Beck has characterized this collective headlong rush into the unknown as one of 'organized irresponsibility' (1998: 15). No one is in control because our social democratic and economic responsibilities have been abnegated in favour of market forces and the alleged universal beneficence of ICTs. We have created a 'world **risk society**', argues Beck, which can only be understood and minimized through 'institutional reform' over the decision-making processes in government, in private corporations and in the sciences (1999: 5). In short, people have to regain control over what Anthony Giddens calls a 'runaway world' (1999a).

Consider one element of risk – the feedback loop. In physics as well as in economics the feedback loop is seen as something inherently *unstable*. If we continue with the economics example, the logic of this instability may become clearer. When everyone is buying and spending and consuming to ever-higher levels, inflation can set it. We live in a world of finite resources. In a market economy too much demand for a finite resource can cause it to rise in price. Rising prices across a whole range of goods and materials leads to demands for higher wages, which puts pressure on employers, forcing them to cut costs, to lay workers off, thereby precipitating a crash or recession.

The resource that we deal with in the information society is, of course, *information* and information is, in theory, *infinite*. This sounds good, doesn't it, like solar energy, maybe, where everyone wins? For the first time in human history we have an economy that is based around an infinite resource. How lucky do you feel? To begin with we have no idea how much information (bytes and bits) is 'out there'. We can hardly even guess the number of web pages, PDF files, HTML documents and hypertext links; the text, voice and data that flow through the network like blood through a hyper-fast circulatory system. We *do* know that this is being added to massively every minute of every day. I add to it and you add to it. The hundreds of millions of people online, banking, shopping, or working with data that is to be posted to the web or sent across the world in the shape of emails, JPEGS, MIDI files, WAV files, MP3 files, spam mail and so on, contribute incalculably to this information build-up. And this is just the Internet! So does all this information that washes around the planet actually matter? If you or I lived in a remote village on an Aegean island, tending sheep and fishing for our dinner, then maybe not. For increasing numbers of us, however, networks and their technologies have become our extensions; they make us part of the network and the network part of us. Networks and the information it both generates and carries are, as McLuhan puts it, 'the medium that shapes and controls the scale and form of human association and action' (1995: 152). To hark back once more to my common refrain: this is why it is important that we call this a network or information *society*. The vast amount of information it generates also accelerates, in terms of its circulation through us and through the network itself. A study at the University of California at Berkeley estimated in 2002 that over the next three years alone more information would be created than was made over the last 40,000 years (Cochrane 2002). Impressive? Take a small corner of what constitutes network interconnectivity: in the UK an estimated 16 billion text messages were sent in 2002 (MDA 2002) Gobsmacking? In fact, the constantly increasing velocity and volume of information may turn out to be a serious problem. David Shenk (1997) believes it is a problem we already own (if have not yet confronted). He calls it 'information overload', the result of instability in the feedback loop. There is already too much information for us ever to be able to consume as individuals, and information overload means that we are increasingly unable to discriminate the good from the bad, the rubbish from the valuable, the useful from the useless. There is just too much of it and it moves too fast, and as Paul Virilio argues, the increase in speed simply heightens the potential for information gridlock (1995a).

Shenk quotes Michael Dertrouzos, director of MIT's Laboratory for Computer Science, as saying that information technology 'is an open duct into your central nervous system' (the 'addiction' metaphor permeates much critical writing on the network society). The point he was making, echoing Virilio's 'gridlock' metaphor, is that information overload 'occupies the brain and reduces productivity' (1997: 30). This is no small irony in a world supposedly made super-efficient through ICTs. What is the logical extension of information overload? Network crash? Society crash? Or lots of little individual human crashes? If we can't make sense of the world any more and no one seems to be in control any longer, what sort of future does an increasingly networked society hold in store? Do we place our fate in the market and its 'invisible hand' to restore the 'equilibrium' at some unspecified point? Do we try to find ways of calculating the risks involved, as Beck argues, through democratic reforms? Or, as Thomas Hylland Eriksen (2001) recommends, do we opt for 'slow time' instead? Read fewer emails; don't use the home PC; read more words on paper instead of the screen and switch off that annoying mobile phone for longer periods? I shall address these and other questions in later chapters.

I want now to turn to those who are seemingly outside the equation, those hundreds of millions in developed and developing countries for whom the network society finds no space. These are the outsiders who have never heard a dial-tone, or have never surfed the Internet; those millions for whom the gentle buzz of a mobile phone in their pocket would be an unimaginable thrill – those who have been deleted from the network society, those on the wrong side of what has been termed the 'digital divide'.

...d . . . the digital divide

Almost as soon as the information technology revolution began to evolve and make itself felt as a major social, cultural, technological and economic 'paradigm shift', people began to notice that the benefits were not flowing evenly and smoothly, either within countries or across the world as a whole. The Digital Revolution was producing what soon came to be termed a 'digital divide'. Indeed, government and academia were surprisingly quick off the mark in this respect. I noted in Chapter 1 that 1995 was an important year in the life of the Internet with the launch of Windows 95 and its bundled free web browser helping to make rates of connectivity soar. In the same year the US government signalled its awareness of an emerging digital divide. The National Telecommunications and Information Administration (NTIA) published the first of five yearly reports called 'Falling through the Net' (NTIA 1995) which documented the extent of this new phenomenon.

The US led the way in identifying the issue and other countries quickly followed suit. Today almost every country in the world has recognized their own digital divide and many have put substantial resources towards efforts that would 'bridge' it. Indeed, so central was access to information technology deemed to be that the United Nations categorized the issue almost as a human rights one. In 1999 Kofi Annan, the UN Secretary General, put in a nutshell the new global thinking on the centrality of information technologies to the human condition. He noted:

> People lack many things: jobs, shelter, food, health care and drinkable water. Today, being cut off from basic telecommunications services is a hardship almost as acute as these other deprivations and may indeed reduce the chances of finding remedies to them. Telecommunications is not just an issue for the telecommunications minister of each country, but for ministers of education, health and many others.
>
> (Annan 1999)

Such universal official interest meant that much research funding has been devoted to the issue since the mid-1990s. Governments, academia and community groups have been industriously involved in defining the digital divide and suggesting solutions for it. One can get an inkling of the scale of the interest by typing 'digital divide' in an Internet browser. On one occasion my Google search engine came up with 667,000 references (in 0.26 seconds). It fetched up 740,000 (in 0.18 seconds) a week later. However, a scan of even a fraction of these websites and a detailed review of the published literature in books and journals reveal that a good deal of the research misses the point and that much well-meaning concern and millions of dollars have been wasted since 1995. A key issue is that much of this literature sees the problem of the digital divide as being one of a 'technology gap'. This is especially prevalent in official governmental thinking. The 'solution', therefore, tends to revolve around ways to bridge this gap, such as through more computers for schools and colleges; extending the network to rural and remote areas; providing free or cheap access to community centres in poor areas; or providing free or cheap computers and Internet access for poor individuals and families in their own homes. Training is emphasized too: give the elderly, the young and the unemployed computer skills, this approach maintains, and their potential will be unleashed.

This thinking was evident in the first *Falling through the Net* report in 1995 – an influential piece of research that was based on the provision of the 'universal service' mentality that grew out of the era of telephony and has helped to shape the general approach in the US and across the world. *Falling through the Net* saw the problem as one of *access to information*, a bifurcation between information 'haves' and information 'have nots'. The report states that 'information "have-nots" are disproportionately found in [the US's] rural areas and its central cities' (NTIA 1995). And each *Falling through the Net* report since has proceeded upon the basis that providing access (the 'universal service' model) to information services is the most effective way to close the digital divide. Generally speaking, then, approaches to the digital divide have been of a 'throw resources at the problem' kind – approaches that hardly have had any impact at all.

Brian Loader (2002) has noted the experience of Britain's UK Online centres, a government digital divide 'solution' that aims to provide Internet access to all. He writes:

> It is scarcely surprising perhaps that the anecdotal picture which is emerging in the UK is of large numbers of grossly underused Online centres packed with state of the art digital equipment and providing formal training which is regarded as irrelevant to the needs of their intended users.

Notwithstanding its rather unimaginative title, a book called *Bridging the Digital Divide* (2002) provides a useful corrective to the 'give them computers' mindset. The author, Lisa Servon, argues that we need to *redefine* what is meant by the term 'digital divide'. The real issue, argues Servon, is not access to ICTs. Lack of access is only a symptom of a much deeper issue, which is 'the problem of persistent poverty and inequality' (2002: 2). She goes on:

> Clearly, the digital divide is much more complex than a mere lack of computers. Simplistic solutions have therefore masked and perhaps even exacerbated the larger problem. When we provide people with computers, we find that not much changes. IT on its own does not function as a ladder out of poverty.
>
> (Servon 2002: 6)

Getting the definition right, Servon argues, is absolutely central. Once we are clear about what the issue is and where the problem actually lies, then we can begin to think about ways that may effectively address it. She goes on to make the point that ICTs can in fact be part of the solution, being able to provide new ways to address the problems of poverty and inequality. However, 'to have any significant effect', she continues, 'technology must be enabled by *effective public policy in cooperation with concerted efforts by the private for-profit and private nonprofit sectors*' (2002: 6, emphasis added).

Servon's book is valuable in that she correctly identifies the nature of the problem, that is to say, that the digital divide is but an indicator of the deeper malaise of poverty and economic exclusion. However, implicit in her argument is the idea that it is simply a matter of goodwill, ranging across the broad front of government, employers and nonprofit organizations. Along with the 'deleted' themselves, these stakeholders would come together to fashion public policy for the information age. This will supposedly help create meaningful jobs that can link with meaningful training opportunities. Such an approach will correspond with easy access to ICTs to empower people, lift them from endemic poverty and bridge the wealth and technology gaps. Logically, this seems straightforward and, given the existence of goodwill among the stakeholders, there would appear to be a good chance of success through such an approach. However, I believe that Servon fundamentally misreads the *nature of capitalism* in the network society.

We discussed in Chapter 1 how the network society evolved from the nexus between the ICT revolution and the rise of neoliberalism as a political, economic and cultural force. Key to this restructuring, as we also saw, was the 'flexibilization' of labour, the free movement of capital, and an end to the state and organized labour as having a lead role in the managing of the economy. *Market forces* were to set the pace and determine the shape of the New Economy. Some of the social and economic effects of neoliberalism are already well known (for example Martin 1998). Let us look, then, at what I see as three major effects of the nexus between neoliberalism and the ICT revolution and then place Servon's stakeholders approach in the context of these.

First is the so-called 'wealth gap'. The gap between the rich and the poor has yawned to almost unprecedented levels in restructured, neoliberalized societies. This fact alone makes Servon's essentially democratic project much harder to take root. Why? Because as the gap widens, more and more people may recall the words of former Chief Justice of the US Supreme Court, Louis D. Brandeis, who said in 1941 that 'We can have democracy in this country or we can have great wealth concentrated in the hands of the few, but we can't have both.' In the US today, 1 per cent of the population owns 40 per cent of the nation's wealth – taking us back to levels of inequality last experienced in the 1920s. Second, the power of the state in most developed countries has given way, in relative terms, to the power of big business and the market. Neoliberal globalization, according to Richard Falk, has meant that 'the states system as the self-sufficient organizing framework for political life on a global level is essentially over' (1999: 35). What he means is that economic globalization, the power of markets, the chaos of stock markets, and freebooting multinational corporations that can shift goods, services, production and capital across increasingly porous national boundaries have become the de-centre of gravity in the New Economy. The state remains the 'pre-eminent political actor', Falk cautions, but it now has to take into account the reaction of the markets when formulating policy. Accordingly, domestically the state has lost a good deal of its power to shape and implement policy that could be seen as anti-market or 'bad for business'. Last, and deeply interconnected to these processes, is the atomization of society. This is the 'restructuring' of citizens and members of communities and societies into individualized consumers, where civic participation is in decline and where 'social capital', i.e. the essence of our positive, social and community-building connections with each other, is being depleted (for example Sennett 1999; Putnam 2000).

Key to Servon's approach is 'effective public policy': the central policy formulating and coordinating role to be played by the state at local, regional and national levels. Here, government would have to play a leading role in providing the right environment for the creation of meaningful jobs of more than short-term duration, with decent salaries, and which encourage the use of ICTs in ways that are useful and significant in people's daily lives. To at least some degree this would entail more regulation and protection of employment, the very things that scare markets and the things that neoliberalized governments at present have no stomach for. 'Effective public policy' in the New Economy also needs to take cognizance of what the markets and big business are prepared to go along with. If this means higher wages, giving workers more rights, making bosses flexible as well as workers, then, again, there is not going to be much enthusiasm. The logic of neoliberal globalization and the ICT revolution has, from its earliest days, been about *replacing* workers and *cutting* jobs, making those who are employed highly *flexible* and their working conditions *uncertain*. In the New Economy this is what makes business 'competitive'. This logic is undemocratic, highly exploitative and has widened the gap between rich and poor to extremely high levels. This logic has also created an immense amount of wealth and excess capacity and so it would be therefore relatively easy to shower the poor and the unemployed with computers and broadband connections – all for free. This has been the general response to the digital divide, something that is easily doable, politically positive and economically painless. And it doesn't work. It will not lift them out of poverty and bridge the digital divide, because the mutation of capitalism that currently dominates our societies and economies actually creates *and depends upon* the circumstances that create the divide.

To begin to tackle the digital divide we need to redefine what the digital divide means and to identify its locus. 'Effective public policy' would start from the premise that the divide stems from an unequal and exploitative economic system and not from a simplistic lack of access to ICTs. Capitalism has always been based upon inequality and exploitation. However, with the rise of neoliberalism, the rule of the markets and the abrogation of the state as ameliorator to the worst aspects of the system, social and economic injustice has steadily increased. Unless and until market and business imperatives are downgraded in favour of social democratic and inclusivist policies to tackle the digital divide, the divide itself can only grow and become more intractable. Those who have been deleted from the digital divide (the majority of humanity on the global scale) will be therefore outside the realms of power, outside the orbit of economic opportunity and without access to the tools for change (ICTs) that, within the context of social power and economic opportunity, would make for a more inclusive and diverse network society.

Wired world wars

The segue from 'digital divide' to 'wired world wars' is not as obscure as may first appear. The divide, as we have just seen, has its locus in the nexus between neoliberal globalization and the ICT revolution and the socially exploitative and repressive dynamics that stem from it. 'Wired world wars' or the *revolutionizing of armed conflict* in the network society, follows logically from the nature of capitalism and the 'the military origins of the information revolution' that Robins and Webster argued to be important dimensions that should not be underestimated (1999: 150). Exclusion and war have been upgraded with new digital features for the information age. I want to use this shortish section to outline how armed conflict has changed through the use of ICTs and then discuss what this may mean for our collective understanding of conflict and how 'wired world wars' are situated within the general configurations of global power in this early phase of the twenty-first century.

The information technology revolution and the evolution of the network society has changed not only the ways in which we do business and how we communicate with each other, but also the ways in which warfare is organized, conducted and understood. As I see it, armed conflict has been revolutionized in at least three different (and fundamental) ways. These are:

- in the *machinery* of war;
- in the ways in which war is *conducted*; and
- in the ways in which war is *represented*.

I shall take up these in their turn. But first we should remind ourselves what forms of conflict have been superseded in the advanced western countries, especially in the US and the western European countries.

In the post-Second World War period, up until quite recently, warfare between nations was tooled, organized and represented along *Fordist* lines. Professional or conscripted mass armies, equipped with standardized gear such as tanks and guns and missiles, were the machinery of warfare; territorial wars of manoeuvre and clashes between opponents seeking victory through overwhelming force were how wars were conducted; and warfare was represented through the media as wars of ideology (capitalism versus communism), or wars to repel perceived aggression (usually territory grabs) by outside forces. For all of this period, major war was avoided because of the nuclear stand-off that existed between the capitalist 'free world' and the 'communist' totalitarian regimes. Nevertheless, the post-war superpowers, the US and the Soviet Union, conducted numerous proxy wars through client regimes all across the world in Africa, South America and Southeast Asia. Where the superpowers did become physically involved in open warfare, such as in Vietnam for the Americans (1965–73) and Afghanistan for the Russians (1979–89), humiliating defeat and a long period of national social and political trauma were the consequences.

In a short space of time this general and ultimately failed framework (from the point of view of the superpowers) has been swept away. Indeed, Castells (1996: 455–6) views the experiences of Vietnam and Afghanistan as:

> . . . turning points in the capacity of states to commit their societies to destruction for not so compelling reasons. Since warfare and the credible threat of resorting to it, is still the core of state power, since the end of the Vietnam War strategists have been busy finding ways still to make war. Three conclusions were rapidly reached in advanced, democratic countries, regarding the conditions necessary to make war somewhat acceptable to society:
>
> 1. It should not involve common citizens, thus being enacted by a professional army, so that the mandatory draft should be reserved for truly exceptional circumstance, perceived as unlikely.
> 2. It should be short, even instantaneous, so that the consequences would not linger on, draining human and economic resources and raising questions about the justification for military action.
> 3. It should be clean, surgical, with destruction, even of the enemy, kept within reasonable limits and as hidden as possible from public view, with the consequence of linking closely information-handling, image-making and war-making.

Information and communication technologies in all their forms fit the bill for this new kind of war-waging (or at least they *appear* to, when war is being reported in the mainstream global media). The 1991 Gulf War against Iraq was the prototype for the new digital warfare. By that time the hardware of warfare was software-driven. 'Smart' computer-guided missiles fitted with digital cameras on their nose cones were now able to give the general population of the advanced countries the ultimate videogame thrill: 'experiencing' the moment when the missile hits its target – be it the roof of an enemy 'command and control centre', or a 'strategic' bridge, or radar tower – or whatever the military briefing officer who appeared on CNN told us what this grainy, soon-to-be-rubble image actually was. No longer do the body bags come home, publicly and persistently, by the planeload as they did in Vietnam. War is now conducted on a higher technological plane. 'Fire and forget', it is called in military parlance. It is conducted, supposedly, through clean, surgical, flexible, intense and devastating strikes by Cruise missiles controlled by men and women in offices thousands of miles from where the ordnance hits – fire and forget. When pilots actually do fly to their targets, they either fly so high in their B52s that they cannot see (or be attacked by) the enemy they are pummelling, or they are in the cockpit of a super-fast jet or Stealth bomber where the targets are sighted on video screens and where computers lock onto them and launch the bombs.

Such 'mediated' war in our highly mediated society has two central dimensions that separate it out from other, more 'conventional' forms of warfare. First is that our highly mediated society allows for highly mediated forms of killing by those in control of the high-tech means of war. Death and destruction are abstracted to an unprecedented degree. The enemy, for those with the technology, is represented as shadows on a radar screen, or as coordinates on an electronic map. They are targets already identified by satellites and stored in Defense Department computers so that someone (a pilot wedged into his cockpit or a staff officer sitting in a comfortable chair in a 'command and control centre' with coffee in hand) has only to perform the martial equivalent of the mouse double-click to set the remote procedure into deadly motion. Second is how this mediated process is itself mediated (represented) as news and as information for us to consume. In the digital wars against Iraq in 1991 and 2003, against Serbia in 1999 and against Afghanistan in 2001–2, the world at large was given a filtered, cleansed and highly ideological window on what happened. These were technologically mediated events brought to you by a controlled and highly mediated media. In the second Iraq war this process reached new levels of sophistication with the innovation of 'embedded media'. Here over five hundred journalists, the vast majority of those who would see, hear and report the war, were 'embedded' with units of the US army, air force and navy. They were escorted at all times by military 'minders', the equivalent of the Red Army commissar, who applied strict rules regarding what they could and could not report. Moreover, as many journalists were later to complain, they knew nothing of what was going on elsewhere, and were only able to give what the Secretary of Defense Donald Rumsfeld himself called 'the soda straw view' of war, a description of a small, disconnected fragment of the big picture (Marshall 2003). Many independent journalists felt this to be a serious restriction of their code of freedom in reporting and went it alone, roaming the countryside and cities in four-wheel drives and relying upon initiative and experience. They did so at their peril. The International Federation of Journalists (IFJ) noted that non-embedded journalists were killed at a higher proportional rate than the US army, at least fourteen by the time the 'main phase' of the fighting was declared over by President Bush on 1 May. Moreover, the IFJ called for a 'war crimes' inquiry into some of these deaths, suggesting that the victims may have been secretly and deliberately targeted by US forces (Marr 2003).

As Jean Baudrillard argued in his (in)famous *The Gulf War Did Not Happen* (1995), this is virtual reality played out with live ammunition and real targets. The 1991 Gulf War (and all the subsequent digital wars), according to Baudrillard, was *simulacra*; a copy of reality, a digital image on our TV screens and on the computer screens of the soldiers, sailors and pilots; a PowerPoint presentation by a military official to CNN, BBC and the rest of the world's media. Baudrillard's point is that war's *actuality* is lost to us through layer upon layer of mediation. The extraordinarily low numbers of allied dead reinforces this unreality, with the subtext of our mediated version of mediated war being that this is war and victory almost without death.

Iraq, Serbia, Afghanistan and then Iraq again in 2003 were the wars of the high-tech against the low-tech, the wars of the digital divide, and the new mode of warfare for the twenty-first century. Indeed Iraq in 2003 represented a higher level of technical sophistication, and a wider digital divide, than ever before. The invasion to oust Iraq from Kuwait in 1991 necessitated a massive ground force of half a million soldiers against a fairly well armed and some-way motivated army. In 2003 less than half that number opposed an ill-equipped and non-motivated agglomeration. The bulk of the destruction was meted out through high-tech air power. The digitally powerless (civilians as well as troops), as a result, stood no chance and died in their thousands, unable to avoid the aerial onslaught (see www.iraqbodycount.net). The majority of the Iraqi army who had the opportunity, sensibly offered little or no resistance and melted back into the civilian population.

Just as the capitalist system driven by neoliberalism and ICTs leave millions digitally divided and 'deleted' in its wake, the high-tech wars being prosecuted by the advanced countries (primarily the US) have left a virtual world of destruction, death and resentment in the Middle East, in North Africa and in Central Asia. On the effects of this military digital divide, Australian media theorist Scott Burchill has argued that 'no amount of technological fetishism will insulate the West from the unintended consequences of its actions around the world' (2003). The major 'unintended consequence' is Benjamin Barber's (1996: 23) 'powerful and paradoxical interdependence', a yawning disconnection *within* the wired world: the high-tech and the low-tech, the rich and the poor, the exploiters and the exploited – McWorld versus Jihad.

The failure of the US security services, despite their vast preponderance in high-tech methods of surveillance, to predict or forestall the World Trade Center and Pentagon Building attacks are but the most dramatic instance to date of the disconnection between worlds. Indeed, the US's hyper-reliance upon ICTs for intelligence gathering at the expense of having 'people on the ground', so-called 'human intelligence', had severe repercussions – what the CIA call 'blowback'. A lack of human intelligence of the areas in question, of the peoples, the languages, the politics and the cultures, was arguably a significant contributing factor to the blindness to the growing al-Qa'ida threat. The result was that the high-tech virtual war became a low-tech reality over the skies of New York and Washington instead of Kabul and Baghdad.

The surveillance society: living with digital 'Big Brother'

I finish this chapter with some discussion on a subject that also flows logically from the sections on the 'digital divide' and the 'wired world wars'. Throughout history, and especially in more concentrated form under capitalism, exclusion and exploitation have always bred and instilled a certain amount of fear on the part of those doing the excluding and the exploiting. Creating social division necessarily creates a social, economic and sometimes cultural 'other'. This 'other' is usually something largely unknown, something possibly subversive and dangerous and therefore something that needs to be monitored and kept in check. This process has been especially acute under neoliberalism. I argue, therefore, that the explosion in ICT-based surveillance techniques such as closed circuit television (CCTV), for example, can be viewed as a symptom of one of the central contradictions of neoliberal capitalism. As Dean Wilson and Adam Sutton (2002: 7) argue,

> CCTV is a microcosm of the cultural contradictions of late modernity; it is very much a creature of its times. In societies that seem inherently risky and unstable – where social and economic relations are free floating and contingent – there is a corresponding impulse to control, segregate, fortify and exclude. Public surveillance is directed at one of the central dilemmas of our society: how to maintain the free-play of market forces while simultaneously governing and controlling social risk.

Philosopher and sociologist Zygmunt Bauman made essentially the same connections in his 1998 book *Globalization: The Human Consequences*. In it he wrote that 'The complex issue of existential insecurity brought about by the process of globalization tends to be reduced to the apparently straightforward issue of "law and order" ' (1998: 5). In other words, the 'inherently risky and unstable' world created through the rule of the market and powered by ICTs is viewed not as an issue that calls for a fundamental rethinking of how our society is structured – but more as one of uncomplicated *criminality* that needs to be detected and punished. Moreover, the reducing of complex civil society issues such as the right to privacy to simplistic rhetoric concerning 'law and order' has been largely successful. CCTVs are either popular or treated with indifference (Webster 1999: 122). People who do voice concerns run the risk of being treated as 'soft on crime' or are subjected to the old disingenuous cliché that 'if you have nothing to hide, then you have nothing to worry about'. CCTV surveillance in shopping malls, in high streets and in 'high crime' areas such as run-down housing estates are indeed used as tools to 'detect and deter crime' (Webster 1999: 116). The efficacy of these, however, is at least questionable, with results from studies tending to be either mixed or inconclusive (see for example Ditton and Short 1999). But there are larger issues connected to civil liberties, especially the citizen's right to privacy and the potential for CCTV and related techniques to be used as tools for social control, political repression and the identification and monitoring of what Charles Raab terms 'suspect social groups' (1998: 157).

The existence of widespread techniques for digital surveillance throughout society can easily slip over into abuses of civil liberties. With both the technique and the laws already in place in advanced 'wired societies' we can see examples where this is happening. In the wake of the attacks on the World Trade Center and the Pentagon Building, we are in danger of entering, in the words of Thomas Hylland Eriksen, 'the paranoid phase of globalisation' (2002: 1). Under the general rubric of 'the war against terrorism', most countries around the world reassessed their internal security measures after the al-Qa'ida attacks; and those countries with the technological sophistication to enable it, turned to ICTs as surveillance tools to provide even greater intelligence-gathering measures than before. As Adam Penenberg (2002) wrote:

> Within hours of the attacks on the World Trade Center and the Pentagon, as federal officials shut down airports and US strategists began plotting a military response, Attorney General John Ashcroft was mobilizing his own forces. In meetings with top aides at the FBI's Strategic Information and Operations Center – during which the White House as well as the State and Defense departments dialed in via secure videoconference – Ashcroft pulled together a host of anti-terrorism measures. Days later, the attorney general sent to Capitol Hill a bill that would make it easier for the government to tap cell phones and pagers, give the Feds broad authority to monitor email and Web browsing, strengthen money-laundering laws and weaken immigrants' rights. There were whispers of a national identity card and of using face-recognition software and retinal scans at airports and in other public spaces. And high above it all would sit an Office of Homeland Security . . .

The paranoia-inducing 'others' in this instance were 'Arabs' or people of 'Middle Eastern appearance'. The point, however, is that it could have been any group and – through various laws enacted in the US and in the European Union in the 'paranoid phase of globalization' – it now, theoretically, *can* be any group or any individual.

Of course the electronic 'surveillance society' was in place well before September 11th. The network that acts as our 'extension' in the wired world leaves myriad traces of our passing through it or acting upon it every day – mostly in ways we are unaware of. The network of networks is the means for cyber-surveillance of the CCTV kind writ large; a digital 'panopticon' that, in potential at least, means that every keystroke we make online, every email (however personal or embarrassing), every phone call or SMS text message, every part of our PDA traffic, every website visited, every search-phrase we put into the search engine, every download, upload and peer-to-peer file swap we make, every JPEG picture we send or receive is vulnerable to relatively easy interception and capture. *Your* business can also very easily be the business of not only your nosey ISP or paranoid boss, but also the concern of state security agencies such as the FBI, the CIA, and their equivalents across the developed economies.

In a globalized world where 'flows' of information represent the lifeblood of the New Economy and are the oxygen of competition between corporations and between states, covert COMINT or communications intelligence is vital. It can provide the means to stay ahead of the game in both the commercial war between corporations for global market domination and the 'war against terrorism' that was launched in the wake of 11 September. As David Lyon notes in his *Surveillance Society* (2002), the age of globalization and the information technology revolution meant that 'surveillance went global'. The actual extent of COMINT systems controlled by a select few rich English-speaking countries only came under a somewhat pale light in the late 1990s. Lyon describes COMINT's rationale as

> the effort to gain access to, intercept and process every important modern form of communication, in every significant sphere and in many countries. Such an important task is supported by the activities of the USA–UK alliance of English-speaking nations and above all the American NSA [National Security Agency].
>
> (Lyon 2002: 95)

Since the 1970s a US-initiated system called ECHELON has electronically managed this system, which extends to 'second-tier' English-speaking countries such as Canada, Australia and New Zealand. To cite Lyon (2002: 96) once more:

> [ECHELON] made possible the continued examination of messages whose volume had become too great for manual classification. 'Watch lists' that compile names that are of 'reportable intelligence interest' are now automated using a key component called a 'dictionary'. These dictionaries store extensive databases on specified targets, including names, addresses, telephone numbers and other selection criteria. Such dictionaries have been found, for example, to intercept every telex message that passes through London every day; thousands of personal, business and diplomatic communications. ECHELON computers also sift through fax and modem data, as well as topics of communication and, since 1995, voiceprints. Pager messages, cellular mobile radio and new satellite communications are also vulnerable to such interception.

I have argued at points throughout this book that the lines between the state, the economy and big business have been increasingly blurred. Knowledge of this fact means that it should come as no surprise to learn that ECHELON also collects commercial intelligence that may give advantage to private enterprise. Indeed, in the UK, as Lyon notes, 'GCHQ (General Communications Headquarters) is *obliged* to intercept foreign commercial communications traffic "in the interests of the economic well-being of the United Kingdom" ' (2002: 96). ECHELON has been linked to the commercial interests of American companies, too. In 1994 the Boeing and McDonnell-Douglas airline manufacturers beat Airbus Industrie in a bid for a large Saudi Arabian order. It was alleged by the French government that ECHELON had supplied intelligence on the Airbus bid that allowed the US companies to gain an unfair advantage. This and other allegations prompted the European Union (EU) to investigate, at French insistence, the extent of 'Anglo-Saxon spying'. The actual extent of industrial espionage will, of course, never be fully revealed due to the convenient excuse of 'national security' that routinely cordons off such matters from public-democratic scrutiny.

On a somewhat less dramatic level, our own little personalized 'data-trails', the traces of our ordinary lives, are also out there in cyberspace. These too can be picked up and analysed not only by government spooks (should they so wish), but by commercial interests who want to discover (or anticipate) something of far more interest to them than our political opinions or our terroristic proclivities – our spending and consuming habits. Lyon (2002) calls it 'consumer surveillance' and it is reflective of a sea change in how consumer capitalism operates in the New Economy. Instead of mass production for mass consumption – the essence of Fordist production systems – 'what was once a matter of mass production and mass merchandising is now increasingly individualised', notes Lyon. 'The trend' he continues, 'is towards one-to-one marketing and personalised techniques such as loyalty "clubs", co-branded credit cards, named and narrow-cast mailshots and targeted advertising on invoices that are customised to the buying patterns of each consumer' (2002: 43).

Many of us will be familiar with these sorts of techniques. Moreover, the network society is every day being consciously constructed to ensure that we do become familiar with, and *blasé* about, 'consumer surveillance'. How, for example, does Amazon.com appear to know who I am, addressing me personally whenever I visit their website? How can it 'suggest' titles of books that I might look at myself if I were in an actual bookshop? One reason is '**cookies**'. A cookie is a line of text that is placed on your computer's hard drive, indicating that you have visited a certain website. This can be accessed by website operators to construct a profile of your web surfing habits, your general interests, the sort of things you would be likely to spend some money on. This data can be used by commercial entities as a way of targeting you for 'consumer surveillance' that leads to 'personalized marketing'. You absent-mindedly look up the price of, say, a pair of specialized cycling shoes on a certain website, and soon afterwards receive spam mail, or pop-up advertisement which just happen to suggest 'great deals' on cycling footwear, or just about anything to do with bikes.

Cookies are now a commercial standard on the Internet. Most of the time we are unaware they are operating, until a website announces that your PC browser is 'not cookie enabled' and therefore bars you from entering unless you 'enable' the browser. Once tagged you will blithely surf the web leaving tiny digital footprints all over the place and be completely ignorant of it. How much of the spam mail we receive has been targeted to you personally; how much is narrowcast mail shots; how much do these databases actually know about you?

In terms of our rights to privacy in the New Economy and network society, we need to ask ourselves some serious questions. Is the potential for ICTs to open up our private lives to the scrutiny of both state and commercial interests a price worth paying for membership of the network society? Is our individual and collective fixing under the gaze of the digital panoptic the cost we must bear to maintain 'law and order'? If so, how is it that life just seems to get more uncertain, more lawless and less orderly?

To get to grips with these issues it is necessary, I believe, continually to remind ourselves of the logics that gave life to the network society and shape it in very substantial ways: those of neoliberal capitalism and the information technology revolution that has been inextricably bound up with it. As we have seen, the blurring of the lines between what is commercial and what is not has meant, in general, that the commercial has colonized more and more of what previously lay outside the realms of the market. Deregulation has been central to this. Leaving much of life to the vagaries of the market has, as argued by Beck (1998), Sennett (1999) and Putnam (2000) among others, increased uncertainty and risk. However, if this chain of causality is not linked to the effects of neoliberalism and marketization, then politicians and those with a stake in the New Economy can point instead to 'law and order' reasons and demand more surveillance in the streets and in our networking habits; more use of 'consumer surveillance' to increase sales and make us ever more open to the scams, manipulations and blandishments of the unscrupulous. Such inattention to a critique of the network will simply drive the economy, culture and society into yet more dependency upon ICTs and market forces. It will bury the democratic rights and obligations of people under the weight and pressure of more information, more automation, more risk and uncertainty and an ever-quickening pace of life.

Further reading

Lyon, D. (2002) *The Surveillance Society*. Buckingham: Open University Press.
Rifkin, J. (2000) *The Age of Access*. London: Penguin.
Servon, L. (2002) *Bridging the Digital Divide*. Oxford: Blackwell.
Shenk, D. (1997) *Data Smog*. London: Abacus.
Slevin, J. (2001) *The Internet and Society*. Malden, MA: Blackwell Press.

4 LIFE.COM

> Our private sphere has ceased to be the stage where the drama of the subject at
> odds with his objects and with his image is played out: we no longer exist as
> playwrights or actors but as terminals of multiple networks.
>
> (Baudrillard (1988: 16)

'The future has arrived; it's just not evenly distributed'
(William Gibson)

What I want to do for most of this chapter is to take the reader through a series of
thought-experiments. These will comprise a fairly gentle (and I think useful) series
of mental exercises, using the power of imagination to give to the discussion in
the previous chapters an element of clarity that can sometimes be clouded by the
combination of theorization and empirical reality.

What do I mean by this – using the *imagination* to augment and understand reality?
Well, concerning the literary genre of science fiction, it has long been argued that what
science fiction is 'really about' is not the future, but that it instead acts as a series of
metaphors for our present condition. Commonly these stem from and play out, consciously or unconsciously, our anxieties about technological change and our fear
of what the future may contain. Consider the 1923 film *Metropolis*, made just five years
after what was then the most destructive and mechanized war in history, with its
overwhelmingly dark and dystopic depiction of an industrialized and coldly automated
society. Fast forward a bit and think of the books and films of the 1950s when the
Cold War was at its most frigid and when the appalling reality of nuclear war was an
enduring (if not wholly incomprehensible) threat. Science fiction was one way of
making the nuclear present more comprehensible. Films such as *The Day the Earth*

Stood Still (1951) have been seen as an anti-atomic war statement. Its not-too-subtle message is that humans can no longer be trusted with the terrifying technologies of destruction they have developed. In *The Day the Earth Stood Still*, a peaceful emissary from another world arrives in a flying saucer with his nine-foot robot-bodyguard. His mission is to make earthlings realize that they are on the point of self-destruction. Demented US generals and politicians respond to this friendly advice with tanks, guns and airplanes. They eventually kill the emissary – to the more-than-mild irritation of his bodyguard who brings him back to life, after wreaking some pretty comprehensive revenge, so he can tell humans that if they (the communists and capitalists?) do not learn to coexist then mutual destruction will be their lot.

The series of Arnold Schwarzenegger *Terminator* films that began in the 1980s are similarly dystopian visions of the future. These revolved around the futuristic 'cyborg', the robot covered in flesh, which represents the final melding of humans with computers and machines. The cyborg metaphor is an important one that has been employed by socialist–feminist theoretician, Donna Haraway, to help make sense of our technological present, and will be taken up shortly.

In literature, the science fiction sub-genre of cyberpunk and its writers such as William Gibson have created new languages and new conceptual categories, which, while set in the future, allow us to articulate and conceptually probe our *current realities*. As Paul A. Taylor has argued, neologisms contained in the dystopian novels of Gibson, such as *Neuromancer* (1984), or Neal Stephenson's *Snowcrash* (1992) provide what Taylor terms 'zeitgeist-capturing qualities' that 'provide fresh insights into the cultural experience of a society increasingly transformed, not only by the extent of technological change in a new informational age, but also its unprecedented pace' (2001: 74). It was Gibson, for example, who coined the term 'cyberspace', a science fiction term that is now used and understood (at some level of sophistication) by everybody from the Nintendo kid playing an online version of *Metroid Prime* to the buttoned-up bureaucrats in the White House who drafted *The National Strategy to Secure Cyberspace* that we discussed in the previous chapter. It was also Gibson, incidentally, who gave us a challenging way to think about cyberspace that was rooted in the real world when he wrote that 'cyberspace is where the bank keeps your money'.

To say that we live in a network society and that it exists *here* and that it exists *now* is one thing; we can also, if we try, reflect upon our own experience of this. However, to *understand* the experience we need to push it a bit further and through a deeper understanding the experience may elicit more meaning. The following few pages are not going to be an indulgence in the realms of futurology, nor do they try (God forbid) to science fictionalize the network society. What I have tried to do is to capture the *zeitgeist* through the delivery of a concentrated dose of the *technological present*, in the form of a couple of imagined scenarios. Essentially this is a literary device that highlights the network society and our place within it. These will not give us a glimpse of the future – instead they will give us an insight into the present. As Peter Fitting noted of the work of Gibson, his writing is 'not so much "about" what lies in store for us as it is a figure for our experience of the present' (cited in Tofts 1997: 22).

There is a certain freedom in thought-experiments: in this case the freedom accorded through bringing together, in the shape of a couple of scenarios, the ICT applications and devices that are transforming our lives and creating a powerfully technologized existence – a hypermediated and networked reality. In everyday life these act upon us so quickly and comprehensively that we almost never have time to register their significance. So what we are also doing in these thought-experiments is to engage in a form of critique, a slight defamiliarization that will afford us the space in which to 'step back' and take stock of the present. This is vital if we are not only to understand the present but also be in a position to have a hand in shaping how the future might unfold. As cyberculture theorist Darren Tofts argues in the context of understanding cyberspace, 'critique needs to be realistically in touch with the contemporary before it can attempt to understand the possible trajectories of the indeterminate future' (1997: 23).

Moreover, an understanding of our experience of the network society will be an indispensable conceptual tool for developing the more politically oriented tasks of self- and community-empowerment in the 'indeterminate future' of the network society: issues that will be discussed in the next chapter.

A day in wired life

Scenario one

Friday, 6:45 a.m. Danny wakes up to a deafening blast of Nirvana's 'Come as you are' emanating from a grunge station on his Internet radio. The radio is linked to his Hewlett Packard Media Centre in the living room through a Bluetooth wireless connection. The Media Centre connection, of course, is 'always on', but the timer on the radio switched the music off when he was out last night and switched it back on again, at full-volume, while he was in a deep sleep. He has to be at work at the marketing company in less than an hour anyway – the full-time job he holds down (just) alongside the full-time study for his business degree. Everyone seems to do both these days. A rude awakening, though. (Danny tired of Nirvana a few years ago and deleted all his MP3s from his hard drive and gave the burned CDs away.) He slams the 'off' button with the knuckle of his forefinger and gets out of bed.

He semi-sleepwalks into the living room and in a reflex action sits down at the Media Centre to check his email. Twenty-four new messages. A quick scan reveals only four are not spam and only two of those he needs to act upon. One is from Anna, his lecturer, a reminder to the class that the year's final essay is due on Monday at 5:00 p.m. The second is from Stuart, his boss at the marketing company, asking if he is available to work on Sunday as someone has fallen ill. There has been hardly any time to do study lately. He did try to read some downloaded articles from class and did a bit of browsing on the Internet, but the essay topic, 'The future for E-commerce', was still only vaguely comprehended. The business websites hyped it continually and people talked about it at work – but so what? Who actually does it and what does it matter? Danny switches on his PDA and makes a note to try to set aside time on Saturday to write it up; he also makes a mental note that it is going to have to be a rush job to meet the deadline. There is just no time in my life to do everything, he thinks.

Sunday is out in terms of doing his essay. The boss's 'request' is more of an order. Stuart tends to view refusal of overtime as almost something personal, as evidence of not being a 'team player', and Danny's contract might not be renewed if he says no. How would he pay for his university fees then? For that matter, how could he afford the payments on the Media Centre and the mobile phone, all of which he would need to get (and try to keep) another job? Danny attaches his PDA to the Internet connection on the Media Centre and downloads some other articles on E-business he has bookmarked from the *Business Week* and *Fortune* websites. Maybe he could quickly read them on the train to work and during his half-hour lunch-break. He had skimmed them earlier and thought them mostly nonsense; stuff glibly penned by business reporters who probably have shares in E-business ventures somewhere. But then, he also muses, at least the words were from someone other than himself and would therefore have to count as research.

He gets dressed and then eats a muesli bar without even having to leave his chair at the Media Centre. As he dresses and eats he puts on a video streaming lecture on 'Consumer Behaviour' from an idiotic part-time 'virtual' lecturer whom Danny's never met. The university website calls it 'distance learning' designed to 'fit with your busy lifestyle'. Danny thinks he's 'distant' only because his job means he can't get to all the classes; and 'learning' is something he doubts he is doing at all. Again, no time. And no point: he can't hear what the talking head is saying when he moves his mouth from the microphone. A joke: they should get actors to do it, he thinks. He clicks 'favourites' on his Internet browser, scrolls down and double-clicks the *onBusiness* website someone has recommended, and half-concentrates on a streaming video item called 'CEO's Upclose', instead.

Danny unplugs his mobile phone from its charger and thumbs it into life. Six voicemail messages have been left. He scrolls down the numbers and sees that there are three from his mother. As he listens to them he makes a note in his PDA to email her as soon as he can. He knows she would rather talk with him, but Danny knows how she goes on and on when on the phone and he's too busy right now. Two from Stuart, hassling him about Sunday no doubt, he thinks, and one from Angie, his super-keen, up-and-coming 'colleague' at work. He listens to her metallic voice rattle on about a 'team building' night she has organized for the group after the shift today. It will be a 'relaxed affair' at the World in a Cup Internet café. *Do* make an effort to come, she intones. Danny makes another mental note to try to get out of it. He remembers that usually at these sorts of things the guys end up playing on the computers and the women drink lattes and plot new ways to make the office an even more terrible place to work in. He has already arranged to go online gaming on Playstation at his brother's house – or was it a night at home doing his essay? Already, he can't remember. It's written somewhere on his PDA.

The half-hour train journey to work is 'wasted' texting some friends and then emailing his mother on the PDA. Until recently, Danny could do some Internet surfing (casual browsing or some university work) on the workplace computer, in between the cold calling he has to do for the marketing company. However, they have installed new software that does what they call 'predictive dialling'. The computer trawls through hundreds of thousands of telephone numbers, dialling each one until someone answers. As soon as the connection is made the call is routed in a split-second to the next available operator who has to pretend that he/ she has made the call and knows whom he/she is speaking to: Good morning/ afternoon/evening, my name is Daniel . . . This little 'efficiency measure' has meant no free time and Danny estimates he's now talking sales for about 95 per cent of the shift.

Just before finishing time Stuart prods him a little too violently between the shoulder blades: could he come in on Saturday too and take a day off during the week, Friday, maybe? Yes, sure, Stuart, he grins. 'What about my essay' he thought, as he smiled? On the way to World in a Cup for the team-building session that he couldn't get out of in the end (Angie will be his boss some day) he calls his classmate Donna and asks her advice about the essay on Monday. Donna says she is also getting pretty desperate and is thinking of submitting a plagiarized essay from Quickpapers.com or something similar.

No way, he thinks. But when at World in a Cup he has a look at the Quick-papers.com site. It all looks quick and easy and he could easily cover his tracks by adding a few riffs from the downloads in his PDA. Who would know? An essay costs only $60.00. He tells himself he needs to think it through. Danny doesn't really want to think of himself as a cheat, but a 'fail' grade is rapidly approaching as the alternative. He leaves the PC and goes to indulge Angie in her little façade and do some team-building instead. As predicted this consists of her conducting a four-hour bellyache about how performance targets are not being met, and that more efficiency measures are needed, a more motivated attitude from staff, etc., etc . . .

Eventually, he gets home and it's already after ten. He remembers reading on a website somewhere that an Internet year is like a dog year, it goes seven times faster. It feels like it, he thinks. This is his last year at university and the whole thing has gone past in a flash; he reflects that he's learned almost nothing other than how to juggle tasks badly because he's always too busy working to pay the fees, the rent, the ICT 'goodies' he couldn't do without – to do a course he isn't really interested in.

At the Media Centre he sheepishly looks at the Quickpapers.com website again and finds a paper called 'E-commerce and globalization' which, from the short description, looks like it will do. He can always do a bit of work to it if he has some spare time over the weekend. Half an hour would do it and then at least some of it would be his own work. Scrolling down the list of generic papers, Danny smiles to himself when he comes across one called 'The Role of Ethics in a Capitalist Economy' – for $55.00. That seems to make up his mind. He goes to the fridge to get a beer and his wallet from the bedroom. Three minutes and a credit card deduction later, the laser printer is silently issuing his 'pass' grade in the form of a seven-page 'E-commerce' essay, with six bibliographic references in it. He can add some more to that from *Business Week* and *Fortune*, he thinks. Danny clicks off the site quickly and with a pang of guilt. Irrationally, he clicks on the 'History' button on his browser and deletes the traces of having visited Quickpapers.com. He swallows some beer to help take his mind off the deception and starts to surf the Internet. A few clicks later and Danny soon finds himself, despite himself, in a grunge chat-room, chatting about how good Nirvana are to ICEBLUE, pUnKtReAtS, expectnosympathy and Dave98 and stays there drinking and chatting until well after midnight.

Scenario two

4:10 a.m. Alison gets up quickly and on the way to the shower she checks the email. Forty-seven messages and all of them addressed to her personally. The spam-filtering programme ensures she does not have to waste time wading through pages of 'unbelievable!' offers of how to make thousands of dollars working from home, or porn site invitations. It's going to be a big day. A 5:00 a.m. videoconference link-up with her company's world HQ and unfortunately for Alison this is the optimal time to have it, given all the time differences involved. A quick look at the names of the email senders tells her that it's mostly about the meeting. Alison is on the bottom rung or thereabouts in advertising; quite good pay, but all work and stress to keep the upper rungs happy. Her company has the contract for the global advertising launch for a new video-game console and it's worth a lot of money and therefore comes with a lot of pressure. Her job at the videoconference is to listen and give a PowerPoint presentation later in the day to those too senior to be aroused at such an hour.

Before the shower, Alison decides to check her stock portfolio quickly. The local markets haven't opened yet and she had already checked just before bed last night.

However, Alison has been obsessed with it ever since taking some big losses (for her) in the 2001 'tech wreck'. Bad tips from Internet shysters who hyped stocks they knew to be worthless. After that she'd decided to do her own stock analysis and day-trading and now spends many hours a week reading up and investing in her favoured industry, biotechnology. She's been doing well recently, although she resents the fact that at 24, she needs to worry constantly about her retirement income.

Twenty minutes and an apple later and Alison is in her car, checking the messages on her mobile. As she gets close to the office, she notices the next message on the list is from Sam, her boyfriend: a cheesy e-card, wishing her luck for the presentation later on. Alison glances at the card on her LED display and deletes it halfway through its little jingle. As she bins it, a call comes through. It's from her boss, Alan. The videoconference has been postponed until the same time tomorrow – a satellite fault or something, he says. No point going home now, she thinks, and gets to the office at 4:55.

The next couple of hours are spent working on her stocks, reading yesterday's business news reports and the various Wall Street analyses on the three biotech firms where she has most of her money invested. As the morning wears on, however, the job begins to take over. Another twenty-three emails have arrived and so they all have to be gone through and responded to; apologetic emails and phone calls have to be sent and made to their clients' local reps, who are also to be briefed on the outcomes of the videoconference; and a review of the four other major accounts she looks after have to be attended to. The latter task is the easy, though time-consuming part of her job and, as usual, involves trawling the Internet for ideas, graphics, angles and clichés to 'appropriate', then 'modify' and then pitch to hopefully unsuspecting clients.

This sort of pretence of research and originality reminds her of the PowerPoint presentation that is now due tomorrow. A textbook from the MBA course the company had enrolled her in came to mind, too. The book was called *Eating the Big Fish: How Challenger Brands Can Compete Against Brand Leaders*, by 'brand guru' Adam Morgan (1999). She's only had time to read the book's Preface, but that contained its little 'hook': what Morgan called 'The Eight Credos of Challenger Brands'. These were:

1. Break with your immediate past
2. Build a lighthouse identity
3. Assume thought leadership of your category
4. Create symbols of reevaluation
5. Sacrifice
6. Overcommit
7. Use advertising and publicity as a high-leverage asset
8. Become ideas-centred, rather than consumer centred

Brilliant. This was the sort of airy-fairy stuff that was essentially meaningless (or could mean anything) but made great pep talk/PowerPoint stuff; the sort of stuff that would give the directors (who would never dream of reading it) a warm fuzzy feeling and make her look like a girl going places. I should have thought of this before, Alison tells herself. The actual videoconference doesn't matter – *this* stuff is what the directors (and the clients) want to hear. A deep mental note is made to use books like this more often. So useful and so time-saving! The book is at home somewhere, but no matter: she's able to download the entire Preface from Amazon.com for free.

Already it's nearly 4:00 p.m. and all she's had is coffee. After writing a 141-word Executive Summary, Alison is feeling pleased with herself and so allows herself time for a sandwich in the park. She takes along her new BlackBerry PDA that Sam bought for her birthday. Some more emails to deal with, mainly routine. The day is shaping up to be a productive one. One message is a positive reply from one of her clients regarding what he calls the 'exciting and innovative' idea she pitched to him this morning as a way to launch their new mobile phone. The concept came more-or-less complete from a website in Slovenia, but no one would be any the wiser when there are a billion websites to choose from. Change a few words here and there. It just gets better, she thinks. The PDA vibrates, signalling another message. It's Sam, sending another 'good luck' e-card, even more inane than the last – people stare at her as 'Tie a Yellow Ribbon Round the Old Oak Tree' jingles absurdly from her BlackBerry.

Another email, this time from Trish, a fellow MBA student she's never met. Trish wants to know if Alison will be taking part in the online group discussion following tonight's 6:30 p.m. lecture. This is their once-a-semester, face-to-face class experience, this one being on 'Leadership Skills for Managerial Behaviour'. What the hell, she thinks, if she feels like it she will join in, otherwise she could just lurk and do some work for another client who is also getting ready to launch a new mobile model. Anyway, there is a guy in her class who works for a rival company. It might be useful, career-wise, to introduce herself. Alison is just about to switch off her BlackBerry and go back to the office when it trembles once more – this time the email is marked URGENT!!! And the text is flashing on and off. It's from Lee, her *confidant* in stock matters and Lee is given to excita-bility. Usually he's telling her the next sure-fire tip but she's already told herself that good background analysis is the only way – not hot tips. Alison grins and switches the BlackBerry off without opening it. She's in too good a mood to panic. Lee can wait.

The next couple of hours before the lecture are taken up with working on the Internet, searching for 'inspiration' for that other mobile phone launch and look-ing over the PowerPoint presentation with a fresh eye. She also decides to really try to impress the directors with some cool graphics which they could then pitch back to the clients, underlining them with the intonation in 'Credo' number two: 'Build a lighthouse identity', in a flashing Bauhaus 93 font to give it that 70s 'retro' look. That will knock them all dead, she imagines.

Alison feels she's on a roll, so she continues with these dual tasks on her laptop and through a wireless link while at the lecture. During the online discussion, which includes a long-winded 'welcome' to 'our MBA colleagues from overseas' from the 'virtual' moderator who is in fact six feet away, Alison quickly gets bored and logs onto her ICQ account. This is her frivolous little vice: chatting to anyone from anywhere around the world. All pretty harmless, although there is a pest from Russia, Makarov666, he calls himself. She had felt a little bit sorry for him in earlier sessions, when he kept referring to his sick daughter and how he's finding it hard to pay the medical bills. Alison doesn't like to delete him altogether, but there's something in his tone that's a bit creepy and he's always leaving her messages. She decides to be brutal (as she's feeling so good) and deletes him while the rest of the class weighs up the pros and cons of Blake & Mouton's Management Grid and Belbin's Team Roles.

The session winds up around ten and Alison goes into a pasta restaurant on the way home for some dinner. She even treats herself to a glass of champagne; it *has* been a very productive day. Only one glass, though, as the charade of the video-conference will have to be performed at 5:00 a.m. tomorrow morning. She's prepared, though, and she'll breeze it. When she gets home finally, it's 11:20 p.m. After a long hot shower, she flips her computer on as dries her hair and looks over the emails. There are 79 in total, as she hasn't checked them for a few hours. Time to have a look at Lee's 'URGENT!!!" mail, she thinks. He wrote:

> Guess you heard. Tried to call a dozen times. That bio stock you have – rumours everywhere that they are about to publish research on very important breakthrough on cancer treatment. Markets are taking it seriously and the prices have been going through the roof!!!
> Cheerio
> ☺☺☺!!!

Alison smiles and thinks of Sam who sends her annoying little messages and compares him with Lee who (for once) seems to have sent her digital gold. Men she hardly ever sees.

Weirdly, Alison feels a sharp pain in her guts. She's a person who, deep down, actually prefers predictability and hates surprises. She needs to check first. She scrolls down her business news bookmarks and goes to her most trusted site – and there it is. The market is taking the rumours seriously, very seriously, especially since the CEO gave a bullish interview to reporters. Her stock has soared all day and she didn't even know it! The overseas markets are driving up the share price right now, and the report says the price is expected to continue its stratospheric trajectory tomorrow when the markets open locally at 9:00 a.m.

There is nothing exaggerated about these short scenarios. Millions of people today lead lives that would echo the digital existences of our fictional Danny and Alison. Indeed, in a short time, these fictionalizations may even read as quaint, as describing a way of life that seems almost sedate and old-fashioned in its pace and in the relatively 'mild' way that ICTs stretch the lives of our protagonists over time and space.

The spaces 'outside' the logic of information technologies and the network society they have created are vanishing in direct proportion to the digitalization of the world that we saw in the previous chapter. The pre-digital spaces of culture and media were also spaces in which identity (individual and collective) could be constructed. This was not an unproblematic process, of course. But within the digital compression of time and space that is the information order, there is much less room for manoeuvre and for negotiation. We have already discussed the effects upon media and cultural identity. It goes deeper, however. Psychologist Kenneth Gergen (1999) has analysed the effects of this intensive and extensive informationization upon the processes of identity construction and conceptions of self. The effect is what he calls 'self-death', and he argues that 'In the fast pace of the technological society, concern with the inner life is a luxury – if not a *waste of time*. We now celebrate protean being. In either case, the interior self recedes in significance'(my italics). When the 'inner life' becomes something that is a 'luxury', and when it 'recedes' to an extent that we are vaguely aware of it, then a certain shallowness of character, of the sense of who one is, becomes inevitable. We inexorably lose touch with our 'inner life' when the immediate constantly clamours for our attention. Concerns, increasingly, become instrumental ones that are organized by and generated through the imperatives of the neoliberal/ICT nexus. In an ever more densely connected world driven by the logic of economic capital, we become disconnected from the disappearing networks of social and cultural capital. These are the 'glue' that binds the sense of identity and self with the wider world on a 'human' level that goes beyond 'business'. In an age of 'self-death' the celebrated 'protean being' that Gergen identifies is simply the (business) creation of a virtue out of a necessity. Accordingly, those who 'celebrate' are not the many millions who are told they constantly have to adapt, or seize the moment, or beat the competition, and so on, but those who make a comfortable living from promoting the ideology itself – Wall Street analysts, motivational speakers, neoliberal economists, free-market politicians and the like. My mental image of the 'protean being' in the network society, vignetted through Danny and Alison, is of the little metal ball in an old pinball machine. The faster you go, the more buffeted about you are, the more 'hits' you take and the more points you might earn. It's only a matter of time, though, before you go down, when the flaps don't propel you back into the chaos anymore and the game is over. Going down in real life may take many forms: depression, anxiety, ill-health, substance abuse, divorce or 'simple' burn-out – when you can't 'cut it' any longer and the next wave of recruits to the network society passes you by with hardly a sideways glance.

There is less time to have regard for those who have fallen. Indeed, in the 'time is money' calculus that has suffused much of culture and society, it is, echoing Gergen, a 'waste of time' to do so. The diversity of temporal rhythms that are already sublimated through the clock and industrialization 'recede' even further as we are synchronized to the time of the network. Time is increasingly harnessed to the 24/7 duration of the network, the flattened, empty and abstracted times of the information society. The age-old psychic and social divisions between work and leisure blur as weekends no longer 'begin' or 'end' – they are vanishing. When you are not chasing work to stay in the game, work follows you around wherever you go and can impinge at any time. To be connected in this sense means not to be set free and to be yourself as Nokia or Vodafone might have us believe, but to be entrapped and psychically disoriented. Under the neoliberalized network society, the 'time-saving' devices of cordless, **wi-fi**, mobile and compact become the digital shackles that are 'always on'. The Microsoft slogan 'Where do you want to go today?' would become heavy with irony if only one had the time to stop and think about it and enjoy the joke.

I suppose that the important point I have tried to make through these vignettes is that we have a complex, yet, at its root, *problematic* relationship with information technologies in the context of the neoliberalized network society. There is little evidence of *control* over the technologies the protagonists use in their lives, or over the wider economic, social, political and cultural dynamics in which these technologies are contextualized. This is because I feel that personal or collective control scarcely exists within the network society. Yes, Danny and Alison are highly 'connected' individuals in a highly mediated society; yes, they have jobs and money and busy lives; but they have had to *adapt* themselves to the tempo and the logic of network information technologies. Their lives (and our lives) are shaped and formed (in ways that may be ostensibly positive) through dynamics and systems over which they (and we) exercise little real sovereignty.

Moreover, as I have tried to show in previous chapters, the network society is a society, a society that does not distinguish between previously discrete realms of life such as work, leisure, home, private and public. They are beginning to comprise one digital space, an interconnected cyberspace that is overwhelmingly oriented towards economic and instrumental tasks. Yes, there are pleasures to be had in this realm and the highly mediated society does not have to feel oppressive. When the inner life recedes far enough through our constant preoccupation with the immediate and the urgent, then unhappiness and dissatisfaction are feelings we experience, but rarely have time to explore – unless forced to seek professional help. And so we want (or think we want) that new PowerMac, we want (or we think we want) a faster processor, a smaller handset with viewable graphics, we want also to be 'always on' to ensure that we do not 'miss out'. However, the more we are connected within the particular structures of neoliberal capitalism, the more tightly we extend ourselves over time and space. Personal and collective sovereignty within that time and space is being correspondingly reduced with each new connection, each increase in speed. Gradually our time is becoming network time, our space network space and our lives network lives. The logic of the network is not about humanism or the well-being of the individual, but about instrumental tasks, formal efficiency, speed, profit and market share.

In the next section I want to move to a discussion on how the network society suffuses our time and space in the way it does. We have discussed the dynamics behind the forming of the network society and I believe these to be largely economic, a dynamic and logic that has 'colonized' other, formerly non-economic, realms of life. But how does this happen in practice, in the real world? Who, or what is ensuring that, as Gibson puts it, 'the future has arrived'? In other words, how does everyday 'life' morph into 'Life.com' on a daily basis?

Bits and atoms

All revolutions come with their own *dramatis personae*, those 'heroes' we discussed in Chapter 1, such as Bill Gates and Steve Jobs, who inspired, motivated, frightened, appalled and amazed those who were swept up in the tidal waves of technological change. These are the elite, the information intelligentsia; those who are in central positions in industry, in the academy and in the media who help not only to shape what the network society will become, but also how we will think about it. They are also a varied bunch. Take someone like Howard Rheingold, a cyberoptimist who feels that networks and ICTs more generally can and do liberate humanity. He feels resentful of 'the shallowness of the critics who say that if you sit in front of a computer and participate in online conversations worldwide you are not leading an authentic life' (Digerati 2002). At the other end of the spectrum, there are those such as Clifford Stoll, a cybersceptic who believes that the network is inherently alienating and argues that 'Rather than bringing me closer to others, the time that I spend online isolates me from the most important people in my life, my family, my friends, my neighbourhood, my community' (Digerati 2002).

Very firmly at the cyberoptimist end of the spectrum, we have Nicholas Negroponte, someone we met briefly in the opening pages of Chapter 1. I want to devote some discussion here to the works and influence of Negroponte as I think they are having a radical effect upon how we interface with ICTs, and this relationship is dramatically shaping the kind of world we live in. What makes Negroponte interesting and authoritative is that he has been able to span the realms of industry, academia and the media. His technology–academic hats are worn as chairperson of MIT Media Lab, which he co-founded with Jerome Wiesner in 1985. The Media Lab, which we shall discuss in some detail shortly, is a hybrid creature that combines very substantial funding from private enterprise with the purported 'ethos' and 'intellectual rigour' of the university – in this case the Ivy League Massachusetts Institute of Technology. His media work was conducted through his columns for *Wired* magazine in the vital years (in terms of the evolution and popularizing of the Internet and the network society) between 1993 and 1998.

Spanning these three important realms with his ideas, Negroponte was thus able to establish himself as a radical and innovative thinker who had caught the cusp of the wave that was propelling the ICT revolution around the world. In 1995 Negroponte published *Being Digital*, a book that sets out what he sees the information technology revolution as portending for human subjectivity. As the title suggests, Negroponte envisions the ICT revolution and the evolution of the network society as the coming together of people and computers, an 'interface that is less about messaging back and forth and more like face-to-face and human-to-human conversation' (1995: 99). What distinguishes Negroponte from others such as Gates (who sees ICTs in purely instrumental fashion), or Rheingold, who views information technologies as ways to enhance what we already have (community, friendship and so on), is that he sees the 'commingling' of 'bits with atoms' as the evolution of something altogether new. For Negroponte, *becoming* digital is nothing less than the evolution of a new form of human subjectivity. Importantly, for Negroponte this is also viewed as an *unproblematic* ontological state. Indeed, it constitutes a massive, technologically assisted step along the path of human progress.

For Negroponte, 'being digital' is a win–win situation; we can only gain through the informationization of our lives to the highest possible degree. In 1998 he expanded upon *Being Digital* in an article for *Wired* (6.12) called 'Beyond digital', where he wrote that

> The decades ahead will be a period of comprehending biotech, mastering nature and realizing extraterrestrial travel, with DNA computers, microrobots and nanotechnologies the main characters on the technological stage. Computers as we know them today will a) be boring and b) disappear into things that are first and foremost something else: smart nails, self-cleaning shirts, driverless cars, therapeutic Barbie dolls, intelligent doorknobs that let the Federal Express man in and Fido out, but not 10 other dogs back in. Computers will be a sweeping yet invisible part of our everyday lives: We'll live in them, wear them and even eat them. A computer a day will keep the doctor away.
>
> (Negroponte 1998)

This is not science fiction of the kind we should find in Gibson's *Neuromancer*, or Stephenson's *Snowcrash*, and where we can impute a critique of the present. It's a critique-free zone. It's futurology, but it's a vision of a future that just may *come to pass*, for a very special reason: it fits with the vision of the future that neoliberal capitalism, augmented massively by ICTs, *wishes* to come to pass. This is 'ubiquitous computing' at its most extreme, where information technologies become literally part of who we are and what we do. We may ask the question: is this so bad? Are 'smart nails' (whatever they might be) or 'intelligent doorknobs', or (and I pause here) even 'therapeutic Barbie dolls' really anything to get worked up over? Well, in themselves, no, probably not. To understand more clearly what I am driving at, let us look more closely at Negroponte's brainchild, MIT Media Lab, what it is, why it is so influential and what role it (and its legion of emulators) plays in the formation of the network society.

MIT Media Lab has been described as 'a genius institution, a place of wild and woolly intellectual endeavour holding nothing back. If the place were a person, it would be a mad scientist, someone who breaks conventional rules and is unafraid to experiment with radical ideas' (Madlin 1999: 35). Intriguingly, though, some of the most conventional of capitalists, blue-suited guys with ties, throw large amounts of shareholder money at it. About 95 per cent of Media Lab's approximately $US35 million annual budget comes from private industry, comprising around 170 corporate sponsors. Many of these sponsors are of the fairly predictable sort and could be placed in the 'usual suspects' category. Corporations such as IBM, Hewlett Packard, Intel, Motorola, Nokia and Swatch would be expected to swell the Media Lab's coffers. More intriguing, however, and pointing to the pervasive influence of ICTs in our society, is a gaggle of not-so-predictable sponsors such as Nike, Lego and Mars, the makers of dog food and chocolate bars, as well as Philip Morris, the cigarette maker. Like its many sponsors, the Media Lab has felt the irresistible urge to expand in the age of globalization. Accordingly, in 2000 it opened MediaLabEurope in Dublin after the Irish government munificently wrote them a cheque for $US55 million and handed them a lease for a permanent facility in a sumptuously renovated ex-Guinness brewery. Moreover, under its 'Digital Nations' programme, the Media Lab also conducts research in South America and in Asia. In 2002 the Australian government was eagerly courting the Media Lab to go down under so as to reflect some of its 'genius' aura toward the relatively laggard domestic ICT industries in the Antipodes.

Why do corporate suits and various governments invest so heavily in such a 'mad scientist . . . with radical ideas'? What is it that the Media Lab does that is so compelling? The Negroponte quotation from 'Beyond digital' cited above gives a bit of a hint. More precisely, it is the Media Lab's mission to 'change the world' through creative and innovative ICT-based products with 'everyday' applications for consumers that is attracting the lavish attentions of big business. In other words, what grips the investor is the vision of computers and microchip technology suffusing almost everything that we do, making it connectable, networkable and, most importantly, commodifiable. With a mile-high reputation and super-funding from corporate America and elsewhere, the Media Lab thus acts as a magnet for the best and brightest faculty and graduate students from diverse disciplines such as computational physics, engineering, linguistics, semiotics and multimedia.

Under the chair of Negroponte, the Media Lab has engaged itself in a wide array of research projects that traverse a whole range of subjects, disciplines and new areas of enquiry. The scope of the research underway by such assorted talent is remarkable and description is perhaps best left to the Media Lab itself:

The Media Laboratory provides a unique environment for exploring basic research and applications at the intersection of computation and the arts. Areas of research include: software agents; machine understanding; how children learn; human and machine vision; audition; speech interfaces; wearable computers; affective computing (a new branch of computing that relates to, arises from, or deliberately influences emotions); advanced interface design; tangible media, object-oriented video; interactive cinema; work in various forms of digital expression, from text, to graphics, to sound; and new approaches to spatial imaging, nanomedia and nanoscale sensing.

(Media Lab Research 2002)

This reads impressively, but it also sounds a lot like geek-speak and would not make too much sense to most people. However, if one dives down to a deeper level of particularity on the Media Lab website (www.media.mit.edu), then the detail (and the Media Lab's ultimate rationale) becomes rather more clear.

MIT Media Lab has several different research streams that come under two formal headings: the 'Research Consortia' and 'Special Interest Groups'. Under the former rubric, there is, for example, the Lifelong Kindergarten research stream. An example of the research done here is the 'Digital Manipulatives' project where traditional kids' toys such as balls, blocks and beads are designed with 'added digital capabilities'. As the website blurb puts it, 'With our new digital versions of these toys, children can learn concepts (such as process, probability and emergence) that were previously seen as too complex for children' (Media Lab Research Consortia 2002). Other high-profile research includes, again in the Media Lab's own words:

Media windshield
The media windshield is a demonstration that changes the use of an automobile windshield to serve multiple purposes. When no one is in the car, it can present information to the outside world; advertising, augmentation of the road signs, even personalized information for a party that is walking by. When the driver gets into the car, it adjusts the audio to be appropriate for their seating arrangement and puts up an Internet interface. When the driver lies back, the windshield can be used as a movie screen for DVD videos. Finally, when the driver is using the car, the windshield can shade the sun and lights, put up virtual signs and annotate difficult-to-see objects.

EyeAre
'The Party Scenario' – everyone wears a unique pair of EyeAre glasses, which can send information back and forth to each other, recording information like to whom you talk and how long your conversation lasts. Every so often you stop by one of several base stations around the room to download the stored information on your glasses and you will be able to find out more information about the people you met, such as their contact information, their business cards, perhaps their

webpages, or allowing you to send them an email, etc. – giving you an easy way to follow up later with your new acquaintances.

(Media Lab Research Consortia 2002)

Now, much of this sounds fairly harmless stuff, fun even (apart, possibly, from the EyeAre party . . .). However, these future-to-come scenarios being worked on by Media Lab 'geniuses' even as you read this do not convey any real sense of what kind of society such gadgets and applications, in their totality, are building. The push by Media Lab and many others constantly to connect and informationalize are symptomatic of a deeper logic (and malaise) that is the push to insert ICTs at every level and in every realm: from the kindergarten, the office and the home, to parties and in the car. Looking at these developments from the wider perspective, as one must when trying to comprehend an interconnected and globalized society, we can see the actual role institutions such as MIT Media Lab play in the network society. The role Media Lab evolved into and grew large upon is that of *digital connector* of the social and temporal interstices of human subjectivity; a filler of the gaps left by the broad meta-dynamics of globalization and the ICT revolution. As we move through the twenty-first century the role of the Media Lab and similar organizations will become increasingly important. Indeed, they are focusing ever more closely on the 'bits to atoms' idea. This was illustrated in their 2001 decision to open, with funding from the National Science Foundation, the Center for Bits and Atoms with the explicit aim to 'explore how the content of information relates to its physical representation, from atomic nuclei to global networks' (*MIT News* 2001). All in all, Media Lab and others in this lucrative field will provide the hardware and software 'solutions' (where, we might ask, is the 'problem' in the kindergarten or at EyeAre-free parties?) that both create Life.com and hold it together. This 'digital stitching' of the fabric of culture and of life will not only help to make possible a world where bits *do* meet and interact with atoms, it will also lay the basis for a world addicted to ICT fixes for almost everything.

And of course it is this kind of world, a commodified and connected **information ecology**, that is the dream of big business. Being connected at every realm in a society driven primarily by commercial imperatives means that the individual is connected to (and helps to comprise) one vast potential market. As Jeremy Rifkin (2000: 55) put it, this kind of ICTs-driven/market-fundamentalist logic is one that will

> . . . relentlessly constitute and reconstitute us as 'focus groups', 'niche markets', 'demographics', 'zones', 'customer profiles' and so on, to be classified, bought and sold just like any other commodity. In the real time information economy we become database-constructed identities that are continually broken down and reformed in tandem with market-competition imperatives.

Seen in such a light, Negroponte and the Media Lab's 'unconventionality', or for that matter the 'hip' and 'cool' aura that surrounds many high-tech New Economy companies more generally, actually turn out to be about very predictable, conventional and conservative things. And they are no less disturbing for all that. Now I am sure that Negroponte honestly believes in the good that can come from his work and his ideas, creating socially useful applications and gadgets that bring 'bits and atoms' together in a form of digital-flesh harmony within an information ecology. However, social harmony and the evolution of a benign, post-human cyborg subjectivity are not at the forefront of the thinking of corporations and their shareholders as they pump millions into such research and development. They expect things that will sell and help contribute to the building of a society that is, above all, consumption-friendly. Wittingly or unwittingly, then, they help to build a life and a society that marketing agencies, multinational corporations and governments find predictable, manipulable and serviceable. Accordingly, every new connection that the Media Lab and others make is the corresponding loss of a space of autonomy, starting with the kindergarten. This is occurring not because ICTs are in themselves alienating, but because the logic that currently drives and creates them, that of neoliberal globalization, most definitely is.

Cyborgs 'R' Us

I want to finish this chapter by digging a bit deeper and questioning philosophically and in terms of current social theory what the 'commingling' of bits with atoms might actually mean. As noted before, science fiction has given us an impression of what being a cyborg entails. It is Arnie Schwarzenegger and his various nemeses in the *Terminator* flicks. Meat and metal, bits and atoms combine in a new form of human. This is a post-human, a development that takes us way beyond whatever Darwin or anyone else could have imagined and into a new phase of evolution that is part technology and part flesh. In the films, though, the troubling part is that the technology, metal and binary parts seem to be the most important bits, the bits in control. This is the cyborg construction, the science fiction image.

As I said at the beginning of this chapter, science fiction does give us a useful way to gain another perspective on our present, as often the genre, through metaphor and fantasy, is grappling with the issues of the present. The image of the cyborg pushes to the limit our concerns with uncontrolled technological development and the evolution of all-powerful computers. This particular image does not exist, of course, and technoscience is nowhere near such a stage – notwithstanding the immense ethical and moral issues that would also need to be overcome. However, Donna Haraway has some unsettling news for those who imagine that the day of the cyborg is way off in some distant dystopic future. According to Haraway, we are already cyborgs, already post-human.

In her book *Simians, Cyborgs and Women* Haraway argues that

A cyborg is a cybernetic organism, a hybrid of machine and organism, *a creature of social reality as well as a creature of fiction* . . . Social reality is lived social relations, our most important political construction, a world-changing fiction. By the late twentieth century, our time, a mythic time, we are all chimeras, theorized and fabricated hybrids of machine and organism; in short, we are cyborgs.

(Haraway 1991: 149–50, emphasis added)

Haraway makes a compelling case for the idea that we are no longer able to maintain the 'fiction' of a duality between what is 'natural' and what is 'man-made'. No longer is it possible to say with any degree of certainty where our bodily flesh ends and technology begins. In fact, so intimate, so tangled and so blurred is our relationship with technology that the 'we are cyborgs' declaration made by Haraway sounds less absurd the more we think about it. Of course, as I said previously, we are not at the Schwarzenegger-*Terminator* phase of post-humanism, but our entanglements with electronic bits, metals, plastics, silicones and *technology* and *technique* in general are as dense as they are irreversible.

For example, think of the pacemaker that keeps the heart muscles of many thousands of people pumping at a rate that keeps them alive; the cochlear implant that allows better hearing; the silicon breast implant that certain women feel they have to have; the hip replacement or knee reconstruction, the contact lenses – the list could go on. Thinking about being a cyborg in this relatively low-tech fashion opens up the way to the fairly obvious conclusion that we may have been post-human for some time, indeed, a very long time. For example, the Etruscans developed dentures over two thousand years ago from ivory fixed in place by gold; and the hypodermic syringe, injecting vaccines for diseases such as rabies and plague, was developed in the late nineteenth century. However, due in large part to the ICT revolution and the profit-seeking imperatives of neoliberal globalization, especially in hugely lucrative areas such as biotechnology, the technical constraints to a more comprehensive 'cyborgization' are being loosened at an unprecedentedly fast pace. It is here, I believe, at the nexus between the technological and economic revolutions, that both the qualitative and quantitative difference has occurred. As humans we have crossed the line at some unknown point into post-humanity due to the neoliberal globalization/ICT nexus. Indeed, there is no 'line' any more (if there ever was one). As Haraway (1991: 64) puts it,

Communications sciences and biology are constructions of natural-technical objects of knowledge in which the difference between machine and organism is thoroughly blurred; mind, body and tool are on very intimate terms.

However, our technical knowledge far outstrips our moral–critical understanding of what this means and where post-humanism is leading us. Castells (1997: 379) makes the same point about the network society more generally when he writes that 'there is an extraordinary gap between our technological overdevelopment and our social underdevelopment'. The cyborg, then, is no longer an abstract or simple metaphor: it is real and is what we are. What makes it 'more' real and 'more' of an ontological state than, say, when the Etruscans first fitted themselves with ivory and gold teeth is the *extensity* and *intensity* of the process brought about by 'communications science and biology' – and the ideology of commodification and marketization that neoliberalism holds as its central credo. In other words, and as this book has consistently emphasized, it is about the effects of digital networks and the *network society* more generally upon the 'natural–technical objects of knowledge'. Hari Kunzru (1997) argues that 'Haraway's world of tangled networks'

> . . . relegate old-fashioned concepts like *natural* and *artificial* to the archives. These hybrid networks are the cyborgs and they don't just surround us – they incorporate us. An automated production line in a factory, an office computer network, a club's dancers, lights and sound systems – all are cyborg constructions of people and machines. Networks are also inside us. Our bodies, fed on the products of agribusiness, kept healthy – or damaged – by pharmaceuticals and altered by medical procedures, aren't as natural as The Body Shop would like us to believe. Truth is, we're constructing ourselves, just like we construct chip sets or political systems – and that brings with it a few responsibilities.

If we accept Haraway's thesis and Kunzru's illustration of it, then we are undoubtedly cyborg and post-human. Indeed we can argue that we are *born* post-human, given the medicalization and technological intervention that go into the processes of genetic modification, conception, pregnancy and birth. It has to be emphasized that being a cyborg does not mean that we are approaching the science fiction realms of becoming a robot. Rather, as Haraway makes clear, the term 'cyborg' denotes a particular form of subjectivity. It is a subject position produced and defined (today) with specific reference to a matrix (the networks) of socio-cultural and political economic practices, which find their base of operation in relation to the neoliberal globalization/ICT nexus.

Having reached this point of understanding we are able to step back from the realm of science fiction metaphor and fantasy that represented the cyborg as something set in the distant and dystopic future, to think and act in the present. Accordingly we can accept 'cyborg' as a particular form of subjectivity and as a reality. From this vantage point we can begin to measure and critique. First we need to be able to acknowledge our responsibilities, both moral and ethical. But how is this possible when we cannot keep up with the pace of technical innovation?

As noted previously, the dystopic theme that runs through much science fiction again indicates that we grapple with a perceived loss of control over technological development. Taking this perspective literally can lead to a position of 'anti-science and technology', arguments and visceral hostilities that are as old as the history of science and technology itself. Today, such a stance is even more insupportable because, as Haraway's thesis of the cyborg would indicate, *we are the irreversible product of science and technology*. The question we need to deal with, rather, is one of control;

that is to say, a question of politics. If the vagaries of the market are left to set the ever-shifting agendas, then a grass-roots politics for empowerment and change will find little purchase. Alienated consumers will spend their time adapting and becoming more flexible: like our protagonists Danny and Alison, continually stretching themselves ever more tautly over time and space simply to survive.

In her highly insightful book *Time*, Barbara Adam considers the nature of subjectivity within the network society. She argues that we are intellectually ill-equipped to understand what she terms the present-day 'human–technology–science–economy–equity–environment constellation' (2004). In other words, we understand our world less because it is a world that is increasingly out of our control, a world where abstract market forces and ICT automation, not democratic formations of people, shape culture and society. Adam continues that in such an environment it is impossible to fully appreciate

. . . that people are the *weakest link* when the timeframes of action are compressed to zero and effects span to eternity, when transmission and transplantation are instantaneous but their outcomes extend into an open future, when instantaneity and eternity are combined in a discordant fusion of all times.

(Adam 2004: 125)

And as the 'weakest link' in the 'human–technology–science–economy–equity–environment constellation', we are open to influences and effects that we have little power over. I believe this is the stage we are at now in the network society. If the 'solution' is a new politics, then today we live in a society where 'the political' is being steamrollered by the nexus between neoliberal globalization and the ICT revolution. Under the weight of the onslaught, we feebly resist, go under, or adapt. Like Danny and Alison, most of us follow the path of adaptation; we make 'flexibility' and 'coping' instead of 'empowerment' our personal politics – the instrumental ability to navigate the harsh social and cultural landscape created by competition and short-termism.

The need for the development of a new politics for the information age will be discussed over the rest of this book. I want to preface that discussion, however, by sketching some preconditions for their creation. First would be an acceptance, as Haraway urges, that we are cyborgs, irretrievably bound up in a world where the dualisms between nature and technology no longer clearly exist – we exist instead at the constantly shifting interface between the two. This acceptance forces upon us a choice between what Haraway terms 'automaton and autonomy' (1992: 139). To choose the latter will necessitate recognition of how power operates in the network society, that is to say, in ways very different from the power relations and politics that dominated in the pre-digital age of Fordism. We need to know where to identify power in society and learn how to develop a form of politics that can contest with it in the pursuit of a democratic civil society with a *subordinate* market economy. It follows from this that we also will have to recognize that the power of the market and the worship of the market in economics and in institutional politics needs to be brought under social-democratic control, where the 'weakest link' can be strengthened and placed in overall control. Last in this far from exhaustive list is the recognition and the acceptance that the world and society as currently formed is only one of limitless ways of constructing our lives and our world. Accordingly, we need to rediscover and reinforce the currently diminished traditions and practices of critique and of a social, cultural and political imagination that has been marginalized by neoliberal instrumentalism.

Further reading

Baudrillard, J. (1988) *The Ecstasy of Communication*. New York, NY: Semiotexte.

Hassan, R. (2003) MIT Media Lab: techno dream factory or alienation as a way of life?, *Media, Culture and Society*, 25: 87–106.

Haraway, D. (1991) A cyborg manifesto: science, technology and socialist-feminism in the late twentieth century, in *Simians, Cyborgs and Women: The Reinvention of Nature*. New York, NY: Routledge.

www.media.mit.edu (MIT Media Lab) See this site for updates on the devices, applications and processes that merge 'bits with atoms' in more and more realms of life.

Negroponte, N. (1995) *Being Digital*. Rydalmere, NSW: Hodder and Stoughton.

Negroponte, N. (1998) Beyond digital, *Wired*, 6.12.

5

CIVIL SOCIETY AND THE NETWORK SOCIETY

The colonization of civil society

Schools promote fast-food/Police wear logos.

(www.captivestate.com)

'Civil society' is one of those important-sounding terms that tend to induce a warm, fuzzy feeling. It connotes something 'good' like motherhood, and something that many people would readily agree that 'we have to have' without really knowing what It is and what It does. Connected to the vagueness of this term is: would we realize if It weren't there any longer? The term 'network society' is in the title of this book, but even without having read this far into it, or even before ever having read any of it, most people would have at least some idea of what the term meant. Civil society is different. Many may venture that is 'about' politics and democracy, or even about 'hard' things such as philosophy, rights and ethics. And they would be right. But how are we to understand It?

I want to take some time here to explain what I see as the essential features of civil society and what it is supposed to do as a function of society in general. In so doing, I do not argue that I have the only, the correct, or the definitive definition. Many will give emphasis to differing aspects; many others would disagree altogether with my 'essential features'. However, as I see it, the fact that you are reading this means the job is half done. You are, like millions more around the world today, thinking about what civil society is; and this thinking and search for knowledge, I suggest, comes from the fact that we are living in the midst of a *crisis* of civil society stemming from the effects of neoliberal globalization and the ICT revolution. So spend some time to read what follows – and read other things too, those listed at the end of this chapter for example, or wherever else your intuition, sense of injustice or curiosity may lead you.

So what is civil society? A contemporary definition by David Held describes the idea fairly clearly. Held (1987: 281) writes that

> Civil society retains a distinctive character to the extent that it is made up of areas of social life – the domestic world, the economic sphere, cultural activities and political interaction – which are organized by private or voluntary arrangements between individuals and groups outside the direct control of the state.

This central idea of civil society and the state as being *separate realms* is in fact a relatively new one. For example, in ancient Greece and Rome the emphasis was different. Around two thousand years ago the Roman political philosopher Cicero, who was influenced by earlier Greek philosophy on the nature of the State, laid down what was to become the classical definition of civil society. In his *De Republica* (On the Republic), Cicero enquired into the constitution of life in organized society. In *De Republica*, Cicero had defined the republic as a 'weal of the people' or a common-wealth. The 'people' was defined as 'an assemblage associated by a common acknow-ledgment of right and by a community of interests' (from Augustine 1950: 699). It is clear from the writings of Cicero and others, and in contrast to the contemporary understanding of the term, that the state and civil society were not separate spheres of life. As Caparini (2002: 2) puts it,

> Civil society [in the time of Cicero] denoted those who lived in a political community and who fulfilled their public and social roles to serve the interests of the political community. In this view the state constitutes an *instrument* of civil society. Similarly, subsequent European philosophers such as Kant, Rousseau and Hobbes saw the most important distinction between society and the state of nature. *It was only with the writings of Paine, Hegel and de Tocqueville that the notion of the necessary separation between the state and the society emerged.*
> (Caparini 2002: 2, emphasis added)

The idea of a separation between civil society and the state, then, came from the eighteenth-century revolution in democratic political philosophy that grew and spread to eventually become part of what became to be known as the Age of Enlightenment. At this time the state came to be viewed as the antithesis of 'free association' or of a 'community of interests'. Increasingly the state began to be associated with forms of absolutism and intolerance that came through monarchical rule, or theocratic dogma, or through oppressive government (or all of these occurring at once – as they did for the unlucky majority in pre-1917 Russia). The idea of separate spheres remained, but the term civil society fell into disuse in the mid-nineteenth century as political philo-sophers turned their attention more to the social and political consequences of a rampaging Industrial Revolution (Carothers 2000). The idea of civil society as a force for liberty and freedom from oppression was resurrected in the mid-twentieth century through the writings of Marxist philosopher Antonio Gramsci. Gramsci argued in his writings, later compiled into the *Prison Notebooks* (1971), that civil society is where 'hegemony' (or a subtle form of domination) is organized. As he saw it, this was the hegemony of the bourgeoisie over the working classes and the inculcation of their capitalist worldview. An important insight from Gramsci is that because domination is being organized from inside civil society itself, i.e. through the ostensibly 'free association' of individuals and institutions and outside the realm of the state, this makes the ideologies of the ruling class seem less overtly oppressive and more amenable to what he termed 'spontaneous consent' (1971: 12).

During the 1960s and 1970s Gramsci's ideas had *practical* application both as a way of conceptualizing how hegemony and power were organized in repressive regimes in South America, Africa and elsewhere, and as a way of organizing left-wing counter-hegemonic strategies against them. During the same period in the west, however, Gramsci's theories were popular mainly in intellectual and academic circles as frameworks for understanding how power, consent and hegemony were organized and maintained in the bourgeois liberal democracies. This academization of the debate on hegemony in the west was arguably a measure of its success for the rule of the bourgeois–capitalist state.

The modern idea of civil society, then, is that it consists of a whole range of non-state spheres such as cultural activities, the media, family life, professional and amateur associations and the market; indeed in almost any sphere of life where people can freely involve themselves without hindrance or interference from the state and state bureaucracies. There can be interaction between the two, however, where in many subtle and not-so-subtle ways civil society can affect the state and *vice versa*. The point is, as Held and Gramsci make clear, that the influence is not *direct* or *overtly* oppressive. Gramsci's theory of 'hegemony' has been especially useful in understanding the nature of this interaction within capitalist societies. Accordingly, a principal reason why the notion of civil society has been historically vague is that these spheres (civil society and the state) can appear to interact fairly well for much of the time, becoming an issue only during periods of economic, social or political upheaval and crisis.

The 1980s and 1990s saw just such a phase of crisis in the liberal democracies in the west – and a resurgence of interest (both in its theory and practice) in what civil society is and does. At its root, as we have seen in earlier chapters, was the economic crisis of Fordism that led to the emergence of social and political upheavals as the neoliberal 'remedy' was implemented. What this period has presented us with is an interesting (and possibly unprecedented) twist to the long relationship between civil society and the state. The nexus between neoliberal globalization and the ICT revolution has spread the theory and practice of the market not only into many other realms of civil society – but deep into the state itself. Accordingly, this growing domination by a single element of civil society begins, in one sense, to correspond to the classical idea of the state being an 'instrument' of civil society – albeit through a very narrow and disproportionately powerful aspect of civil society: the market. And the logic of the market, through its growing hegemony over the state and the rest of society, the 'invading of the public by the private' as Klein (2002: xx) terms it, is marginalizing or colonizing those non-market sectors that give civil society its pluralistic ethos and diversity, or what Held calls its 'distinctive character'.

So, not only are many other spheres of civil society becoming commodified through neoliberal globalization and the ICT revolution, but the state too has become 'captive' to its logic. The privatization of public utilities, the placing of public servants on commercial employment contracts and the demand from politicians from Thatcher and Reagan onwards that the state should be run 'efficiently' like a business in the marketplace has altered the nature of the state in ways that have no precedent.

British social activist George Monbiot makes no bones about the extent of this colonization. In his book *Captive State* (2000: 4–5) he writes that

> Corporations, the contraptions we invented to serve us, are overthrowing us. They are seizing powers previously invested in government, and using them to distort public life to suit their own ends . . . the provision of hospitals, roads and prisons in Britain has been deliberately tailored to meet corporate demands rather than public need . . . urban regeneration programmes have been subverted to serve the interests of private companies [and] planning permission is offered for sale to the highest bidder.

He continues the litany of colonization of the state by the market, in the form of

> . . . the corporate takeover of British universities, and the resulting distortions of the research and teaching agendas . . . the corporate takeover of schools, the neglect of health and safety enforcement and the deregulation of business with the increasing regulation of the citizen . . . corporations have come to govern key decision-making processes within the European Union and, with the British government's blessing, [have] begun to develop a transatlantic single market, controlled and run by corporate chief executives.

While Monbiot concentrates on the annexation of the British state by global capitalism, Naomi Klein, in her hugely successful *No Logo* (2000), has given us the broader perspective of the commodification of the rest of the world by neoliberal globalization and the ICT revolution. Civil society and the state are now both oriented toward and dominated by the logics of free markets, of selling, of profit and of consumption. *No Logo* shows how the world is becoming a 'web of brands' where at kindergarten, in the school, on television, in the university, in the street, almost everywhere we turn, the processes of commodification have got to that space before us, colonized it, and now want to sell it back to us. This has left us, according to the capitalized themes in Klein's book, with: NO SPACE, NO CHOICE and NO JOBS. The alternative to these, and this comprises the final section of her book is NO LOGO – the emerging dynamics of which we shall discuss shortly.

A pernicious effect of the colonization of civil society by neoliberal globalization and the ICT revolution is a decline of participation in the political process. The symptoms will be recognizable to many in the western liberal democracies.

Young people, especially, now tend to show a lack of faith in the political process through not bothering to vote at election time. The malaise seems to be most acute in that self-styled bastion of freedom and democracy, the US. In 1996 the voter participation rate in that country fell to below 50 per cent, the first time it had sunk that low since 1924, and the second lowest rate since 1824. There has been a steady drop since the early 1970s and the period represents the longest and largest decline of voter participation in the US's history. Research conducted by the Committee for the Study of the American Electorate (CSAE) showed that over the last thirty years voter turnout has declined considerably, producing a series of historic lows (Anderson 2000). This trend concerns the political parties who need to get people out on polling day (but only on polling day) and so 'registration drives' have been a feature of recent elections in the US.

There is a similar trend in Britain. The 2001 'landslide' re-election of Tony Blair's New Labour, for example, was achieved by a 'mandate' from only 25 per cent of those forty-four million persons eligible to vote. This translated as a 42 per cent of the total votes cast, nearly eleven million votes, and in fact the lowest number polled by a winning party since 1929. It was a victory for the 'Stay at Home Party', according to the political analyst for the *Daily Mail*, Edward Heathcoat Amory. As Richard Heffernan wrote in his analysis of the 2001 election, 'The fall in turnout of the magnitude witnessed in 2001 may reflect a rise in voter hostility, ignorance or simply plain indifference to the political process' (Heffernan 2002). Moreover, survey after survey continues to indicate public cynicism and/or apathy regarding the political process and the politicians who make it happen. This cynicism infects not only the average voter, but also those who comment on the process; a cynicism that often bleeds over into biting sarcasm regarding the democratic 'mandate' of governments elected through a minority of the electorate. As Tom Nairn observes in his book *Pariah* (2002), the Labour Party in 2001 was 're-elected by an overwhelming quarter of the UK electorate'.

A corollary to the apathy that confronts institutional politics is a decline in what Held (1987: 281) calls the countless 'private or voluntary arrangements between individuals and groups outside the direct control of the state'. These 'arrangements' are in many ways what constitute the lifeblood of civil society and form the 'social capital' that can make civil society dynamic and diverse. As Manfred B. Steger notes, the underlying cause of what Robert Putnam in his *Bowling Alone* (2000) calls 'the killing of civic engagement' is '. . . excessive commercialism and the socially destructive effects unleashed by neoliberal capitalism' (2002: 276). The principal task of Steger's essay is to take issue with Putnam for not giving any emphasis to the effects of neo-liberalism. He has a very good point, as the thrust of my argument thus far in this book would indicate. However, I think Steger himself omits to include a co-dynamic, without which neoliberalism would have probably remained a right-wing fantasy: the ICT revolution. Globalization, in its project of shrinking time and space for the prime benefit of profit, simply could not have occurred at the rate of intensity and extensity that it did without the 'enabling' effects of ICTs.

The colonization of large tracts of civil society and the state has had, almost needless to say, a profound effect upon the Left across the world. As Slavoj Žižek (2002: 13) writes, 'The Left is undergoing a shattering experience: the progressive movement is being compelled to reinvent its whole project.' The 'old' spaces in which the progressive forces within civil society operated have been either wholly or partly colonized; and the political spaces where reform or revolution could be developed and organized have been marginalized and/or left to implode. Many people have realized this and so the reorganization and 'reinvention' Žižek speaks of is happening today, and has been going on since at least the early 1990s. The social, political and economic disruptions that have flowed from a hegemonic neoliberalism have ensured this and the motivation is for a new politics and for new forms of political organization that can reclaim a civil society free from the domination of neoliberal capitalism.

We are only at the beginning of the process of reinvention, and so I want to spend some time in the next section tracing the contours of the new politics that are emerging. More precisely, I want to look at the coalition of a free-floating rage into what has been called by the mainstream press the 'anti-globalization movement'.

A global political movement for the age of globalization

Politically speaking, we have been here before – that is to say, we have seen a worldwide movement developing out of the dissolution of social capital in the wake of free-booting free markets. The phase of *laissez-faire* free-market capitalism that dominated in Britain during the nineteenth century undermined the existing complex social relations that had been developing for hundreds of years. As Steger (2002: 267) notes, this

> . . . left ever-larger segments of the British population without an adequate system of social security and communal support. Most people caught in these free-market dynamics experienced a strong sense of alienation and loneliness that contributed to a decline of civic engagement and the weakening of the social bond.

This violent and predatory form of capitalism, the mutation that produced the first phase of imperialism, eventually forced people to resist and to organize. This led to the formation of trade unions and political parties that sought to protect workers' rights and to reform the worst aspects of the *laissez-faire* system – or try to overthrow it altogether. Accordingly, across the world, trade unionism and social democratic (and eventually even conservative) parties became the counterbalance to the forces of social chaos and hyper-exploitation that would result from capitalism left to its own devices. This form of social movement politics evolved, grew, consolidated and eventually atrophied during the period from around 1850s until the 1970s (Wallerstein 2002: 29).

This historical counterbalance to untrammelled capitalism was upset with the rise of neoliberalism and its mission to reintroduce a more *laissez-faire* system. It took a decade or so of neoliberalism and its policies of economic restructuring along free-market lines to bring global resistance to something like a critical mass. The decade of the 1990s thus saw a growing interest in the idea of the civil society and what it was meant to represent. This 'reawakening' was accompanied by a rejection of the 'old' mechanisms of institutional party politics that seemed unable (or in many cases unwilling) to stop or resist the neoliberal onslaught that was sweeping the world.

Respected intellectuals such as Anthony Giddens and politicians such as Tony Blair and Bill Clinton have attempted to harness this growing disaffection through articulation of what came to be known as the 'Third Way' (Giddens 1999b). The idea was to make the market economy less harsh, and give it a 'social democratic' dimension that would ameliorate the worst excesses of capitalism. However, many soon realized that the Third Way, especially as envisaged by Blair, Clinton and kindred politicians, left the central tenets of neoliberalism intact. For instance, the continuing round of free-trade agreements designed to prise open every sphere of every economy, notwithstanding their vulnerability to global competition, were seen as sacrosanct. Similarly, the multilateral instruments of neoliberal globalization such as the World Trade Organization (WTO), the World Bank and the International Monetary Fund (IMF) were unthreatened by Third Way policies. Also untroubled by Third Way thinking was the global stock market, a 'techno-economic system' as Castells terms it, which is set up in such a way that it 'allows for the geographic redistribution of investment so that, while economies [may] suffer, most global investments do not' (2000: 60). The unwillingness of Third Way adherents to challenge what were perceived to be the most socially, environmentally and culturally destructive aspects of neoliberalism meant that for most people alienated by neoliberalism, the Third Way offered nothing.

Unless one has spent the last twenty years reading only *The Economist* and the *Wall Street Journal*, watched only *Big Brother* on television and savoured nothing more challenging than Hollywood's offerings in the cinema, then the negative effects of neoliberalism's 'techno-economic system' will be recognized and understood on at least some level of comprehension. The idea that we live in an uncertain, unfair and unravelling world is becoming increasingly evident. On the geo-political front, the United Nations is suffering a deep crisis of identity and legitimacy. In a unipolar world, where the US tries to assert its cultural, political, economic and military dominance, insecurity is at levels not seen since the 1930s. On the economic front, as I write, Argentina is being wracked by economic and social crises where millions have slid into poverty and unemployment. Corporate collapses continue with Enron and WorldCom being only the most spectacular in recent years, overshadowing, in terms of media space, lots of others known mostly (and acutely) to their ex-employees and creditors. But the evidence mounts daily and is available to those increasing numbers who question what is going on. I could go on *ad nauseum*, adding to the list of macro and micro disasters that neoliberalism has delivered over the last couple of decades. Instead I'll leave it to members of what the authors themselves call 'global civil society' (a much more accurate term than the 'anti-globalization movement' label, as we shall see) to articulate the main social, cultural, economic and environmental costs of neoliberal misrule. The group is called the International Forum on Globalization, and in 2002 it published a book called *Alternatives to Economic Globalization* (Cavanagh *et al.* 2002). In it they write that

> The U.N. Food and Agriculture Organization (FAO) reports that the number of chronically hungry people in the world declined steadily during the 1970s and 1980s but has been increasing since the early 1990s. The U.S. Department of Agriculture estimates that by 2008 two-thirds of the people of sub-Saharan Africa will be undernourished, and 40 percent will be undernourished in Asia.
>
> In a world in which a few enjoy unimaginable wealth, two hundred million children under age five are underweight because of a lack of food. A hundred million children die each year from hunger-related disease. A hundred million children are living or working on the streets. Three hundred thousand children were conscripted as soldiers during the 1990s, and six million were injured in armed conflicts. Eight hundred million people go to bed hungry each night.
>
> This human tragedy is not confined to poor countries. Even in a country as wealthy as the United States, 6.1 million adults and 3.3 million children experience outright hunger. Some 10 percent of U.S. households, accounting for 31 million people, do not have enough food to meet their basic needs. These are some of the many indicators of a deepening global social crisis.
>
> On the environmental side, a joint study released in September 2000 by the United Nations Development Programme (UNDP), the United Nations Environmental Programme (UNEP), the World Bank, and the World Resources Institute assessed five ecosystem types – agricultural, coastal, forest, freshwater, and grassland – in relation to five ecosystem services – food and fiber production, water quantity, air quality, biodiversity, and carbon storage. It was found that of these twenty-five ecosystem–service combinations, sixteen had declining trends. The only positive trend was in food and fiber production by forest ecosystems, which has been achieved at the expense of species diversity.
>
> Human activity – in particular, fossil fuel combustion – is estimated to have increased atmospheric concentrations of carbon dioxide to their highest levels in twenty million years. According to the Worldwatch Institute, an environmental think tank, natural disasters, including weather-related disasters such as storms, floods, and fires, affected more than two billion people and caused in excess of $608 billion in economic losses worldwide during the decade of the 1990s – more than the previous four decades combined. Three hundred million people were displaced from their homes or forced to resettle because of extreme weather conditions in 1998 alone.

It becomes more imperative to rethink human priorities and institutions by the day. Yet most corporate globalists, in deep denial, reiterate their mantra that with time and patience corporate globalization will create the wealth needed to end poverty and protect the environment.

(Cavanagh *et al.* 2002: 6–7)

Since the beginning of the 1990s more and more people have simply refused to believe the mantra any longer. Importantly, they are also beginning to realize that globalization itself offers the means to resist it. Individuals, groups and communities are now beginning to experiment with 'ubiquitous computing' in ways that run counter to its intended role under neoliberalism.

The UN-sponsored Rio Earth Summit in 1992 provided the inspirational example of how ICTs could work for the growing networks of non-governmental organizations (**NGOs**) around the world. More than one thousand NGOs were registered at the so-called Global Forum that convened parallel to the Summit. Some thirty-five thousand NGO delegates gathered to express their environmental and social concerns to the world leaders at the Summit and to the world's media who were covering it. The Global Forum saw the first mass use of ICTs to interconnect and network such an enormous gathering, enabling delegates to share information quickly, debate, construct agendas and plan strategies for the future. As Shelley Preston (1994) noted, 'These on-site information exchange services were unprecedented.' Distribution among delegates of a document entitled *Computer Communications and the 1992 UNCED: Alternative Technology for Communication and Participation by NGOs* was intended as a primer on ICTs and their significance for NGOs. Preston went on to write that 'One of the most significant documents to emerge from the Global Forum was the *Communication, Information, Media, and Networking Treaty*, which declares the right of communication as a basic human right' (Preston 1994). Word of the success of the 'experiment' in Rio quickly spread as homeward bound delegates fanned out across the world, disgusted by the official Summit and enthused by the possibilities inherent in ICTs for the constitution of an alternative civil society. The message did not take long to catch on. As John E. Young of the Worldwatch Institute later commented, 'As of mid-1993, thousands of environmental activists and organizations around the world [were] using commercial and nonprofit computer networks to coordinate campaigns, exchange news, and get details on the proposals of governments and international organizations' (1993: 21).

In 1994 the significance of ICTs for the conduct of direct action and overt political and ideological struggle was made apparent by the Zapatista insurgency in Chiapas Province in Mexico. The Zapatista movement arose to represent the rights of indigenous workers and peasants in Chiapas Province who felt that neoliberalism in the shape of the North American Free Trade Agreement (NAFTA) was destroying their culture, environment and economy. Were it not for the innovative use of ICTs by their leader 'Subcommandante Marcos' in promoting their struggle against the Mexican government and military, then the Zapatista movement may well have remained an obscure rebellion that was quietly, but no doubt viciously, crushed. However, through use of the fax, the laptop, email and the Internet, the movement connected rapidly with sympathetic groups and movements around the world. The Zapatista struggle (especially in respect of its inventive use of ICTs as a weapon) was picked up by sections of the media and became a *cause célèbre* in the struggle against the worst aspects of neoliberal globalization. In July 1996, in a bold show of international solidarity, over 3000 activists from over 40 countries around the world gathered in Chiapas to take part in what came to be known as the 'First Intercontinental Gathering for Humanity and Against Neoliberalism' (Flood 1996). Delegates at the meeting called for the creation of the 'Intercontinental Network of Alternative Communication'. Their spokesperson was Subcommandante Marcos, whose statement (cited in Leal 2000: 7) read:

> Let us start a communications network between all our struggles, an intercontinental network of communication against neo-liberalism, an intercontinental network for humanity. This intercontinental network will seek to tie together all the channels of our words and all the roads of resistance. This intercontinental network will be the means among which the different areas of resistance will communicate. This intercontinental network will not be an organized structure, it will have no moderator, central control, or any hierarchies. The network will be all of us who speak and listen.

By this time the 'anti-globalization movement' was beginning to take some sort of shape. Groups of people from all around the world were now intensively communicating, sharing ideas, inspiring each other to organize and to strategize both locally and globally. The late 1990s saw many movements evolve and connect, disconnect, grow in strength or fade away in an amorphous and yet always expanding network of alternative civil society. They see the enemy as neoliberalism and their weapons of choice as ideas, protest, communication and information. To be sure, the 'anti-globalization movement' was comprised not of a single mind, or ideology. It was peopled by anarchists, socialists, trades unionists, farmers, unemployed, low-waged workers, students, intellectuals, environmentalists and more. What brought them together, however, was a shared feeling of an economic system gone wrong; one that seemed to be run in the interests of big business first, with anything left over to 'trickle down' to the rest of humanity. These groups also began to focus on what were viewed as the organizations and corporate symbols of global economic oppression such as the World Economic Forum (WEF), the WTO, the IMF, the World Bank – and their neoliberal cousins in the private sector such as McDonald's, Borders, Gap, Nike or Shell Oil. This shared focus between so many disparate groups would have been impossible without the intercommunication made possible by ICTs and through such websites as www.indymedia.org – and by falling physical transportation costs – another effect of neoliberal globalization that was being turned against it.

The demonstrations at the WTO meeting in Seattle in 1999 marked a new phase in the development of a politics for the age of globalization. An estimated 50,000 people gathered for a week of meetings, sit-ins, 'happenings' and battles with riot police armed with tear gas, rubber bullets and truncheons. The protests succeeded in taking almost all the attention away from the 'real' business of the WTO meeting, which ended rather dismally, without a *communiqué* or an agenda or schedule for more talks. This unheard-of level of disruption of the 'legitimate' business of neoliberal globalization caught officials napping. Politicians, WTO officials, business leaders as well as the majority of mainstream media were almost as one in branding the protestors as anti-trade, or anti-business or, in the one that seemed to stick – anti-globalization.

However, as Naomi Klein (2002: 3–6) wrote at the time in an article that appeared in the *New York Times*:

> This is the first political movement born of the chaotic pathways of the Internet. Within its ranks, there is no top-down hierarchy ready to explain the master plan, no universally recognized leaders giving easy sound-bites and nobody knows what is going to happen next. But one thing is certain: the protestors in Seattle are not anti-globalization; they have been bitten by the globalization bug as surely as the trade lawyers inside the official meeting. Rather if this new movement is 'anti' anything, it is anti-corporate, opposing a logic that what's good for business – less regulation, more mobility, more access – will trickle down into good news for everybody else ... The face-off is not between globalizers and protectionists, but one between two radically different visions of globalization. One has had a monopoly for the past ten years. The other has just had its coming-out party.

Far from ending the 'party' at its beginning, before it got too noisy and troublesome – as the politicians, business leaders and mainstream media commentators wished – the party simply grew and went on the road. It got bigger, more inclusive and was held at venues all around the world, wherever the symbols of neoliberalism such as the WTO or the World Bank or WEF had agreed to meet. An indication of the alarm the 'anti-globalization' movement was beginning to cause in elite circles is that various politicians, right-wing journalists and others tried to link it to various terrorist groups. Predictably, this unimaginative propaganda trick failed to connect, and probably did as much as the 'chaotic pathways of the Internet' to swell grass-roots support for issues that millions could see were being ignored. Accordingly, Seattle snowballed into Prague, which became Washington, which morphed into Quebec, which travelled to Melbourne, which rolled on to Porto Alegre, Salzburg and Barcelona. These venues were just the beginning of a new social and political development, where global civil society spectacularly, brazenly and regularly interrupted the 'legitimate' business of neoliberalism.

The Group of Eight (G8) intergovernmental summit held in Genoa in July 2001 attracted half a million 'anti-globalization' protestors. However, the summit organisers had learned the lessons of Seattle and were ready for the demonstrators. Genoa city centre (designated the 'red zone' for that weekend by city authorities) bristled with surface-to-air missiles, swarmed with armed helicopters, and was barricaded by roadblocks and was occupied by 15,000 riot-trained *carabinieri*. So heavily tooled up were the Italian authorities that violence seemed inevitable. And so it transpired. Even mainstream media accounts depicted the police action as brutal as well as incompetent. ABCNews.com reported at least 150 protestors and police were hospitalized (ABCNews 2001). And in images that were to flash around the world and disseminate across the network, police shot dead an unarmed protestor, Carlo Guiliani.

Far from being strangled at birth as the authorities in countries around the world fervently hoped, the global civil society movement has grown immeasurably. No longer can the high priests of neoliberalism simply gather in opulent surroundings, detached from the real world, and plan the next steps in the creation of a world that reflects their values, prejudices and worldviews. They now have to be helicoptered in to meetings, or travel in buses with blacked-out windows and shielded by phalanxes of riot police; or – in a further twist of desperation – forced to convene in remote places such as Doha in the desert state of Qatar in the Arabian Gulf.

As many activists are beginning to realize, however, the ostensible 'success' of grass-roots activism on a global scale may be masking serious and ultimately debilitating problems. The most obvious issue confronting the global civil society movement is: 'where to from here?' Inconveniencing (and basically this is what it amounts to) corporate CEOs, senior trade negotiators and World Bank economists when they try to get together is one thing. The important and substantive elements of their work go on. The increasingly pressing questions are: how to change, or halt, the course of neoliberalism, not just inconvenience it? Further, and devilishly tricky questions flow from this. For example, how does such an amorphous and polyvocal thing as the global civil society movement articulate and implement the policies, strategies, ideologies, programmes and plans required to enable change? Indeed, a central issue is: do the many and varied activists within this new global civil society *want* to become organized in the traditional ways? Part of the problem is that some do and many others don't. How, then, to go forward, when the idea of 'going forward' is itself seen by many as problematic? How is it possible to reconcile the strengths of the movement, such as difference, pluralism and diversity, with the achievement of aims that normally require hierarchies, strategies and programmes? Activist and writer Michael Hardt posed the problem with some acuity in the aftermath of the World Social Forum in Porto Alegre, Brazil, in January 2002, where eighty thousand 'delegates' gathered. He noted that

> The [Porto Alegre] Forum was unknowable, chaotic, dispersive. And that overabundance created an exhilaration in everyone, at being lost in a sea of people from so many parts of the world who are working similarly against the present form of capitalist globalization . . . The encounter should, however, reveal and address not only the common projects and desires, but also the differences of those involved – differences of material conditions and political orientation. The various movements across the global cannot simply connect to each other as they

are, but must rather be transformed by the encounter through a kind of mutual adequation … What kind of transformations are necessary for the Euro-American globalization movements and the Latin American movements, not to become the same, or even unite, but to link together in an expanding common network? The Forum provided an opportunity to recognize such questions and differences for those willing to see them, but it did not provide the conditions for addressing them. *In fact, the very same dispersive, overflowing quality of the Forum that created the euphoria of commonality also effectively displaced the terrain on which such differences and conflicts could be confronted.*

(Hardt 2002: 113–14, emphasis added)

I think that the final sentence encapsulates the contradiction that faces the global civil society movement. The many and varied effects of neoliberal globalization have brought together an enormous diversity of people who want to resist it. However, if the effects of neoliberal globalization are so diverse, stretching across so much of the world, how are people able to confront their differences to be able not only to resist neoliberal globalization effectively, but also to change it?

The next section will look at the mechanics of this political dilemma and then discuss how individuals and groups are, in theory and in practice, attempting to overcome it.

The politics of technopolitics

The seriousness of the political issues facing the growing number of people who oppose neoliberal globalization cannot be underestimated. To be able to resist and to change neoliberalism, what is required is nothing less than the development of a whole new way of conducting politics and political struggle. As Emir Sader (2002: 87) argues, the logic emanating from the global civil society movement '… points towards an *entirely new* ideological, political and geographic design'. As I intimated earlier, things cannot simply go on as they are as far as the movement is concerned. 'Where to from here?' will unavoidably become a dominating issue as the movement is forced to become, at least for a period, more reflective and introspective. Why? Because sooner or later, if central political questions are not confronted, then the presently fresh and vibrant civil society movement will simply run out of steam. Innovative use of ICTs harnessed to a rage against the new world order being shaped by corporations has enabled a movement to grow and to come together to make its voice heard in venues from Seattle to Genoa to Porto Alegre. The movement has been inspirational, motivational and exhilarating. Equally, it has also been, to use Hardt's terminology, 'unknowable, chaotic, dispersive'. However, the reality is that thus far the movement has only been a minor irritant, a flea on the corporate body of neoliberal globalization. The work of creating one big marketplace that stretches from Tierra del Fuego to

Anchorage, and from Dublin to Dunedin and back up to Delhi, goes on pretty much unimpeded. The novelty of a travelling show of protestors, providing mainly spectacle and valuable crowd control practice for riot police will soon wear pretty thin. Sympathizers around the world, and most especially the activists themselves, whose energy and commitment levels need to be considerable, will require to see tangible returns on all this emotional, intellectual and physical investment. Simply hoping that things can go from strength to strength is therefore not an option if one looks analytically at the movement and the global political context it works within.

In trying to unpack these issues, Michael Hardt has looked at the political and ideological composition of the global civil society movement, particularly as it was constituted at the Porto Alegre Forum that convened in January 2002. He noted that there are 'two primary positions in response to today's dominant forces of globalization'. These are, he goes on to write, that either

> one can work to reinforce the sovereignty of the nation-states as a defensive barrier against the control of foreign and global capital, or one can strive towards a non-national alternative to the present form of globalization that is equally global. The first poses neoliberalism as the primary analytical category, viewing the enemy as unrestricted global capitalist activity with weak state controls; the second is more clearly posed against capital itself, whether state-regulated or not. The first might rightly be called an anti-globalization position . . . the second, in contrast, opposes any national solutions and seeks instead a democratic globalization.
>
> (Hardt 2002: 14)

In 'old style' politics, this sort of fundamental political and ideological chasm would be more or less irreconcilable. The logic of hierarchy, of 'party line' and of discipline and party loyalty that were the mainstays of the politics of modernity simply do not have the flexibility necessary to reconcile such radically divergent worldviews. However, as we have seen, the 'politics of modernity' are exactly what millions across the world have been turning away from, and have been attempting to articulate alternatives to, for over a decade. This disaffection has opened up the space for a new politics based on a shared antipathy towards neoliberalism and a willingness to use ICTs as the organizational glue that holds it all together.

As the global civil society movement has demonstrated, a new-style politics based upon a shared antipathy towards neoliberalism and held together in time and space by networks – a **technopolitics** – is now possible. Global civil society's rise to the level of a critical mass has shown the potential (at least) of the development of spaces (virtual and actual) where anarchists can make common cause with trade unionists, socialists with NGOs, ecologists with farmers, intellectuals with church groups and so on. But of course, such developments will neither be easy nor smooth, and the extent of the difficulties is only just being realized and theorized. The ideological, geographical and structural problems to be overcome are considerable, notwithstanding the immense strides forward that the nascent global civil society has already taken. As Hardt notes, those who hold to the 'national sovereignty' position were the 'most visible' and 'dominant' at the Porto Alegre Forum. For them, 'national liberation' from the yoke of transnational neoliberalism was the primary goal (2002: 115). This position gives priority to the strengthening of the state against neoliberal globalization and the power of Wall Street. This 'national sovereignty' position was to be found among those from both developed and developing countries. Their mode of organization, as Hardt observes, was much more traditional and hierarchical and linked to the dynamics of the activists' own domestic structures of political parties, trades unions and other political institutions. The non-sovereign 'alternative globalization' position may have been numerically superior at Porto Alegre, but was less represented in official plenary sessions and so on, where all the 'decisions' get made and *communiqués* developed. The 'alternative globalization' position, according to Hardt, could be said to be more representative of those participants in the protests from Seattle to Genoa: those involved in the 'happenings' and the more specific 'anti-capitalism' protests. The mode of organization utilized here depended more upon an amorphous 'horizontal network-form' that privileged the building of networks to the building of parties or traditional movements (2002: 115).

Importantly, these divisions do not correspond to the geography of North and South, of developed and developing regions and economies. Rather, the fact that they span the globe indicates that they are *an effect of globalization* and the forms of communication made possible by ICTs and the evolution of the network society. The real division, as Hardt (2002: 116) notes, is

> . . . between two different forms of political organization. The traditional parties and centralized campaigns generally occupy the national sovereignty pole, whereas the new movements organized in horizontal networks tend to cluster at the non-sovereign pole. [Moreover] within traditional centralized organizations, the top tends toward sovereignty and the base away. It is no surprise, perhaps, that those in positions of power would be most interested in state sovereignty and those excluded least. This may help to explain . . . how the national sovereignty, anti-globalization position could dominate the representations of the [Porto Alegre] Forum even though a majority of the participants tend rather towards the perspective of a non-nation alternative globalization.

As Hardt sees it, the future of the global civil society movement depends upon whether they choose between modes of organization based upon 'parties or networks'. That is to say, between hierarchical modes based upon national sovereignty or upon horizontal modes based upon borderless networks; and between the binary politics of opposition and the politics of unity within a limitless diversity. Almost by definition, most of the people attracted to the global civil society movement are seeking a new politics. And at least intuitively, many also realize that power and the politics of real change in the network society will be contested within the network itself. In other words, ICTs as well as ideas will be the tools for the formation of a new politics. Hardt (2002: 117), as a passionate advocate of networks over parties, states the case for the former with some eloquence:

> How do you argue with a network? The movements organized within them do exert their power, but they do not proceed through oppositions. One of the basic characteristics of the network form is that no two nodes face each other in contradiction; rather they are always triangulated by a third, and then a fourth, and then by an infinite number of others in the web. This is one of the characteristics of the Seattle events that we have had the most trouble in understanding: groups which we thought in objective contradiction with one another – environmentalists and trade unions, church groups and anarchists – were suddenly able to work together, in the context of the network of the multitude. The movements . . . function something like a public sphere, in the sense that they can allow full expression of differences within the common contexts of open exchange. But that does not mean that networks are passive. They displace contradictions and operate instead in a kind of alchemy, or rather a sea change, the flow of the movements transforming the traditional fixed positions; networks imposing their own form through a kind of irresistible undertow.

Fine words indeed, but theorists and activists are only just beginning to think in these terms. There is a long way to go before a technopolitics armed with this sort of flexibility, inclusivity and power can develop – and this is before it can take on neo-liberalism as an alternative and plausible form of politics for the networked society.

Nevertheless, many individuals and groups, theorists and activists, in theory and in practice, are determined to realize the goal of the formation of a new political order for the network society. They realize, either intuitively or from a thought-out position, that a new form of politics will need to develop out of the radically changed circumstances that neoliberal globalization and the ICT revolution have brought about. In a world where there is 'no outside' of the network society any longer, as Lash (2002: 10) has put it, then Hardt and others (as we shall shortly see) are laying the foundations for the modelling of an alternative politics in networking, in communications and in media.

Further reading

Hardt, M. (2002) Porto Alegre: today's Bandung?, *New Left Review*, 14, March–April: 114.

Klein, N. (2000) *No Logo*. London: Flamingo.

Klein, N. (2002) *Fences and Windows*. London: Flamingo.

Lasn, K. (2000) *Culture Jam: How to Reverse America's Suicidal Consumer Binge – And Why We Must*. New York, NY: HarperCollins.

Monbiot, G. (2000) *The Captive State*. London: Macmillan.

6

TACTICAL MEDIA

It must not be forgotten, that even in industrialised countries, during times of repression, there have been snipers and guerrillas.

(Aron 1968: 215)

In a post-Fordist world driven by globalizing competition, powered by ICTs, and where, as Giddens has observed 'no one is in control' (1997: 4–5) any longer, the once-monolithic field of the political has shattered into a million pieces. People, also in their millions, have been organizing to develop an alternative politics for these new, networked, postmodern times. In the main, they have been forced back upon their own devices, as it were, to their own resources to rethink old ideas in the context of the new circumstances; or, probably more prevalently, they are groping along in the dark for what 'feels' better, more empowering, fairer, more inclusive, more diverse and more democratic. It is here, in the chaos of where 'no one is in control', that new forms of technopolitics are being forged and that new ways of political organization are being tested, rejected, modified, developed and articulated.

Media theorists and activists Geert Lovink and David Garcia are at the cutting edge of the formation of a technopolitics. In network time it seems like aeons ago, but it was only in 1996 that they published a document called the *ABC of Tactical Media*. The essay has found various homes on the Internet and is easily traceable and downloadable. In it they argue that people should embrace the network society, but in ways that undermine and subvert the domination of it by neoliberalism. Activists, users, programmers – anyone who interacts with ICTs as a daily and integral part of their lives – should (must) learn to use this media 'tactically', they argue. So what is 'tactical media'? Lovink and Garcia (1996) write that

> Tactical media are what happen when the cheap 'do it yourself' media, made possible by the revolution in consumer electronics and expanded forms of

distribution, are exploited by groups and individuals who feel aggrieved by or excluded from the wider culture.

The drive to use media tactically stems from what they see as the 'crisis' of the dominant system and through increasing 'criticism and opposition' to it. The authors take their intellectual cue from Michel de Certeau and his book *The Practice of Everyday Life* that was first published in English in 1984. In this de Certeau analysed the ways in which we 'make do' in our everyday life through our use and consumption of the products and practices of commodity culture. We do more than 'make do', however, according to de Certeau. Inside the oppressive 'product-system' as he calls it, people strive consciously or unconsciously to secure for themselves areas of personal and collective autonomy through their interaction with the everyday world that surrounds them. For de Certeau, these 'ways of operating' or 'tactics' amount to a kind of resistance; or, as he puts it, 'ways of reappropriating the product-system, ways created by consumers, [and which] have as their goal a *therapeutics for deteriorating social relations . . .*' (1984: xxiv, emphasis added).

This 'tactics of practice' was thus for de Certeau a highly political process. It constituted a mild form of *guerrilla* warfare, and involved the development of 'ruses', of an 'increased deviousness', and of the cunning of the 'poacher'. However, having its goal as a form of 'therapeutics' does seem a rather passive objective. And as Lovink and Garcia see it, the stakes are now much higher today than when de Certeau wrote. Accordingly, they have replaced the goal of 'therapy' with one of the forming of a new politics for the construction of a new world – a new 'everyday life' where people themselves seek to control and shape it, as opposed to an amelioration of the system's worst aspects. In only a couple of decades our world has become a mediatized world, where 'ubiquitous computing' suffuses much of everyday life. Accordingly, what are now most readily 'to hand' in everyday life, and what comprises much of our culture, are ICTs. What we must become *au fait* with, and tacticians of, then, is media and communications technologies. Recognizing this, Lovink and Garcia build upon, and make more radical, de Certeau's work to develop their own theory (and practice) of *tactical media*. In keeping with the *guerrilla* metaphor and of 'hit and run' practices, they make the observation that

> Tactical media are based on a principle of flexible response, of working with different coalitions, being able to move between the different entities of the vast media landscape without betraying the original motivations. Tactical media may be hedonistic, or zealously euphoric. Even fashion hypes have their uses. But it is above all mobility that most characterises the tactical practitioner. The desire and capability to combine or jump from one media to another creating a continuous supply of mutants and hybrids. To cross borders, connecting and re-wiring a variety of disciplines and always taking full advantage of the free space in the media that are appearing because of the pace of technological change and regulatory uncertainty.

In an essay from 2002 (this time authored with Florian Schneider), Lovink ups the ante, and if anything becomes even more extreme in the theory and practice of tactical media. In this, I think, the writers sense and reflect a radicalism that has emerged within the global civil society itself and a willingness to use ICTs in new ways to achieve their own individual and collective ends. 'This is the golden age of irresistible activism', they write, one where 'current forms of activism attempt a redefinition of sabotage as social practice, but not in the usual destructive sense, rather in a constructive, innovative and creative practice' (2002: 315–16). This innovation and creativity, they argue, emanates from a global civil society movement 'without organs and organisation' (2002: 315).

Within this amorphous energy Lovink and Schneider identify three layers of ICT activism that have emerged over the last decade, and function still in a rudimentary fashion. First is _networking within a movement_. These are the basic elements required to help create the movement and to make it work. It consists of using the Internet to share and collect information, to build websites that act as 'toolboxes' for the activists themselves through the use of mailing lists, email and so on. The second level is what the authors term _networking in between movements and social groups_. This is a move upwards in complexity and a move outwards to connect with other groups and movements. This form of second-level activism is defined by 'campaigning and connecting people from different contexts. It means joining forces, collaborative and cooperative efforts, creating inspiring and motivating surroundings in which new types of actions and activities may be elaborated' (2002: 316). The third level of ICT-based activism is what Lovink and Schneider term _virtual movements_. This means:

> Using the Internet _vice versa_ as a platform for purely virtual protests, which refer no longer to any off-line reality and which may cause incalculable and uncontrollable movements: E-protests like online demonstrations, electronic civil disobedience or anything which might be seen as digital sabotage as a legitimate outcome of social struggle: counter-branding, causing virtual losses, polluting the image of the corporation.

If the theory is developing apace, then forms of practice are attempting to catch up. Consciously or unconsciously, individuals and groups all over the world are now acting as media tacticians in their everyday lives. They are finding many creative and innovative 'ways of using the products used by the dominant economic order', as de Certeau put it, to carve out their own sovereign spaces within the information-based order. The critical point is that instead of doing this as a form of 'therapy' they are turning these products (ICTs) against that order itself.

Tactical media in action

We have already seen examples of the first two layers of Lovink and Schneider's three layers of net activism. The evolution of a global civil society was (and still is) fundamentally dependent upon the use of ICTs in these ways. They are the basis upon which new groups and movements will form and coalesce, and will represent the future of net activism in the years to come. However, level three in the authors' taxonomy is especially interesting as it incorporates the first two as necessary technological and organizational stages, but then moves the struggle onto a different plane – to the plane of symbols and representations, of semiotics and of logos. In many ways this level of 'virtual movements' activism can, if underpinned by these other levels, act as the most important terrain of struggle. This is because, being virtual (largely screen-based), this form of activism deals with what people *see* in a visual world, what information and communication technologies they *use* in a mediatized world, and what they *consume* in a consumer society. People can 'do it themselves' through following examples they find in virtual movements, or they can contribute their own ideas for others to follow; or, when necessary, they can act as part of a virtual collectivity – or a physical collectivity – as and when required by members of the group itself.

   Think software. Linux is a computer operating system (OS) that was developed in the early 1990s by a (then) computer science student and hacker-nerd, Linus Torvalds. He wrote the OS as an 'open source code' that could be used and modified in whatever new and innovative ways the programmer could devise – for free. As it grew and became more complex and useful through the additions and modifications made by other hackers in the so-called 'open source movement', Linux adopted what is called the 'copyleft' system. This 'general public licence' (GPL) is at the core of the open source movement and permits users to sell, copy and change copylefted programs. The finished product can then be copyrighted. However, you must pass along the same rights to sell or copy your modifications and for others possibly to change them further. You must also make the source code of your modifications freely available. With potentially hundreds of thousands of hackers continually modifying and (one would think) improving the code, the GPL system acts as a sort of Darwinian 'natural selection' through which applications that best suit their contexts or environments are the most successful (Moody 1997). The dynamism from this global hacker community has ensured that Linux has become a viable alternative (and thus a possible challenge) to the monopoly in PC operating systems enjoyed by Microsoft. In terms of numbers it is difficult to estimate the number of users of a system that is freely distributable and copied endlessly across the network, but one guesstimate has put it at around 18 million. And as Linux becomes more popular, so too will it become more 'institutionalized', and even more popular. For example, in mid-2003 in Germany, the Munich municipal government decided – to the not-inconsiderable chagrin of Microsoᶠ· cancel its Microsoft contract and begin using Linux-based open source sc instead (Naughton 2003); the PC giant Hewlett Packet (owner of Compaq) has dᴇ

This is the key!!

to install the Linux OS as 'the operating system of choice for the emerging server appliances market' (Hewlett Packard 2002); and Motorola has installed Linux copyleft software in all its 3G mobile phones.

The somewhat unassuming Finn Torvalds is not your average activist. He probably didn't go to Seattle or Genoa. He seems to be a very mainstream guy with a good job and a flair for writing code. 'Radical social activism', quite probably, does not appear on the 'Interests' section in the CVs of many of the hackers and programmers who contribute to the ongoing evolution of Linux, either. Nevertheless, their combined actions *are* political *and* subversive in that they have taken on the power of monopoly with the fundamentally democratic objective of open source coding. In other words, they are using the tools of the system and turning them against it.

Culturejamming

Rather more your average activists, but just as immersed in ICTs, and hypertuned to their possibilities for challenging the *status quo*, are the 1960s Situationist-inspired Adbusters. Consisting of a website (www.adbusters.org) and the magazine *Adbusters*, they are committed to subverting ('polluting' in Lovink's terminology) the corporate symbols of neoliberal capitalism and exposing corporate malfeasance and hypocrisy wherever they find it. They organize online and paper-based campaigns such as the yearly 'Buy Nothing Day' where consumers are urged to try and spend a single day of the year without supporting global capitalism through buying; or 'TV Turnoff Week' where the idiot box in the corner gets switched off – or preferably thrown out. As a medium that privileges the visual over the aural, their website and magazine uses powerful artworks and logos, images that punch the message home. Today, I looked at their website which opened with a single picture, no text, of a Mercedes-Benz sports car. This once-flash car had obviously been in a bad collision with a wall or a tree. But look closely at the beaten-up personalized licence plate on this terminally damaged plutocrat's plaything and you see the twisted letters JOY. Ironic statements such as this have made adbusters.org and *Adbusters* magazine powerful tools for activists across the world to use in their personal or collective projects of resistance.

'**Culturejamming**' is their *metier*. This is the project to subvert (or to halt) what they see as the 'branding' of America. This is the 'brand bombing' that Klein describes in her *No Logo*. Kalle Lasn, editor of *Adbusters* magazine, argues that 'branding' is nothing less than the colonization of the spaces of the diversity within American culture and rendering it prey to homogenizing corporate capital. In 2000 Lasn wrote a book called *Culture Jam: How to Reverse America's Suicidal Consumer Binge – And Why We Must*. In it he argues that under the influence of neoliberal globalization we find ourselves

> . . . adrift at a historically significant time . . . Most of us are now detached from
> the natural world. We can barely remember the last time we drank from a stream,

smelled wild skunk cabbage or saw the stars from a dark remove, well away from the city. We can't remember the last time we spent an evening telling stories, instead of having Jerry or Oprah or Rosie tell stories to us. We can't identify three kinds of tree, but know how much Mike Tyson received for his last fight. We can't explain why the sky is blue, but we know how many times Susan Lucci has been passed over for a daytime Emmy Award.

(Lasn 2000: 4)

Lasn sees this 'separation from nature' by consumer culture as a 'malaise' that is rendering society spiritually empty and culturally shallow. What Adbusters and *Adbusters* magazine try to do is to show where the real spiritual and cultural vacuum lies – in the consumer culture that suffuses everyday life. As I said, irony is a weapon they resort to a lot. And so an example of 'counter-branding' is to take the brand name 'Adidas', and acronym it as 'All Day I Dream About Suicide'. This speaks to the immense pressure put upon youth by massive brand bombing, to buy and to be seen in whatever it is the Adidas 'coolhunters' have deemed 'cool' for this summer or winter, for sport or for leisure, and so on. Politically and culturally, the work of activists such as Adbusters and Naomi Klein, among others, is having an effect – at least in terms of their raising awareness on certain issues. Who now is not at least dimly conscious of the fact that Nike or Gap, for example, quite apart from being 'cool' also have significant public relations 'challenges' concerning labour exploitation in developing countries; or that McDonald's or KFC have similar problems concerning the nutritional (and ethical) value of their product as well as the environmental costs in bringing it to your mouth? A measure of their success is that these and many other global icons can now be mentioned, and with no incongruity, in the same breath as death-dealing cigarette manufacturers or the most rapacious oil companies.

Warchalking

As the network becomes more wireless-based and its nodes increasingly mobile and ubiquitous, then potential tactical media opportunities continually present themselves. '**Warchalking**' emerged in 2002 when small groups of people and individuals began to realize that they could hitch a free ride on business or institutional wi-fi hotspots. It was discovered that hotspots give off a wireless Internet signal that can spill over into public spaces. Someone with a laptop or PDA and the appropriate link and a networking card can therefore enter what is in effect an open network as opposed to the private hardwired Local Area Network (LAN) that it is intended to be by its owners. 'Appropriate link' can be something as basic (and ingenious) as a Pringles crisp can attached to a cable, acting in effect as an aerial to receive the network signal.

The term 'warchalking' is a neologism, but it references the pictographic language developed by 'hobos' during the 1930s Great Depression in the US. A crude system of signs served as a form of communication between itinerants who would chalk their coded symbols on walls, pavements and so on, to signify if, say, the police in a particular town were hard on the homeless, or if there was a doctor who wouldn't charge a fee in a particular house, and so on. The term was coined by London web designer Matt Jones, who set up a devoted website (www.warchalking.org). In addition to chalking on buildings and so on to signify an open hotspot, people can also use websites like www.warchalking.org to post messages informing where a free spot of surfing on the Internet may be had. One such post, by 'Fletch', runs:

> I have a new favorite location. Starbucks in Borders, Oxford Street is just a bit too busy and touristy. What I needed was something a bit more chilled – a better place to be seen! Now I admit that Starbucks is not really cool, but those sofa's are oh so comfy . . . So my new favorite location is Starbucks Notting Hill Gate (next to Oxfam). The hotspot has the unlikely name of 'futon' eminating (sic) I deduce from the futon shop next door, you need to sit in the front half of the store to get good reception (at least you do with my vaio internal antenna.) Coolest of all, when the weather gets better you can sit out on the street and get your laptop stolen in a driveby!
>
> (Accessed 25 April 2003)

It is not known if 'Fletch' was inadvertently logging to the wi-fi service that Starbucks provides (for a fee) in some of its establishments, or he/she was in a wi-fi free Starbucks and picking up the signal from somewhere else. A futon shop somehow seems less likely than a Starbucks to be an Internet hotspot. I don't suppose it matters. What is interesting is the phenomenon of going poaching in cyberspace itself. It remains to be seen, however, how popular warchalking will become. It's not exactly revolutionary, and smacks more than a little of selfishness and ironic trendiness: 'a better place to be seen' to 'get your laptop stolen'. Also, it's a bit like riding on public transport for free – you can make a good case for it if you are poor, but if everyone does it then fares will go up, or taxes increase, and if these don't work then public transport availability may decrease. Ambulating around London, or New York, or Sydney with a few thousand dollars worth of hardware looking for a free-ride hotspot does not make all that much practical sense, anyway. In mass demonstration situations such tactics may well prove unworkable, or far too slow compared with mobile phones and text-messaging. Moreover, community groups who advocate free community-based networks are unenthused by it. One quoted on the ZnetUK technology site, when asked if warchalking was a good thing, said: 'I am one of those people trying to seriously encourage community networking and if that activity is seen to be some sort of cracker plot it will be damaged' (Loney 2002).

Like fare evasion, warchalking may foreground a David versus Goliath element that may obscure what it is you are really doing. Moreover, linking it back, somewhat romantically, to grim economic times, when to be a 'hobo' does not remotely approximate today's laptop and PDA-equipped warchalkers, may be stretching the underdog analogy a little too far. It also taxes the imagination to find a place for it within Lovink and Schneider's tactical media classification. Warchalking may turn out to be a crash-and-burn fad, or it may be the beginnings of something big, but hitchhiking on a corporate server in a Starbucks or at an obscure corner in a big city central business district appears to be primarily an individualistic enterprise for the emerging digital proto-*lumpenproletariat*. What it does have going for it, I believe, is that it shows that individuals, no matter how deeply commodified and colonized by the logic of the neoliberal/ICT nexus, will always create spaces of at least partial autonomy for themselves. Moreover, there is at least a slither of subversion and creativity here, no matter the motivation. Warchalking, then, may not be the beginnings of a digital insurrection, but it is just one dimension of life in the network economy that exhibits a techno and cultural savvy that *may* help form the basis for a richer and more communitarian-oriented expertise or cultural competence in future tactical media struggles.

Digital direct action

In what is a combination of *all three* levels of Lovink and Schneider's ICT activism, the Ruckus Society represents a more radical and direct action version of what Adbusters are trying to achieve, and what warchalking is in nascent, undeveloped and potential form. It has distinct anarcho-environmentalist leanings, but this Oakland, California-based organization involves itself in civil society struggles that range across the board. Using ICTs as its organizational glue, it draws together people from across the US and the rest of the world to learn the non-violent tactics of global civil society activism. Through the Internet, email lists and bulletin boards it advertises periodical 'training tech-camps' where activists physically convene to acquire the skills of resistance through ICTs. In what is a fundamental attempt to create a new civil society, Ruckus Society volunteers can attend these 'camps' to learn the skills of media activism. In a centrifugal action they are then expected to return home to their own community organizations to pass on what they have learnt.

The emphasis they place upon ICTs as a weapon for social justice and social change is striking. Take the 'tech toolbox action camp' that was held in Occidental, California from 26 June to 2 July 2002. The bulletin board notice for this event stated that 'The camp will offer a place for activists to evaluate and learn how they might employ technology in their work and campaigns, side by side with those who are already doing so' (Ruckus 2002a). Among the topics the participants covered at the camp were:

- Online organizing;
- Independent media;
- Tactical communications for nonviolent direct action;
- Secure collaboration;

- Electronic surveillance and counter-surveillance;
- Legal workshops for tech activists;
- Culture jamming and creative messaging.

And, as noted, after their training, participants are encouraged to 'go home and translate what [they have] learned into action at the local level' (Ruckus 2002b).

Consciously or unconsciously, what the growing number of groups such as the Ruckus Society and Adbusters seem to have realized, and what warchalkers exhibit notwithstanding their motivation, is the importance of the 'media savvy' and 'techno savvy' dialectic we discussed in Chapter 2. It is not enough, as I noted then, to be simply technologically skilled within the network society. To have any chance of personal and group empowerment, one must also develop and hone a media savvy, too. Media savvy is the ability to understand the cultural, economic and social contexts within which ICTs have been conceived, developed and implemented, under the aegis of neoliberalism. It affords the space to 'step back', evaluate, interpret and critique. They will be able to think about ICTs and their actual and possible uses in society. Moreover, a honed media savvy feeds back into the techno savvy, allowing critique to do its work upon the ways we can use ICTs themselves, in ways that can be truly innovative, creative and geared toward alternative and 'unintended' uses. To connect a media savvy with a techno savvy, then, is to create the cultural competencies that comprise the basic survival kit for Life.com, as well as the weapons and tactics that can help change it. This techno-cultural dialectic echoes, powerfully, the necessary 'desire and capability' of the media tactician that Lovink and Garcia described earlier in their *ABC of Tactical Media* (1996). They noted that 'desire and capability' are the underpinning of the media tactician, the ability to create a 'continuous supply of mutants and hybrids . . . to cross borders, connecting and re-wiring . . .' to subvert the neoliberal network. Such 'desire and capability' is thus the *imagination* to desire alternatives and the capacity to *make them happen* – which constitutes the *sine qua non* for the guerrilla in the jungle of the network.

It is easy to see how virtual groups such as Adbusters and groups that are both physical and virtual such as the Ruckus Society can complement each other, and have many different crossovers. People can and do belong to both, as well as to other groups such as Greenpeace, Friends of the Earth and various other political and community organizations. Their interconnections are many, varied and growing. They form a network of networks that stretches from the local to the global and is held in tension through the common goal of opposing the rule of neoliberal globalization. Such groups also, I believe, are taking the first steps toward overcoming the central political dilemma that Hardt identifies: that tension between the 'national sovereignty' activists and the 'alternative globalization' activists. The key, it seems to me, are ICTs themselves and their potential to reconcile these positions by being able to be both local and global at the same time. Both positions stress the need to work locally in the first instance, and this will help strengthen local and national identity. This form of 'rhizomic politics' will always place the local before the global and form the basis for a democratic 'national sovereignty'. However, both positions must also recognize that 'globalization' cannot be dismantled. It is not possible to go back to the forms of regionalism and the relative cultural, economic and political insularism that existed prior to the 1970s. Much that neoliberalism has brought us cannot be so easily uninvented. The argument, then, is more accurately about the *forms* that globalization might take, with the emphasis on the plural. A grass-roots 'rhizomic politics' that is predicated upon ICT networks and their potential for social change is the ideal place to make this work. The democratic activism and politics of the local can, through 'networks of networks', achieve the 'step up' to the global through deep and constant interconnectivity by individuals, groups and movements throughout the world. Such 'strength through networks' cannot but have an effect upon the way neoliberalism currently considers the planet as its own space to be marketized and commodified in its own image. If this can be made to work as 'the next step forward', or at least as the beginning of an answer to the question: 'where to from here?', then the neoliberal clerics in Wall Street and in the WTO and IMF and so on will be forced to listen to the voices of those who are just beginning to find them.

Further reading

Lovink, G. and Garcia, D. (1996) *The ABC of Tactical Media*. http://www.timesup.org/Times.UP/ABC.html

Jordan, T. (1999) *Cyberpower: The Culture and Politics of Cyberspace and the Internet*. New York, NY: Routledge.

Manovich, L. (2001) New media: a user's guide, Sarai Reader: http://www.sarai.net/journal/pdf/100–108%20(user%27s).pdf

www.adbusters.org (Website devoted to network-based activism influenced by Situationism).

www.ruckus.org (US-based Internet activism influenced by a blend of non-violent direct actions, anarchism and environmentalism).

7 | A NETWORKED CIVIL SOCIETY?

> Today there are no longer pessimists and optimists. There are only realists and liars.
>
> (Virilio 2001: 221)

So where are we today? The preceding chapters have discussed the effects of the double revolutions of neoliberal globalization and of information technology upon media and upon the dynamics of cultural production. As we have seen, media industries and cultural production have been digitized and globalized to the extent that there are little or no spaces 'outside' the information order in terms of where the dynamics of power to shape the world are. We have seen also the effects of this nexus upon the processes of politics and the functioning of civil society. We saw that a new global civil society is trying to emerge and free itself from the constrictions of the neoliberalized network society. And it is trying to do this with the tools of the network society itself, with ICTs in general and the network of networks that comprise the Internet. Finally, it is through a new and re-energized technopolitics, I tried to argue, that we might see the best chance for changing the dominance of the present neoliberal order.

So where are we going? Irritatingly, the future is not predictable. We get only inklings, some of which may become insights in the light of subsequent events. Moreover, relying upon trends and trajectories to guess what may happen, as do many stockbrokers, economists and sundry others whose business is prediction – is predictably hazardous. As Walter Laqueur (2002) wrote about such predictology in politics,

> One of the most common mistakes committed by intellectuals in politics is to assume that certain recognised evolving trends will culminate in the near future. These thinkers underrate the enormous obstacles and ignore the retarding factors that inevitably prolong such evolutions.

We have already identified some tends in the emerging civil society movement, but, following Laqueur's advice, I am not going to make any assumptions or draw any over-hasty conclusions regarding what these may portend. What I want to do in this final chapter is to look realistically and with a cold eye at the 'state of play' in these early years of the twenty-first century. We are looking, fundamentally, at two competing forces in the evolution of a new civil society. Both are dialectically linked in that one influences the other in either a positive or negative way. What I want to draw out here is how that dialectic is balanced.

The first force is, of course, that of neoliberal globalization and the information technology revolution; the second force, the *antithesis* of the neoliberal/ICT revolution nexus, is the global civil society movement. After describing the salient elements of these dual dynamics in their turn, I will finish with some discussion that will try to impute some meaning into them. In so doing, the reader will have gained some under-standing of the 'state of play' and enough of an inkling into what needs to happen to have a broad, diverse and multicultural global civil society; one that grows from within and helps to develop the network society in ways that are based upon democracy as well as social and economic justice.

Neoliberal globalization today

Echoing Laqueur's *caveat* once more, I argue that the 'evolving trends' of neoliberalism with which this book has been much concerned are not about to 'culminate in the near future'. Rumours concerning the death of neoliberalism are somewhat premature. The ideological project that began in the early 1980s to transform the world into a market economy continues to power ahead. It does so notwithstanding the disasters, economic, social and cultural, it has left in its increasingly broad wake. And it does so, according to the late Pierre Bourdieu, because:

> The neoliberal programme draws its social power from the political and economic power of those whose interests it expresses: stockholders, financial operators, industrialists, conservative or social-democratic politicians who have been con-verted to the reassuring layoffs of *laissez-faire*, high-level financial officials eager to impose policies advocating their own extinction because, unlike the managers of firms, they run no risk of having eventually to pay the consequences.
>
> (Bourdieu 1998)

When those who are in power are the ones likely to run least risk, then general lessons in fiscal and social rectitude tend not to sink in. Accordingly, the national economic and social disasters of Mexico in 1994–95, of Indonesia and Thailand in 1997–98, or Russia in 1998, and of Argentina in 2002–03 are viewed as mere hiccups. Even when disasters are closer to home, away from the silent and largely unseen miser-ies of the developing world, the lessons are ignored or wilfully dismissed. The bursting of the dotcom bubble in 2001 meant, for millions in the developed world, the loss of jobs, savings and retirement income. Around the same time, the veils of corporate secrecy were pulled back slightly to reveal the scandals of Enron, WorldCom and others. Here, straightforward crookedness on the part of senior executives was compounded by the fact that they stole or misappropriated the funds of yet more millions of ordinary people; those same people told by those same CEOs and Wall Street gurus that the stock market and corporations such as Enron or WorldCom were the surest way to 'grow' your money. A handful of imprisonments aside, those who wield 'political and economic power' live on to secure yet another deal, make yet another acquisition, strip yet another asset. At the same time they vigorously lobby the WTO, the World Bank or the IMF to give them the freedom (financial or regulatory) to spread the creed of neoliberalism deeper and wider still.

The WTO is an essentially non-accountable and opaque multilateral organization, and has been at the forefront of neoliberalizing the world. It acts as the 'legitimizing' body for multinational corporations and free-market economies. Since at least 2000 a big effort has gone into what the WTOs website terms 'the further liberalization of the global services market' (WTO 2003). This is in fact the mopping up of any remaining pockets of resistance to neoliberalism around the world and the selling off of the remainder (usually in the poorest of the poor countries) of state-owned utilities such as water, telecommunications and electricity. In justification, the WTO repeat the now predictable *laissez-faire* mantra that selling off the public infrastructure of developing countries will provide 'better service', 'lower prices and better quality' (WTO 2003). However, in June 2000, Bolivian demonstrators who begged to differ were shot, clubbed and gassed by riot police for their temerity in protesting about the 200 per cent rise in water charges by the new utility owners, International Waters of London. No one had asked them if selling their water to a British multinational – which would then sell it back to them at a profit – would be a good idea. Campaigners from the World Development Movement argue that despite the outrage such 'better services' provoke, the trend to 'liberalize' every last vestige of public ownership left in the world is being pushed harder and harder by the WTO. The inevitable outcome of a wholly privatized planet is that multinationals would be free 'to charge for providing [essential services] to some of the 1.2bn people living on less than a dollar a day' (Elliot 2003).

This ongoing conquest of the public and social realms by private interests has, as we have seen, cultural consequences, too. Indigenous cultures and ways of life, in every country and across every continent, are being commercialized and/or westernized. Africa is probably the region in the world most marginal to neoliberal globalization, and yet that continent's multifarious cultures are being relentlessly colonized in the same way as those in any other region. As Nigerian journalist Wole Akande (2002) argues, '[our] culture – whether it is music, food, clothes, art, sport, images of age or youth, masculinity or femininity – has become a product [to be] sold in the market place'. If the culture is not for sale, or is unsaleable, then it is marginalized or obliterated. This ongoing cultural imperialism means, inevitably, that we begin to share the same cultural values, extract similar cultural meanings, and think and choose within similar (culturally narrowed) boundaries: Coke or Pepsi, McDonald's or Burger King, *Friends* or *Sex and the City*, Nike or Adidas, a Ford or a Toyota, and so it goes on, everywhere. In the same essay, Akande quotes the Chairman of Coca-Cola who, no doubt inadvertently, puts the case for the prosecution very neatly when he said that 'People around the world are today connected by brand-name consumer products as much as by anything else.'

Notwithstanding all this, it would be a mistake, I think, to imagine that the continued domination and expansion of the 'neoliberal programme', as Bourdieu calls it, is evidence of a positive, vibrant and robust social, cultural and economic force. Fear and uncertainty are the business of neoliberal business. In Chapter 3 we discussed Beck's concept of the risk society, whereby the increasing complexity of industrialized science and technology, what is now a market-oriented 'technoscience', is creating risks and hazards we are less able both to anticipate and to deal with effectively. In this context, consider the 1990s BSE (Bovine Spongiform Encephalopathy) scares in Britain and elsewhere; consider the foot-and-mouth holocaust in that same country during 2001 when millions of cattle and sheep were shot, burned and/or bulldozed into vast pits; consider the murky science and vague popular understanding of global warming and its potential multifaceted and devastating risk effects upon environments and societies everywhere; consider too, if one can take all these at once, the equally fuzzy debates around genetically modified foods and whether we are planting (literally) a time bomb in the human food chain. The logic of competition and acceleration within the network society means that what Beck called the 'sensory-organs of science', which help society anticipate and plan for risk, have been dulled, leaving us blind to what is ahead of us, and to the time bombs planted in our past (Beck 1992: 162). Blindness to risk does not mean that we are not acutely aware of it – far from it. The invisibility of risk has merely made the world a more paranoid place (another dimension of Eriksen's (2002: 1) 'paranoid phase of globalization') and this feeds directly into the paranoia underpinning market competition.

Consider, as well, the SARS (Severe Acute Respiratory Syndrome) virus that brings the paranoias of personal risk and economic risk into one bleak focus. SARS is thought to have emanated in South China in 2003 from the intensified 'soup of chemicals and viruses' that is free-market agribusiness in developing countries (McDonald 2003). This acronym-for-a-tautology is undoubtedly a killer, albeit one that pales into insignificance when compared with numbers of victims of, say, tuberculosis, or even common influenza. It is more than likely that the virus will be contained and become dormant. However, oxygenated by the media, the virus thrived and grew with an impressive virulence in the mindscape of fear and that uncertainty that is the global economy. Economies and societies in the Asian region in particular were gripped by a fear bordering on the irrational. And in a tightly interconnected world, the medico-social quickly spills over into the economic. In a move of unusual speed and panic, the Chinese government sacked the Mayor of Beijing in April 2003 for not being more open with the public, the media and the financial markets. As well as constructing a vast 'quarantine camp' it closed food markets, Internet cafes, cinemas and other places of public gathering in the attempt to stop contagion. At the time of writing, forty-eight people had actually died in China (Armitage 2003). The World Health Organization (WHO) issued travel warnings to a host of countries in Southeast Asia – and even the city of Toronto in Canada, where several deaths had been recorded. Taiwan closed its borders to China, Hong Kong and Canada in what was deemed a 'drastic' measure to stop the spread of the infection (Laurance 2003). Such measures could, in themselves, be seen as prudent, and may limit the spread of the virus. But in the age of globalization nothing can be considered in isolation. SARS had a feverish *economic* knock-on effect. In a global system of 'flows' that revolves around the interconnection of people, of markets, of capital and of technology, such rational public health measures, irrationally, are bad news. In normally sober and level-headed Singapore, to take just one example, Prime Minister Goh Chok Tong fretted in a BBC interview, just as the media panic was taking hold, that

> I would say [that] if we can contain the virus, then we can also contain the paranoia, the fear about this spreading. If we can't contain this and this gets out of hand, then, of course, you are going to have a very big problem, not just on people's behaviour and livelihood, but on the whole economy.
>
> (Bottomley 2003)

It is clear, then, that the structures of neoliberalism, of market rule, stand upon constantly shifting sands. Nothing is certain and much is unknown. SARS will come and go; Argentina will get off its knees at some stage – but what next, and where? The whole edifice creaks and splinters and threatens collapse, in whole or in part, at any time.

A worldwide social system based upon cut-throat competition, widespread corruption, a chaotic stock market and the cults of short-termism and of speed cannot offer security and predictability. Neoliberalism has taken on its own momentum, that of 'the market', which is supposed to keep everything in balance. Unsurprisingly, 'balance', social, economic, cultural or otherwise, has not been a noticeable feature of the last twenty years of neoliberal rule. What keeps it in place, then? A major element in its continued shaky existence is, as Chapter 1 explained, ideology. It is the doctrine of the free market, perpetuated by those in positions of power and influence and who have most to gain by promoting a system that works (first and foremost) for them. Their creed (which can hardly sustain the merest scrutiny or critique) is massively augmented by a lack of sufficiently powerful countervailing arguments for an alternative system of economic and social organization. In short, for the mass of humanity that struggles daily within a system of unfairness, and has learned implicitly or explicitly that you are on your own and must 'sink or swim', there seems to be no other imaginable way. This, the present system teaches us, is simply a hard fact of life.

Countertrends from the networked civil society

Recall, if you will, the words from the quotation by Willia
argued that there are always people who will not accep
hegemonic ideology. Increasing numbers of people are .
for what it is: a system that is destructive of economies, ot .
businesses, of ecologies and of individuals. Karl Marx argued tha.
class creates the seeds of its own destruction, its own 'gravediggers' as he p.
proletariat). What Marx wanted to illustrate was the operation of the dialectic, whu.
the nature of capitalism causes it unavoidably to produce its own antithesis. The vital
question for us is how this antithesis will develop within the network society. The
major example of the network society's antithesis, or dialectical opposite, is, of course,
the global civil society movement itself. And coming from a diversity of regions and
circumstances, these potential 'gravediggers' comprise a much broader stratum than
the classic Marxist working class. All sorts of issues and all sorts of people from all
walks of life are now being motivated by the depredations of increasingly unfettered
market rule.

Take the anti-genetic modification (GM) movement, a movement whose activists
span the globe and whose spheres of concern link with other environmental, cultural,
social and political movements that comprise the emerging global civil society. During
the 1990s, free-market liberalism together with advances in molecular biology and
information technologies combined to produce a handful of presumptuous multinational corporations who assumed they could change the genetic structure of the
world's staple food crops – with no thought as to how ordinary people, consumers,
might feel about it. The introduction of genetically modified foods such as soybean, for
example, where the long-term effects upon the environment and upon those who eat
the stuff are unknown, became one of the red-hot issues that galvanized people in the
early 2000s. The actions of multinational bioengineering firms such as Monsanto, Du
Pont and Novartis revealed what many felt about globalization but were possibly
unable to articulate until this particular 'line' had been crossed. Unsolicited tampering
with our food supply in the name of profit helped to open a Pandora's box of issues
ranging from science and technology, to sustainable development, to the operation of
the market itself. As the business magazine *Red Herring* succinctly put it,

> If health fears about the marriage between farms and pharmacy have attracted the
> most attention, the real issue is deeper, and, in a way, much more serious. It is a
> historic debate about the extent to which a few multinational corporations control
> the world's food supply. To broach that rather philosophical issue – which at its
> heart is a critique of globalism, capitalism, and modern reliance on science –
> opponents of GM foods have aimed their attacks where they know they can get
> easy support: at the kitchen table. As a result, the promising technology has stalled.
> (Cukier 2000)

technology with the potential to liberate the world from hunger is now in trouble because those who owned the technology behaved as though people were unimportant, or important only as passive consumers. As John Berger (2003) wrote, corporations

> pretend to be saving the world and offering its population the chance to become their clients. The world consumer is sacred. What they don't add is that consumers only matter because they generate profit, which is the only thing that is really sacred.

The logic of the market compels corporations to act in this way. Thinking and concerned people, however, were not impressed, and, through global campaigns organized in large part through the Internet, email, list servers and so on, succeeded in severely denting the global GM ambitions of a few corporations. Supermarket chains, grocers, farmers and food producers such as Heinz and Gerber rapidly saw what was at stake with such a groundswell of anger and began to slap the 'GM free' label to their baked beans and apple purée. However, the battle over 'control of the world's food supply' is not yet over, and will remain an important test of how the global civil society movement will develop in the early decades of the twenty-first century.

In many ways food goes to the heart of neoliberal globalization. This is because it forms such an important part of what and who we are, and we are beginning to feel deeply uneasy about how 'market forces' cause it to be produced and distributed. Consider once more the BSE and foot-and-mouth disease nightmares in Britain; or read the horrifying realities of the hamburger industries portrayed in Eric Schlosser's *Fast Food Nation* (2001). A backlash is underway, a repercussion inspired in no small part by a diversity of techno-activists who campaign against the environmental, social, health and cultural costs of feeding the 45 million who walk or drive through a McDonald's (and this is only McDonald's!) every day (see for example www.mcspotlight.org). Consumers are finally gagging on that calorie-laden, salt-filled and fat-soaked repast; not necessarily on its taste, but on how it reaches you and what it might do to you. In December 2002 McDonald's posted its first-ever corporate loss. As a result, the company said that it would close 175 outlets worldwide and lay off hundreds of staff. Business analysts, predictably thinking within the square, were blaming the slight sag in the Golden Arches on increased competition from rivals such as Burger King, Wendy's and the allegedly 'healthier' options such as Subway (Hospitalitysite.com.au 2003). Doubtless this has something to do with it. But also, could the turning away from burgers and fries be a result of a deeper resentment, a sickening (literally and figuratively) with the industrialization, technologization, homogenization and globalization of food? Could it also be, as Schlosser puts it regarding the popularity of his book *Fast Food Nation*, that people were gradually awakening to the contradiction between the rhetoric of the free market presented by supporters of enterprise in public discussion and the reality of how their businesses operate'? 002).]

This worldwide 'consciousness raising' regarding issues of science, technology and neoliberal globalization did not come about through dramatic *exposés* or sustained 'public interest' campaigns in the mainstream mass media. The media, acting as the so-called 'fourth estate', guardians of democracy and the public interest, have become a part of the neoliberal network society (Ainger 2001). To all intents and purposes, they now act as propaganda arms of the free market and big business of which they are an integral part. Ignacio Ramonet, Editor of *Le Monde Diplomatique* and professor of Communications at the University of Paris, states the issue clearly. He writes that

> The media for a long time was the resource of the citizenry, known as the fourth power, the power to oppose decisions of the government that would have harmful effects on people. The fourth power no longer has this power.
>
> (Cited in Seneviratne 2003)

Ramonet goes on to say that instead of acting as the guardian of people's rights within civil society, the 'fourth power is now exploiting and oppressing them'. The dilemma, he poses to us is: 'How can we tackle this when the protector of the people has transformed into its enemy?' (Seneviratne 2003). For almost a decade, the millions who now comprise the global civil society have been creating, almost by default, a 'fifth estate' through networks of networks. It is here that the 'enemy' is being confronted. Words and ideas that are questioning and progressive found no space in the occupied fourth estate, and so alternative texts and opinions were forced to find – or to create for themselves – other outlets. Crucial books that became best sellers such as *No Logo* (Klein 2000), *Fast Food Nation* (Schlosser 2001) and Thomas Frank's *One Market Under God* (2000) did so not because of slick marketing and an immense advertising campaign, or by being picked up early by sympathetic mainstream media wanting to air dissenting views. They sold by the truckload because they struck a deep chord around the world with both techno-activists and those who simply had had enough of brand bombing, rapacious oil companies, hamburgers without end, spineless government, chaotic stock markets, arrogant corporations and thieving CEOs. Networks of people read and spread the words and the ideas contained in these books and others, with the mainstream media picking them up later, wanting to know what all the fuss was about.

The 'fuss' may be fairly easily explained, I think. It is about alternative dreams, visions and vocabularies that now move in different circuits. These do not flow through mainstream media, or through Labour Party branch meetings or through 'town hall assemblies' so mythologized by Democrats and Republicans, or through local councils or regional governments or national parliaments. The 'fuss' flows through self-organizing and amorphous networks. These virtual channels of communication flicker and buzz twenty-four hours a day with critiques of the present order, and ideas for ways to assemble a different society. They constantly meld theory with practice to produce the new strategies and tactics, art and literature, science and technologies that can help make this happen. This evolving global civil society is constantly experimenting, adapting, rejecting and accepting the ways and means of doing something innovative and creative – something, anything, different. And nobody really knows where it is all leading. Scary?

Conclusion

Uncertainty is wondrous.

(Wallerstein 1997)

If you had been offline for six months prior to mid-February 2003, or, indeed, if you had never sent or read an email or browsed the Internet in your life, then there is a good chance the huge worldwide protests against the then-approaching war in Iraq would have seemed to have been conjured up out of thin air. Mainstream media said almost nothing about it. Yet, it has been estimated that anything from ten million to twenty million people marched in cities across the world over the weekend of 14 to 16 February. Whatever the true figure was, its undoubted immensity prompted Noam Chomsky to say that 'there's never been a time . . . when there's been such massive opposition to a war before it was even started' (Perrone 2003). Others said it was the biggest mass mobilization in history. In London, up to two million people marched, and there were dozens of smaller (though sizeable) demonstrations all over Britain. Demonstrations took place in cities across the US, with some of the largest being the four hundred thousand participating in the New York protest and the quarter of a million strong gathering in San Francisco. Surveying the global scene, the online magazine *ZNet* wrote that

> The *Los Angeles Times* reports that at least a million people showed up for the largest ever march in London, two million rallied in Spain, 500,000 in Berlin, and 200,000 in Damascus, Syria. Another couple of million demonstrated in Rome, and over 150,000 turned out in Melbourne, Australia according to Associated Press.

(Engler 2003)

Really!?

This was practically all organized online. The mainstream media turned up mainly to cover the event for evening news 'vision' and the morning newspaper full-colour spreads. Hundreds of groups had been connecting, sharing information, passing on tips, planning and meeting physically and virtually for weeks prior to the weekend of protest. Websites such as Indymedia.org acted as the hot nodes in the information networks, giving shape, content and voice to the broad parameters of opinion that the anti-war movement contained. They provided advice on how to get to the nearest demonstration, how to get involved, how to arrange to speak, how to download flyers, print your own anti-war literature and so on. An activist from Stop the War Coalition explained to the mainstream media newspaper the *Guardian* how this was done:

Using mailing lists and its website, the central office communicated with a rapidly growing network of local groups that provided much of the movement's organisation. Those local groups communicated with their members and the wider movement through their own mailing lists, group text messages and local websites.

(Alexander 2003)

This constant buzz of digital activity was augmented by **webloggers**. These are the creators and contributors to thousands of personal websites that helped to connect people even more tightly. In the rash of anti-war weblogs that sprang up people were able to publish their ideas, have them critiqued or slandered, or supported. All in all the anti-war protests constituted a stunning example of what networked global civil society is capable of: online organizing leading to massive offline direct action. These demonstrations were the first tangible proof of the potential that many knew the Internet (and ICTs more generally) to have when put to positive use. People across the planet were able to overcome obstacles of language, distance and ideology to co-ordinate themselves to be at a prearranged space at a prearranged time to share in a collective physical and political experience. It had never been done on such a scale before.

Exhilarating, yet somehow hollow. Something was missing. What was missing was the 'appropriate' government and media response. In the 1960s and 1970s mass demonstrations against the Vietnam War drove Presidents Johnson and Nixon (especially the latter) to demented distraction. As late as 1989, filling the streets still had the ability to fell regimes, ideologies and entire systems, right across eastern Europe. However, in February 2003, much of the mainstream media reported the demonstrations either neutrally or with hostility. More importantly, governments felt strangely unruffled by the prospect of millions of hostile citizens at their doorsteps. George W. Bush ignored them, Tony Bair patronized them, Spain's prime minister, José María Aznar, was unmoved by them, and John Howard, prime minister of Australia, abused them, calling them a 'mob'. Millions took to the streets and governments didn't even blink. What is happening?

The essence of this institutional sanguinity regarding mass political protest will become more evident in the years to come. But what I believe we witnessed was the critical mass of global civil society hitting, almost immediately, its seminal critical juncture. This is because the age of neoliberalism and the dawning of the network society itself have brought us to an historical point in time, a point where the 'old' ways of doing things are no longer appropriate and 'new' ways have not yet formed into recognizable and effective patterns. In other words, in this phase of interregnum, history, power, the shape of the future – and how we get there – is still all up for grabs. Thus the disconnection in the political process was revealed graphically in the governmental responses to the anti-war demonstrations in early 2003. It was considered by George W. Bush *et al.* that the millions across the world who demonstrated on that February weekend did not matter. Those who shivered in the streets of New

York or sweated in the boulevards of Melbourne were written off as ones who didn't vote, or if they did then it was for marginal parties such as the Greens or Ralph Nader; they were the ones judged to be concerned only with a single issue or a mish-mash of ideas and politics that could not possibly challenge the all-encompassing dogma of neoliberal values and free-market policies.

In this phase of momentous historical change it is only through struggle that a new and more democratic world system can emerge. What is clear is that the *forms* of struggle will have to change. The global civil society has proved it can fill the streets with millions of concerned and angry people, citizens who want something other than what they are told they have to have. However, mass demonstrations, the virtual becoming the physical and the political, are now not enough. Our new relationships with time and space and with technology demand that we develop new languages and new ways of understanding our place in this digital ecology. We need to create new narratives; new stories to both reacquaint us with our past and help make sense of our present. This will give us new perspectives on what needs to be done. Theory and practice go hand-in-hand in the network society. Fortunately vast numbers of the emerging civil society realize this. They are constantly developing both a media savvy and techno savvy (the theory and practice) that the 'tactician' or 'guerrilla' needs. Such flexibility means that people can learn new tactics for localized political struggles and new strategies for global ones. Old habits (such as marching in the streets) can quickly be downgraded as a priority, and something new tried. And if that fails, then try something else.

An inestimable advantage for global civil society is that neoliberalism has a very ordinary and predictable vision for media, culture and society in Life.com. E-business, e-education, e-entertainment and e-shopping just about sum it up. The network society, notwithstanding all the business-theory hype, was never intended to be truly inventive and creative. It was formed and shaped with profit and efficiency in instrumental tasks in mind. When neoliberalism gave over the functioning of society to the market and computerized automation, then innovation and originality became marginalized and redundant to the job at hand. ICTs are eminently capable of processing and distributing information, copying, simulating and scheduling; only humans are capable of creativity. To be creative in meaningful ways that can help fashion different worlds, we need to regain control of both the market and ICTs.

The colossal investment that went into the building of the network society during the crazy years 1995–2001 had instrumental and profit-oriented outcomes as the principal goal. The dotcom bubble has burst, of course, but the frenzied economic activity of the period has built an enormous capacity in global communications. This is also a massive capability for rebuilding upon the shattered communities, blasted economies, and blighted lives that the 'neoliberal programme' has bequeathed. Economist Robert Brenner has analysed the nature of the dotcom bubble in the US, and, as with any boom in capitalist history, *overproduction* eventually becomes a factor leading to the inevitable bust. The dotcom boom was no different. Brenner (2003: 54) writes that

Thanks to the unregulated product and financial markets, everyone was [expanding]. In 2000 no fewer than six US companies were building new, mutually competitive, nationwide fibre-optic networks. Hundreds more were laying down local lines and several were also competing on sub-oceanic links. All told, 39 million miles of fibre-optic line now criss-cross the US, enough to circle the globe 1566 times. The unavoidable by-product has been a mountainous glut: the utilisation rate of telecom networks hovers today at a disastrously low 2.5–3 per cent, that of undersea cable at just 13 per cent. There could hardly be clearer evidence that the market – and especially the market for finance – does not know best. The consequence was an amassing of sunk capital that could not but weigh on the rate of return for the foreseeable future, in the same way as did the railway stock built up during the booms of the 19th century.

In computer engineer *patois*, unused capacity is called '**dark fibre**'. This is the cabling and the fibre optic wires that are in place, but not in use; they are called 'dark' because fibre optics send information by way of light pulses and so when they are not in use, they are 'dark'. As the above Brenner quotation shows, there is a lot of it about. But this is private, unused space, so beware of the dogs for now. The open Internet itself is becoming increasingly privatized and commercialized, with 'the romantic libertarian' angle that was used to sell it in the early years giving way to the e-business, e-education, e-entertainment and e-shopping instrumentalized world I just mentioned. So, if you're not buying please leave, is the unstated message. However, anticipating the tremendous growth of the global civil society movement, with its activists, artists, designers, engineers and critics, Geert Lovink, in his book *Dark Fiber* (2002), argues that this will

> . . . result in a demand for a public infrastructure which will utilise the often unused Internet capacity (called 'dark fiber') for multiple educational and creative purposes. In the conceptual vacuum which the dotcom era has left behind, a rich and critical Internet culture has hit the surface, offering sustainable and imaginative alternatives to both corporate and government attempts to contain the Internet.

History does not get stuck in a rut. Nor has it come to an 'end' as Francis Fukuyama famously argued (1992). It is always open-ended and subject to the balance of social forces that help shape it at any particular phase.

In other words, it is up to us, and it is incumbent upon us to seize the opportunities that struggle and the operation of the dialectic will always present. The actual unused network capacity, the vast surplus of silent dark fibre acts as a looming metaphor for the latent promise that the network of networks represents. Dark fibre is the potential play-space for humanity. It is the space for the proliferation of new ideas and cultures that are bursting to be given more room. 'Free bandwidth for all!' can be the catchphrase. It can be the media-rich environment in which to experiment, to theorize and criticize, to frame agendas and formulate tactics and strategies for new worlds. Taking over the network society from the restrictive and ever-tightening grasp of the free market and turning it into a public space (light fibre?) would be the first step in the long path through this historical transition. Taking over the network society is not (necessarily) about the abolition of capitalism. It is about personal control and free will (fundamental neoliberal tenets, by the way); it is about being able, as communities and nations and cultures, to realize fundamental social political and economic change; it is about embracing the network and our network fate, our digital *amor fati*, as Scott Lash terms it after Nietzsche (2002: 10); and it is about believing in ourselves and our cultural competence to help craft something better, something else. This constitutes a sort of revolution of the imagination. Terry Eagleton (2003: 17) expressed this process wonderfully. He wrote that

> The flights of fancy that get in the way of seeing the situation straight are vital to imagining an alternative to it. If the romantic conforms the world to his desire, and the realist conforms his mind to the world, the revolutionary is called on to do both at once.

We don't know what these 'flights of fancy' may bring for our cultures and societies, but if it is democratically constructed it will be self-reflexive, and if our society can openly and effectively critique itself, then it can change. Scary?

We can end here with a quotation from Immanuel Wallerstein (1997: 3), a historian and economist who sees the thrill and the wondrousness of such uncertainty – and of the unlimited potential of humanity.

> In human social systems, the most complex system in the universe, therefore the hardest to analyse, the struggle for the good society is a continuing one. Furthermore, it is precisely in periods of transition from one historical system to another one (whose nature we cannot know) that human struggle takes on most meaning. Or to put it another way, it is only in such times of transition, that what we call free will outweighs equilibria. Thus, fundamental change is possible, albeit never certain and this fact makes moral claim on our responsibility to act rationally, in good faith and with the strength to seek a better historical system.

Fundamental change, or revolution, as Wallerstein would readily admit, is not about fundamental rupture or cataclysmic break. As I remarked at the end of the Introduction of this book, human social systems are marked by *continuities*, where a basis for a better, more democratic future is not a distant ideal, but is always immanent in the ongoing present. An understanding of the newly forming dynamics between media, cultural production and political activism within the network society, and how these continuities are emerging through these dialectics, is a step towards playing an active role in their future development.

Further reading

Langman, L., Douglas M. and Zalewski, J. (2002) Cyberactivism and alternative globalization movements, in Wilma A. Dunaway (ed.) *Emerging Issues in the 21st Century World-System*, pp. 218–35. Westport, CT: Greenwood Press.

Lovink, G. (2002) *Dark Fiber: Tracking Critical Internet Culture*. Cambridge, MA: MIT Press.

www.indymedia.org (Global network of regional net-based organizations devoted to local–global direct action campaigns.

www.zmag.org (Internet-based outlet for radical journalism giving opinion and analyses not usually available in mainstream media. Includes writers such as Robert Fisk, Noam Chomsky, Edward Said and John Pilger.)

GLOSSARY OF KEY TERMS USED IN THE BOOK

ARPANET: Advanced Research Project Agency Network. ARPANET was the network that became the basis for the **Internet**. It was funded mainly by US military sources and consisted of a number of individual computers connected by leased lines and using a packet-switching scheme.

Birmingham School: Formed around a group of researchers at the Centre for Contemporary Cultural Studies at the University of Birmingham, England. The Centre was a Neo-Marxian school of thought, most notably associated with Stuart Hall. Research carried out at the Centre from the 1970s continued in the post-Gramscian tradition of studies of hegemony and ideology.

Broadband: Refers to telecommunication in which a wide band of frequencies is available to transmit information. Because a wide band of frequencies is available, information can be multiplexed and sent on many different frequencies or channels within the band concurrently, allowing more information to be transmitted in a given amount of time.

Civil society: In the modern sense, civil society connotes those areas of culture, politics, private life, the economy, media and so on that are outside or apart from the power of the state and its bureaucracies.

Cookies: A message given to a web browser by a web server. The browser stores the message in a text file. The message is then sent back to the server each time the browser requests a page from the server. The main purpose of cookies is to identify users and possibly prepare customized web pages for them.

Cultural competence: In sociology Pierre Bourdieu first used the term in his book *Distinction* (1986). It is described as a social function to legitimize social differences, that is to say, the 'cultural sophistication' of those who 'possess the code' to decide what is 'vulgar' in art or in literature. In media and cultural studies the term was used by John Fiske (1987) to describe a critical attitude brought to the reading of media forms, in his case, television. It is closely linked to the terms **techno-** and **media savvy** competences and is used to convey a level of autonomy and critical distance within the mediated world of the network society.

Culturejamming: Situationist-inspired subversion to the commodification of culture by corporate capitalism. See www.adbusters.org and *Adbusters* magazine.

Cyberspace: A term coined by science fiction writer William Gibson to describe his computer-generated virtual reality in which the information wealth of a future corporate society is represented as an abstract space. The word has come to be used as a very generalized term to cover any sense of digitally created 'space', from the Internet to virtual reality.

Cyborg: Describes the increasing and complex intermeshing between the human body and technology. This can range from the low-tech of a hearing aid, to the high-tech of genetic engineering through DNA manipulation, to the science fiction of *Robocop* or Arnie Schwarzenegger in the *Terminator* films.

Dark fibre: Dark fibre is optical fibre infrastructure (cabling and repeaters) that is currently in place but is not being used. It is referred to as 'dark' fibre because optical fibre conveys information in the form of light pulses so when unused they are 'dark'.

DARPA: Defense Advanced Research Project Agency. DARPA provided funds and oversight for a project aimed at interconnecting computers at four US university research sites. By 1972, this initial network, now called the **ARPANET**, had grown to 37 computers. **ARPANET** and the technologies that went into it, including the evolving Internet Protocol (IP) and the Transmission Control Protocol (TCP) led to the **Internet** that we know today.

Dialectics: The word *interaction* is sometimes used as a synonym for dialectic and this captures the dynamic of the dialectic – but there is more. The word dialectic is derived from the Greek word for open-ended dialogue or debate. A debate begins with a proposition (thesis), then the examination of a contrary view (antithesis), and then arriving at a new view that incorporates elements of both sides (synthesis). In the Marxist tradition this basic philosophical framework was developed, passing through Hegel's more spiritual meaning, into what was called 'dialectical materialism' (the application of this reasoning to real-world criteria). For Marx this was in the dialectic of history that was being played out in the struggle between the bourgeoisie and the proletariat that would eventually be resolved in the 'synthesis' of communism. In cultural studies, the dialectic has been imbued with a critical element, or the arrival at synthesis through critical reflection, or what Fredric Jameson called 'stereoscopic thinking' – the ability to think through both sides of the argument (1992: 28).

Digital divide: Stems from critique of the nexus between **neoliberalism** and the **ICT** revolution, and argues that free-market-based distribution of the fruits of information technologies will always leave behind those with the inability to pay. As information technologies spread across much of society, then those who cannot afford them are increasingly disadvantaged.

Dotcom: Businesses, or in many cases business plans, that emerged in the 1990s using the Internet as the basis for production, distribution and content. The term emerged from the widespread use of a business's Internet domain name, such as Salon.com (spoken as 'Salon dot com') as their trading name also.

Dotcom bubble: Frantic investing in Internet-based businesses during the mid- to late 1990s caused a spiral of rising stock market prices even for businesses that had never made a cent in profit, and, upon close scrutiny, were unlikely ever to. On the back of this speculative bubble the **NASDAQ** shot from 751 in January 1995 to 5048 in March 2000. A month later, when the bubble was deemed to have 'burst', the **NASDAQ** had lost 35 per cent of its value and thousands of **dotcoms** had evaporated.

Embedded ideology: From Postman (1993) and argues that technologies come pre-coded with an ideological bias. That is to say, they reflect the dominant values of a particular social system. In other words technologies are not 'neutral'.

Fordism: A stage in the development of twentieth-century capitalism characterized by mass factory-based production for mass consumption in a mass market. Also characterized in the 'high Fordism' phase (1945–73) as the operation of the 'social contract' between capital, labour and government in the organization of the 'strategic heights' of the economy such as shipbuilding, steel, heavy engineering and so on.

Frankfurt School: Group of German philosophers and sociologists who moved to the US to escape Nazi repression in the 1930s. Its leading theorists, such as Theodor Adorno, Max Horkheimer and, more peripherally, Walter Benjamin, pioneered theories on the nature of cultural production in industrial society.

Global civil society movement: Loose world-wide coalition of diverse groups, including **NGOs**, social movements, trades unions, political parties, religious groups and so on that arose to confront neoliberal globalization and the effects they were having upon their local constituencies.

Globalization: In its economic context it is closely linked to the idea of the **New Economy**. Globalization is characterized by the opening up of markets and borders to economic competition, and drastically deregulating economies more generally, making them susceptible to 'market forces'.

GUI: Graphical User Interface. A software program that generates a graphical representation of a computer operating system. The most popular GUIs are Microsoft **Windows** and the Apple Mac OS X.

Hegemony: Describes the process of domination of subordinate classes and groups through the elaboration and penetration of ideology (ideas and assumptions) into the common sense and everyday practice of those subordinate classes and groups (see Gitlin 1981: 253).

ICTs: Information and Communication Technologies. Literally, any device or application, hardware or software, such as a PC, mobile phone, scanner or personal digital assistant (**PDA**), that is connectable in theory or in practice to the network of networks that comprises the contemporary high-tech information society.

Information ecology: The construction of an information-based environment through individual and collective use of ICT-based devices and applications in increasing realms of culture, society and the economy. A central development stemming from the processes of **informationization**.

Informationization: The processes of the suffusion of increasing realms of culture, society and the economy with the logic of computing. In this book it is used in the context of a historical trend emanating from the nexus between neoliberal globalization and the ICT revolution.

Internet: A matrix of networks that link computers and servers together.

Media savvy: See **techno savvy**.

Mirror-site: A replica of an original website that is contained in a different server. Mirror-sites can reduce the load on individual sites when traffic is heavy, allowing for faster access and more ease of access.

MIT Media Lab: Institution founded by Nicholas Negroponte and Jerome Wiesner in 1985. Funded through corporate sponsorship, the Media Lab conducts research that aims to integrate ICTs into many realms of culture, economy and society.

MP3: Motion Picture Export Group Layer 3. Digital format for encoding sound, widely used for sharing music files over the **Internet**.

NASDAQ: National Association of Securities Dealers Automated Quotation. It is a virtual, computer-driven equities trading system for over 3600 communications, biotechnology, financial services and media companies. It began trading in the US in 1971.

Neoliberalism: Ideology that argues the innate superiority of the 'free market' as the principal means for organizing economic life. Arose as a re-reading (or misreading) of Adam Smith's *Wealth of Nations* 1776, which argued that the hidden hand of market forces would bring an economy into an 'equilibrium' of supply and demand. *Contra* Smith, however, neoliberal fundamentalists aim to bring the logic of the market to every realm of society. Neoliberalism underpins both **globalization** and the **New Economy**.

Network society: A historical trend whereby the dominant functions of society, that is to say its economic, cultural and media processes, are increasingly organized around networks. ICT-based networks have become, as Castells puts it, 'the new social morphologies [organizing structures] of our societies' (1996: 469).

New Economy: 1990s term used here to describe the mode of production that arose from the restructuring of **Fordism**. New Economy features are that its dynamics are based upon **ICT** networks, flexible production, flexible labour, **globalization**, and **neoliberal** market principles.

NGOs: Non-governmental organizations.

PDA: Personal Digital Assistant. An **ICT** device that acts as a digital personal organizer and is connectable to the **Internet** to download and upload information.

Risk society: Term coined by Ulrich Beck (1992) to argue that, as modern industrial society becomes increasingly complex and all-encompassing, it is characterized by an increased creation and distribution of risks such as chemical pollution, 'mad cow' disease, etc., that remain invisible until the damage is done.

Social capital: The term has been around since at least Bourdieu (1983) but brought to prominence by Robert Putnam (2000). It refers to features of social organization such as networks, norms and social trust that facilitate coordination and cooperation for mutual benefit.

Tactical media: Term coined by Lovink and Garcia (1996), and refers to the use of ICTs in ways that are culturally empowering, innovative, creative and subversive of the dominant logic of ICTs under the neoliberalized **network society**. Closely connected to **cultural competence, media savvy** and **techno savvy**.

Technological determinism: A theory that argues that technology is the primary driver of human history, and that individuals, groups and society in general are directly shaped by technological developments. More sophisticated accounts argue that the relationship is more complex and that, at certain stages of history (such as the Industrial Revolution and, as this book describes, the ICT revolution and neoliberal globalization nexus), technology can become a powerful determinant.

Technopolitics: Used here to refer to the politics of the **global civil society movement**, whose organization and communications are based around **ICTs**.

Techno savvy: A level of expertise with **ICTs**. Used in this book to describe the elements (along with **media savvy**) that comprise a form of **cultural competence** *vis-à-vis* information technologies. It is not enough merely to be techno savvy, but is also necessary to understand the cultural, historical, ideological and economic contexts of the information technologies being used. Techno savvy and media savvy and the cultural competence they engender give a level of sovereignty and autonomy (creative freedom) with the tools of the information order.

URL: Uniform Resource Locator. The Internet address of a website, such as www.amazon.com

Warchalking: Practice of chalking coded symbols to signify the presence of a wireless hotspot in a public place, where people with a laptop computer and a wireless card can log on to the Internet via a private network or ISP account.

Weblogging/blogging: Also 'Web log'. Refers to a Web page that serves as a publicly accessible personal journal for an individual. Typically updated daily, blogs often reflect the personality of the author. Usually contain links to similarly themed Web logs.

Weightless economy: Term coined by Jeremy Rifkin to describe capitalism in the **New Economy**. For Rifkin, information and access to it, not buildings and real estate, comprise the essence of capitalism today in the 'cyberspace of networks' (2000: 35).

Wi-fi: Wireless fidelity.

Windows: The Graphical User Interface (**GUI**) for PC-based operating systems.

3G: 'Third Generation' of mobile phones that are connectable to the **Internet** to send and receive data, graphics and sound.

REFERENCES

ABCNew.com (2001) Protestor killed in Genoa, http://abcnews.go.com/sections/world/
 DailyNews/genoa010720_protests.html

Adam, B. (1995) *Timewatch*. Cambridge: Polity Press.

Adam, B. (2004) *Time*. Cambridge: Polity Press.

Adorno, T.W. and Horkheimer, M. ([1944] 1986) The culture industry, in *Dialectic of
 Enlightenment*. London: Verso.

Ainger, K. (2001) Empires of the senseless, *New Internationalist*, 333, April, www.progres-
 sive.org/mccl.199.htm

Akande, W. (2002) The cultural drawbacks of globalization, *The Yellow Press*,
 http://www.globalpolicy.org/globaliz/cultural/2002/1110cult.htm

Alexander, A. (2003) A revolution for revolt, *Guardian Online*, http://www.guardian.co.uk/
 online/story/0,3605,898666,00.html

Anderson, K. (2000) United States of apathy?, BBC online news, http://news.bbc.co.uk/1/hi/
 in_depth/americas/2000/us_elections/vote_usa_2000/597444.stm

Ang, I. (1996) *Living Room Wars: Rethinking Media Audiences for a Postmodern World*.
 London: Routledge.

Annan, K. (1999) Opening ceremony address: ITU Telecom, http://www.itu.int/telecom-wt99/
 press_service/information_for_the_press/press_kit/speeches/annan_ceremony.html

Appadurai, A. (1990) Disjuncture and difference in the global cultural economy, in
 M. Featherstone (ed.) *Global Culture: Nationalism, Globalization and Modernity*. London:
 Sage Publications.

Armitage, C. (2003) The shadow of death in a ghost city, *The Australian*, 28 April.

Arnold, M. ([1869] 1960) *Culture and Anarchy*. London: Cambridge University Press.

Aron, R. (1968) *Progress and Disillusion*. London: Pelican.

Augustine, Saint (1950) *The City of God*, trans. Markus Dods. New York, NY: Modern Library.

Barber, B. (1996) *Jihad vs McWorld*, New York, NY: Ballantine Books.

Baudrillard, J. (1988) *The Ecstasy of Communication*. New York, NY: Semiotexte.

Baudrillard, J. (1995) *The Gulf War Did Not Happen*. Sydney: Power Publications.

Baudrillard, J. (2003) *The violence of the global*, ctheory, http://www.CTHEORY.NET/TEXT_file.asp?pick=385

Bauman, Z. (1992) *Intimations of Postmodernity*. London: Routledge.

Bauman, Z. (1998) *Globalization*. Cambridge: Polity Press.

BBCWorld.com (2002) *Technology Leapfrog*, http://www.bbcworld.com/content/template_clickonline.asp?pageid=666&co_pageid=2

Beck, U. (1992) *Risk Society. Towards a New Modernity*. London: Sage Publications.

Beck, U. (1998) The politics of the risk society, in J. Franklin (ed.) *The Politics of Risk Society*. Cambridge: Polity Press.

Beck, U. (1999) *World Risk Society*. London: Polity Press.

Berger, J. (2003) Written in the night: the pain of living in the present world, *Le Monde Diplomatique*, February.

Bottomley, D. (2003) Interview with Mr. Goh Chok Tong, 23 April: http://app.sprinter.gov.sg/data/pr/2003042201.htm

Bourdieu, P. (1983) Forms of capital, in J.C. Richards (ed.) *Handbook of Theory and Research for the Sociology of Education*. New York, NY: Greenwood Press.

Bourdieu, P. (1986) *Distinction: A Social Critique of the Judgment of Taste*. London: Routledge.

Bourdieu, P. (1998) The essence of neoliberalism, *Le Monde Diplomatique*, http://mondediplo.com/1998/12/08bourdieu

Brenner, R. (2003) Towards the precipice, *London Review of Books*, 25(3), February.

Burchill, S. (2003) Public amnesia and hypocrisy needed to justify war on Iraq, *Sydney Morning Herald*, 10 October.

Campbell-Kelly, M. (2003) *From Airline Reservations to Sonic the Hedgehog: A History of the Software Industry*. Cambridge, MA: MIT Press.

Caparini, M. (2002) Civil society and democratic oversight of the security sector, paper to the Fifth International Security Forum, Zurich: http://www.isn.ethz.ch/5isf/5/Papers/Caparini_paper_V-2.pdf

Carey, J. (1992) *The Intellectuals and the Masses*. London: Faber and Faber.

Carothers, T. (2000) Think again: civil society, *Foreign Policy Magazine*, Winter edition.

Castells, M. (1996) *The Rise of the Network Society*. Oxford: Blackwell.

Castells, M. (1997) *The Power of Identity: The Information Age – Economy, Society and Culture*. Oxford: Blackwell.

Castells, M. (2000) Information technology and global capitalism, in A. Giddens and W. Hutton, (eds) *On the Edge: Living with Global Capitalism*. London: Verso.

Castells, M. (2001) *The Internet Galaxy*. New York, NY: Oxford University Press.

Cavanagh, J., Mander, J., Anderson, S. *et al.* (2002) *Alternatives to Economic Globalization*, San Francisco, CA Berrett-Koehler.

Charney, H.S. (2000) Building a competitive advantage in the Internet economy, *Telexpo 2000*: http://newsroom.cisco.com/dlls/tln/exec_team/charney/ppt/pres_032800.pdf

Chomsky, N. (1997) What makes mainstream media mainstream, http://www.zmag.org/chomsky/articles/z9710-mainstream-media.html

Chomsky, N. (2001) *September 11*. New York, NY: Seven Stories Press.

Chomsky, N. and Herman, E.S. (1994) *Manufacturing Consent*. London: Vintage.

Cochrane, N. (2002) Managing the store, *The Age* (Australia), 5 November.

Computer Industry Almanac (2002) http://www.c-i-a.com/pr032102.htm (accessed 24 July 2002).

Cukier, K. (2000) Seeds of doubt, *Red Herring Magazine*, http://www.redherring.com/mag/issue77/mag-seeds-77.html

de Certeau, M. (1984) *The Practice of Everyday Life*. Berkeley: University of California Press.

Diamond, J. (1999) *Guns, Germs and Steel: The Fates of Human Societies*. New York, NY: W.W. Norton and Co.

Digerati (2002) http://www.edge.org/digerati/index.html

Ditton, J. and Short, E. (1999) Yes, it works – no, it doesn't: comparing the effects of open-street CCTV in two adjacent town centres, *Crime Prevention Studies*, 10: 201–23.

Dumett, S. (1998) Evolution of a wired world, *Pretext Magazine*, March, www.pretext.com/mar98/story3.htm

Eagleton, T. (1991) *Ideology*. London: Verso.

Eagleton, T. (2003) Kettles boil, classes struggle, *London Review of Books*, 20 February.

Elliot, L. (2003) EU's secret plans hold poor countries to ransom, *Guardian Online*, http://www.guardian.co.uk/business/story/0,3604,902296,00.html

Ellul, J. *The Technological Bluff* (1990) Grand Rapids, MI: William B. Eerdmans Publishing Company.

Engler, M. (2003) New York against the war, *ZNet* www.zmag.org/content/showarticle.cfm?SectionID=51&ItemID=3102

Eriksen, T.H. (2001) *Tyranny of the Moment: Fast and Slow Time in the Information Age*. London: Pluto Press.

Eriksen, T.H. (2002) The paranoid phase of globalization, *Open Democracy*, 25 October, http://www.opendemocracy.net/debates/article-6-27-279.jsp

Falk, R. (1999) *Predatory Globalization: A Critique*. Cambridge: Polity Press.

Featherstone, M. and Lash, C. (eds) (1999) *Spaces of Culture*. London: Sage Publications.

Fiske, J. (1987) *Television Culture*. London: Methuen.

Flood, A. (1996) Report on the first intercontinental gathering for humanity against neo-liberalism, http://flag.blackened.net/revolt/andrew/encounter1_report.html

Foster, W. and Goodman, S.E. (2000) The diffusion of the Internet in China, *Center for International Security and Cooperation* (CISAC), Stanford University, November. http://mosaic.unomaha.edu/china_2000.pdf

Frank, T. (2000) *One Market Under God*. London: Secker and Warburg.

Fukuyama, F. (1992) *The End of History and the Last Man*. Harmondsworth: Penguin.

Garnham, N. (1990) Contribution to a political economy of mass communication, in F. Inglis (ed.) *Capitalism and Communication: Global Culture and the Economic of Information*. London: Sage Publications.

Gates, B. (1995) *The Road Ahead*. New York, NY: Viking.

Gates, B. (1999) *Business @ the Speed of Thought*, New York, NY: Warner.

Gauntlett, D. *et al.* (2000) *Web.Studies*, New York, NY: Oxford University Press.

Gergen, K. (1999) Self-death by technology, *The Hedgehog Review*, Autumn, 1.

Giddens, A. (1997) Excepts from a keynote address at the UNRISD Conference on globalization and citizenship, *UNRISD News*, 15: 4–5.

Giddens, A. (1999a) *Runaway World: How Globalisation is Reshaping Our Lives*. London: Profile Books.

Giddens, A. (1999b) *The Third Way: A Renewal of Social Democracy*. Malden, MA: Polity Press.

Gitlin, T. (1981) *The Whole World Is Watching*. Berkeley, CA: University of California Press.

Given, J. (2001) *Media Ownership in Australia*, http://www.cem.ulaval.ca/CONCAustralie.pdf

Gleick, J. (1999) *Faster: The Acceleration of Just About Everything*. New York, NY: Abacus.

Golding, P. and Murdock, G. (2000) Culture, communications and political economy, in J. Curran and M. Gurevitch (eds) *Mass Media and Society*. London: Arnold.

Gramsci, A. (1971) *Selections from the Prison Notebooks*. London: Lawrence and Wishart.

Haahr, M. (2001) Dreams of an accelerated culture, *Crossings*, 1(1), http://crossings.tcd.ie/issues/1.1/Haahr/

Hall, S. (1997) The centrality of culture, in K. Thompson (ed.) *Media and Cultural Regulation*. London: Sage Publications.

Hall, S., Hobson, D., Lowe, A. and Willis, P. (1981) *Culture, Media, Language*. London: Hutchinson and Co.

Haraway, D. (1991) A cyborg manifesto: science, technology and socialist-feminism in the late twentieth century, in *Simians, Cyborgs and Women: The Reinvention of Nature*. New York, NY: Routledge.

Haraway, D. (1992) *Primate Visions*. London: Verso.

Hardt, M. (2002) Porto Alegre: today's Bandung?, *New Left Review*, 14, March–April: 114.

Harvey, D. (1989) *The Condition of Postmodernity*. Oxford: Blackwell.

Hassan, R. (2000a) The space economy of convergence, *Convergence*, 6(4): 18–36.

Hassan, R. (2000b) Globalization: politics, culture and society in the space-economy of late-capitalism. Unpublished PhD thesis, Swinburne University.

Hassan, R. (2003a) *The Chronoscopic Society: Globalization, Time and Knowledge in the Network Economy*. New York, NY: Lang.

Hassan, R. (2003b) Network time and the new knowledge epoch, *Time and Society*, 12(2), September.

Heffernan, R. (2002) New developments in British politics, http://www.palgrave.com/politics/dunleavy/explanations.htm

Held, D. (1987) *Models of Democracy*. Stanford, CA: Stanford University Press.

Herman, E.S. and McChesney, R.W. (1997) *The Global Media: The New Missionaries of Corporate Capitalism*. London: Cassell.

Hewlett Packard (2002) HP's linux strategy, http://www.hp.com/wwsolutions/linux/about-_linux_hp/strategy.html

Hospitalitysite.com.au (2003) Golden arches sag, www.thehospitalitysite.com.au/articles/d6/0c0134d6.asp

Huntingdon, S. (1993) The clash of civilizations, *Foreign Affairs*, 72(3): 22–69.

IDA Singapore (2001) *Survey on Broadband Usage in Singapore*, http://www.ida.gov.sg/Website/IDAhome.nsf/Home?OpenForm

Iyer, P. (1996) Postmodern tourism: an interview with Pico Iyer, *Insight and Outlook*, www.scottlondon.com/insight/scripts/iyer.html

Jameson, F. (1992) *Late Marxism: Adorno, or, the Persistence of the Dialectic*. London: Verso.

Jameson, F. (1996) Five theses on actually existing marxism, *Monthly Review*, 47(11): 9.

Kellner, D. (2002) Cultural studies, multiculturalism and media culture, www.gseis.ucla.edu/faculty/kellner/papers/SAGEcs.htm

Kellner, D. (2003) Preface, *Media Spectacle*. London: Routledge.

Klein, N. (2000) *No Logo*. London: Flamingo.

Klein, N. (2002) *Fences and Windows*. London: Flamingo.

Kundera, M. (1996) *Slowness*. New York, NY: Harper Perennial.

Kunzru, H. (1997) You are Cyborg, *Wired*, 5.02.

Laqueur, W. (2002) A failure of intelligence, *The Atlantic Online*, www.theatlantic.com/issues/2002/03/laqueur.htm

Lash, S. (2002) *Critique of Information*. London: Sage Publications.

Lasn, K. (2000) *Culture Jam: How to Reverse America's Suicidal Consumer Binge – And Why We Must*. New York, NY: HarperCollins.

Laurance, J. (2003) Taiwan closes border to curb spread of infection, *Independent*, http://news.independent.co.uk/world/asia_china/story.jsp?story=401067

Leal, P. (2000) Participation, communication and technology in the age of the global market, *Forest, Tree and People* (Newsletter) Number 40/41, http://www-trees.slu.se/newsl/40/40leal.pdf

Lee, L. (2000) Boo hoo!, *Salon*.com, http://dir.salon.com/tech/log/2000/05/18/boo/index.html

Leer, A. (2000) *Welcome to the Wired World*. Edinburgh: Pearson Education.

Loader, B. (2002) A paper for community and information technology: the big questions, 16 October, Monash University, Melbourne, Australia, http://ccnr.net/searchconf/loader.htm

Loney, M. (2002) Warchalking: London wi-fi guerrillas take tips from hobos, *ZnetUK*, http://news.zdnet.co.uk/story/0%2C%2Ct269-s2118000%2C00.html

Lovink, G. (2002) *Dark Fiber: Tracking Critical Internet Culture*. Cambridge, MA: MIT Press.

Lovink, G. and Garcia, D. (1996) *The ABC of Tactical Media*, http://www.timesup.org/Times.UP/ABC.html

Lovink, G. and Schneider, F. (2002) The cities of everyday life, in *Sarai Reader 2002*, http://www.sarai.net/journal/02PDF/07cybermohalla/cybermohalla.pdf

Lunenfeld, P. (2000) Introduction, in P. Lunenfeld (ed.) *The Digital Dialectic*. Cambridge, MA: MIT Press.

Lyon, D. (2002) *The Surveillance Society*, Buckingham: Open University Press.

McChesney, R. (1993) *Telecommunications, Mass Media and Democracy: The Battle for the Control of U.S. Broadcasting*, 1928–1935. Oxford: Oxford University Press.

McChesney, R.W. and Herman, E.S. (1997) *The Global Media: The New Missionaries of Corporate Capitalism*. London; Washington, DC: Cassell.

McChesney, R. (1997) The global media giants, *Extra!* November/December Issue, www.fair.org/extra/9711/gmg.html

McChesney, R. (1999) The big media game has fewer and fewer players, *The Progressive* 63(11), www.progressive.org/mcc1199.htm

McDonald, H. (2003) China's unsafe farming practices may be breeding more than pigs, *Sydney Morning Herald*, 7 April, http://www.smh.com.au/articles/2003/04/06/1049567564240.html

McKenzie, D. and Wajcman, J. (eds) (1999) *The Social Shaping of Technology*. Buckingham: Open University Press.

McLuhan, M. (1964) *Understanding Media*. Aylesbury: Abacus.

McLuhan, M. (1995) *Essential McLuhan*. London: Routledge.

Madlin, N. (1999) MIT Media Lab: the birthplace of ideas, *Photo District News*, 19(2): 53.

Marr, M. (2003) Iraq war takes toll on journalists (Reuters report), Globalaware.org, http://www.globalaware.org/noticeboard/journalists.html

Marshall, S. (2003) Accuracy of battlefield news often hazy, *USToday* online, http://www.usatoday.com/news/world/iraq/2003-04-07-fogofwar-usat_x.htm

Martin, H.P. (1998) *Global Trap: Globalisation and the Assault on Democracy and Prosperity*. Sydney: Pluto Press.

Marx, K. and Engels, F. (1975) The manifesto of the Communist Party, in *Selected Works*. Moscow: Progress Publishers.

Mattelart, A. (1979) *Multinational Corporations and the Control of Culture*. New Jersey, NJ: Humanities Press.

Mazzocco, D.W. (1994) *Networks of Power*. Boston, MA: The Free Press.

MDA (Mobile Data Association) (2002) http://www.mda-mobiledata.org/resource/hottopics/sms.asp

Media Lab Research (2002) http://www.media.mit.edu/research/

Media Lab Research Consortia (2002) http://www.media.mit.edu/research/group.php?id=14

Meiksins-Wood, E. (1998) Work, new technology and capitalism, in R. McChesney, E. Meiksins-Wood and J. Bellamy Foster (eds) *Capitalism and the Information Age*. New York, NY: Monthly Review Press.

MIT News (2001) NSF awards $13.75M to MIT Media Lab to create Center for Bits and Atoms, http://web.mit.edu/newsoffice/nr/2001/bitsandatoms.html

Monbiot, G. (2000) *The Captive State*. London: Macmillan.

Moody, G. (1997) The greatest OS that never was, *Wired*, 5.08, http://www.wired.com/wired/archive/5.08/linux.html?topic=&topic_set=

Nairn, T. (2002) *Pariah: The Misfortunes of the British Kingdom*. London: Verso.

Naughton, J. (2003) Germany 1–Microsoft 0, *London Observer Online*, 22 June, http://www.observer.co.uk/business/story/0,6903,982275,00.html

Negroponte, N. (1995) *Being Digital*. Rydalmere, NSW: Hodder and Stoughton.

Negroponte, N. (1998) Beyond digital, *Wired*, 6.12, http://web.media.mit.edu/~nicholas/Wired/WIRED6-12.html

Nguyen, D. and Alexander, J. (1996) The coming cyberspacetime and the end of polity, in R. Shields (ed.) *Cultures of Internet*. London: Sage Publications.

Nielsen Net Ratings (2002) Half a billion people now have domestic Internet access, http://www.eratings.com/news/2002/20020306.htm

Noam, E. (1996) Media concentration in the US, www.vii.org/papers/medconc.htm

NTIA (1995) Falling through the Net, http://www.ntia.doc.gov/ntiahome/fallingthru.html

Omahe, K. (1990) *The Borderless World*. New York, NY: Harper Perennial.

Ong, W. (1982) *Orality and Literacy: The Technologizing of the Word*. New York, NY: Methuen.

Penenberg, A. (2002) The surveillance society, *Wired*, 9.12.

People's Daily Online (2002) http://english.peopledaily.com.cn/200210/17/eng20021017_105229.shtml

Perrone, J. (2003) Working the web: anti-war coverage, *Guardian Online*, www.guardian.co.uk/online/story/0,3605,898664,00.html

Postman, N. (1993) *Technopoly*, New York, NY: Vintage.

Preston, S. (1994) The Rio Earth Summit and beyond, *A Chronicle of International Affairs*, 3(2), http://www.fiu.edu/~mizrachs/Nets-n-NGOs.html

Public Broadcasting Service (2001) Microsoft proposes deal to settle private cases, http://www.pbs.org/newshour/updates/november01/microsoft_11-21.html

Putnam, Robert D. (2000) *Bowling Alone: The Collapse and Revival of American Community*. New York, NY: Simon and Schuster.

Quarterman, J.S. (2002) Monoculture considered harmful, *First Monday*, 2, February, http://firstmonday.org/issues/issue7_2/quarterman/index.html

Raab, C. (1998) Privacy, democracy, information, in B. Loader (ed.) *The Governance of Cyberspace*. London: Routledge.

Reich, R. (2002) *The Future of Success*. London: Vintage.

Rheingold, H. (2000) *The Virtual Community: Homesteading on the Electronic Frontier*. Cambridge, MA: MIT Press.

Rifkin, J. (2000) *The Age of Access*. London: Penguin.

Robins, K. and Webster, F. (1999) *Times of the Technoculture*. London: Routledge.

Rossetto, L. (1998) Change is good, *Wired*, 6.01.

Ruckus (2002a) Tech toolbox action camp, Bulletin Board posting, www.ruckus.org/techcamp.html

Ruckus (2002b) Media information, http://ruckus.org/training/media.html

Sader, E. (2002) Beyond civil society: the Left after Porto Alegre, *New Left Review*, 17, September–October.

Schiller, D. (1999) *Digital Capitalism*: Cambridge, MA: MIT Press.

Schlosser, E. (2001) *Fast Food Nation*. London: Allen Lane.

Seneviratne, K. (2003) Global media: it's time to create a fifth power, http://www.ipsnews.net/fsm2003/27.01.2003/nota26.shtml

Sennett, R. (1999) *The Corrosion of Character*. New York, NY: Norton.

Servon, L. (2002) *Bridging the Digital Divide*. Oxford: Blackwell.

Shenk, D. (1997) *Data Smog*. London: Abacus.

Silverstone, R. (1999) *Why Study Media?* London: Sage Publications.

Slevin, J. (2001) *The Internet and Society*. Malden, MA: Blackwell.

Sloan, W. (2002) Great firewall of China does more harm than good, *Bangkok Post*, 24 September, http://www.bangkokpost.net/News/24Sep2002_news38.html

Stallabrass, J. (1996) *Gargantua: Manufactured Mass Culture*. London: Verso.

Steger, M.B. (2002) Putnam, social capital and globalization, in S. McLean and D. Schultz (eds) *Social Capital*. New York, NY: New York University Press.

Stewart, F. (2001) Meeting the online challenge, *Australian Financial Review*, 21 March: 11.

Sulston, J. (2002) Heritage of humanity, *Le Monde Diplomatique*, November.

Taylor, P.A. (2001) Informational intimacy and futuristic flu: love and confusion in the matrix, *Information, Communication and Society*, 4(1): 74–94.

Thompson, E.P. (1968) *The Making of the English Working Class*. Harmondsworth: Penguin.

Tofts, D. (1997) *Memory Trade: A Prehistory of Cyberculture*. Sydney: Interface Publishing.

Tomlinson, J. (1999) *Globalization and Culture*. Cambridge: Polity Press.

US Government (2002) *The National Strategy to Secure Cyberspace*, http://www.whitehouse.gov/pcipb/cyberstrategy-draft.pdf

Virilio, P. (1995a) *The Art of the Motor*. Minneapolis, MN: University of Minnesota Press.

Virilio, P. (1995b) Speed and information: cyberspace alarm!, CTHEORY.NET, http://www.ctheory.net/text_file.asp?pick=72

Virilio, P. (1997) *Open Sky*. London: Verso.

Virilio, P. (2000) *Information Bomb*. London: Verso.

Virilio, P. (2001) The one who really scares me, interview with Dorothea Hahn, 'The Cities of Everyday Life', Sarai Reader 2001, http://www.sarai.net/journal/02PDF/9-11/06virilio_interview.pdf

Wallerstein, I. (1997) Uncertainty and creativity, http://fbc.binghamton.edu/iwuncer.htm

Wallerstein, I. (2002) New revolts against the system, *New Left Review*, November–December.

Wark, M. (2001) Abstraction, in H. Brown *et al.* (eds) *Fibreculture*. Melbourne: Arena Publishing.

Weber, J. (2002) The ever-expanding, profit-maximizing, cultural-imperialist, wonderful world of disney, *Wired*, 10.02, February.

Webster, W. (1999) Closed circuit television and information age policy processes, in B. Hague and B. Loader (eds) *Digital Democracy*. London: Routledge.

Weiser, M. and Seely Brown, J. (1997) The coming age of calm technology, in P.J. Denning and R.M. Metcalfe (eds) *Beyond Calculation: The Next Fifty Years of Computing*, pp. 75–87. New York, NY: Copernicus.

Welch, D. (2002) Interview with Erich Schlosser, *Powell's.com Interviews*, www.powells.com/authors/schlosser.html

Welsh, I. (2001) *Glue*. New York, NY: Random House.

Whitehouse, D. (2002) Internet to reach South Pole, http://news.bbc.co.uk/2/hi/science/nature/2211507.stm

Williams, R. (1958a) Culture is ordinary, in A. Gray and J. McGuigan (eds) *Studies in Culture: An Introductory Reader*. London: Arnold, 1997.

Williams, R. (1958b) *Culture and Society*. New York, NY: Harper Torch Books.

Williams, R. (1974) *Television: Technology and Cultural Form*. London: Fontana.

Williams, R. (1979) *Politics and Letters*. London: Verso.

Wilson, D. and Sutton, A. (2002) *Open-Street CCTV Surveillance in Australia: A Comparative Study of Establishment and Operation*. Melbourne: Criminal Research Council Report.

Winner, L. (1997) Mythinformation, in G. E. Hawisher and C. L. Selfe (eds) *Literacy, Technology and Society*, Upper Saddle River, NJ: Prentice-Hall.

Winston, B. (1998) *Media, Technology and Society*. London: Routledge.

Wired (2002) *Encyclopaedia for the New Economy*, http://hotwired.lycos.com/special/ene/index.html?word=intro_one

World Trade Organization (WTO) (2003) http://www.wto.org/english/tratop_e/serv_e/gats_factfiction3_e.htm

Wrolstad, J. (2002) Tech giants announce national Wi-Fi network, http://www.newsfactor.com/perl/story/20176.html

Young, J. (1993) *Global Network: Computers in a Sustainable Society*. Washington, DC: Worldwatch Institute.

Žižek, S. (2002) Revolution must strike twice, *London Review of Books*, 25 July: 13.

INDEX

SPORT, CULTURE AND THE MEDIA
SECOND EDITION

David Rowe

This was the first book to comprehensively analyse two powerful cultural forces of our times; sport and the media. This new edition examines the latest developments in the sports media, including:

- Expanded material on new media sport and technology developments
- Updated coverage of political economy, including integration of large entertainment corporations and sporting organizations
- New scholarship and research in the field, recent sports events, new media texts and theory such as postmodernism, reception and spectatorship

This is a key text for undergraduate students in culture and media, sociology, sport and leisure studies, communication and gender.

Contents

Preface: Immersed in Sport – Part 1: Making Media Sport – Understanding Sport and Media: A socio-historical approach – Working in Media Sport: The discipline of sports journalism – Money, Myth and the Big Match: The political economy of the sports media – Part 2: Unmaking the Media Sports Text – Taking Us Through It: The 'art' of sports commentating and writing – Framed and Mounted: Sport through the photographic eye – Screening the Action: The moving sports image – Afterword: Sport into the Ether(net): New technologies, new consumers – Glossary – References – Index.

240pp   0 335 21075 9 (Paperback)   0 335 21076 7 (Hardback)

MEDIA AND AUDIENCES

Karen Ross and Virginia Nightingale

- How has the concept of 'the audience' changed over the past 50 years?
- How do audiences become producers and not just consumers of media texts?
- How are new media affecting the ways in which audiences are researched?

The audience has been a central concept in both in media and cultural studies for some considerable time, not least because there seems little point exploring forms of increasingly global communication in terms of their content if the targets of media messages are not also the focus of study. This book ranges across a wide literature, taking both a chronological as well as thematic approach, in order to explore the ways in which the audience, as an analytical concept, has changed, as well as examining the relationships which audiences have with texts and the ways in which they exert their power as consumers. We also look at the political economy of audiences and the ways in which they are 'delivered' to advertisers as well as attending to the ratings war being waged by broadcasters and the development of narrowcasting and niche audiences. Finally, the book looks ahead to the future of audience research, suggesting that new genres such as 'reality TV' and new ICTs such as the Internet are already revolutionizing the way in which research with audiences is taking place in the twenty-first century, not least because of the level of interactivity enabled by new media.

Contents

Series Editor's Foreword – Introduction – Early Theories of Audience – Measuring and Moulding Audiences – News, Politics and Public Opinion – The Cause and Effect Debate – Fan Audiences – Audiences and Cultural Action – Audience Research in the 21st Century – Glossary – Bibliography – Index.

288pp   0 335 21166 6 (Paperback)   0 335 21167 4 (Hardback)

RETHINKING CULTURAL POLICY

Jim McGuigan

- What are the possibilities and limitations of public policy in the cultural field under late-modern conditions?

Issues of cultural policy are of central importance now because forms of media are growing at an astonishing rate – new media like video games and chat rooms as well as modified older forms such as virtual access to museums, libraries and art galleries on the Internet. The digital revolution gives rise potentially to a culture of 'real virtuality' in which all the cultural artefacts of the world, past and present, may become instantly available at any time.

This innovative book charts the decline and renewal of public cultural policy. It examines a wide range of contemporary issues and blends a close reading of key theoretical points with examples to illustrate their practical import.

This is the perfect introduction to the area for undergraduate students in culture and media studies, sociology of culture, arts administration and cultural management courses, as well as postgraduates and researchers.

Contents

Why Cultural Policy Matters – Discourses of Cultural Policy – Cultural Policy Proper – Cultural Policy as Display – The Rhetoric of Cultural Development – Culture and Government.

192pp   0 335 20701 4 (Paperback)   0 335 20702 2 (Hardback)

Open up your options

 Education

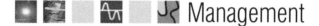 Health & Social Welfare

 Management

 Media, Film & Culture

 Psychology & Counselling

 Sociology

Study Skills

for more information on our
publications visit **www.openup.co.uk**